WOMEN ON THE FRINGE

GROUNDBREAKING WOMEN IN THE PARANORMAL

DENISE A. AGNEW   MARIE D. JONES

NICOLE STRICKLAND

CONTENTS

Introduction
Women Walking On The Fringes Of Reality

The women portrayed in this book are as diverse and unique as snowflakes, yet all share one thing in common: at one point in their lives, they had a knowing that there was more to life than what their five senses told them. They all experienced a specific time or event when they just knew that what we call the "paranormal" was real. They all decided to set out on a path to discover all they could about the world of the paranormal, in whatever direction or form that took for them and never looked back.

Some came to the field later in life, or after not having much of an interest, while others have been interested and involved in some aspect of the paranormal for decades. History once defined women's role in these studies mainly as psychics and mediums, and they still dominate in these areas, but for a long time, certain aspects of paranormal research have come with a "male" branding, most likely due to the proliferation in recent times of television shows that feature male casts, with an occasional woman on the team, usually in the form of a psychic or medium. But the "hard research" seemed to always fall to the men. Women were looked upon as sensitive, intuitive, and emotional as if these traits somehow did not play into our understanding of how ghosts or anything paranormal behaved.

Yet times have changed and today there are as many, if not more, females out in the trenches doing the work of researching, investigating cases and reports out in the field, collecting and sharing data, and forming ideas and hypotheses about what the paranormal is, where it comes from, and how it manifests in our level of reality. Their "feminine" talents and gifts are appreciated and incorporated into the body of their research along with raw data and scientific methodologies, because the truth is, all of it matters. There are all-female ghost-hunting teams, Bigfoot teams, and UFO groups run by women, but ultimately the combination of male and female skills and abilities is what the field most needs to truly understand the depth and breadth of what we are dealing with.

The word "paranormal" itself has expanded. Once thought to only focus on ghosts and apparitions, namely due to a proliferation of popular movies and TV shows signifying such, we now use it as an umbrella term for a wide array of topics from ghosts to psi abilities to UFO and alien abductions to cryptids and Bigfoot sightings to unknown anomalies and the Alaska Triangle and Skinwalker Ranch and shadow people and uncategorizable locations and events of high strangeness. Anything above and beyond the normal, that is.

Cattle mutilations. The Bermuda Triangle. Strange disappearances. Bizarre zones of activity. Time distortions, dilations, and missing time. Parallel universes and alternate dimensions. Poltergeists and cryptids and aliens, oh my! It's no longer just about ghosts, although they continue to remain a mainstay of paranormal studies. The field has also expanded to include research into near-death experiences, remote viewing, zones of high strangeness, quantum physics and the paranormal, and government coverups of UFOs and the existence of aliens. Nothing is off limits and for the women on the fringe, that is just how they like it.

For all of these things, there are groundbreaking women doing groundbreaking research into the fringe sciences, if you will, and presenting their findings in the form of investigative journalism, books, radio shows, podcasts, blogs, speaking events, lectures, and any other way they can find to communicate what they are learning. Women are generous and rarely keep their findings to themselves for egoic purposes, something some of their male counterparts have often been accused of.

The women in this book do not look at their paranormal pursuits as a hobby, they are serious and passionate and all in. They don't care what others think of them, they do what they do because it is who they are and a reflection of how they perceive the world they live in. These women forge ahead despite challenges, problems, negative attitudes of others, erroneous public perceptions, and lack of funds and resources that their more famous counterparts may have access to.

They do it because they love it, it's in their bones. The "paranormal" to them is as real and vibrant and alive with possibility as the normal world, maybe even more so.

Come meet the women on the fringe. For every woman who contributed, there are ten or a hundred more who for whatever reason could not, but their stories share a common thread. They are explorers of the final frontier. Not space or the vast oceans, but the world of the unseen and how it links to the seen, how it influences and affects all of us, and how there may be, right now, entire realities filled with entities and energies dancing at the edges of our own noses we cannot see with our eyes, but are there, nonetheless.

Chapter 1

Meet The Authors/How We Found The Fringe

DISCOVERING MY TRUTH IN THE PARANORMAL

DENISE A. AGNEW

When I was invited to participate with Marie D. Jones and Nicole Strickland in forming this book on women in the paranormal, I was instantly excited and humbled. Yes, I've been interested in the paranormal since I was a wee child. The women in this book have been boots on the ground, striving daily to understand the wild world that is the paranormal. The advances they've made in bringing the paranormal to the forefront, to research, to investigate, and to enlighten the public at large impresses me. I'm delighted to give you a small look into how the paranormal has been a part of my life since the beginning.

It's taken a long time for me to recognize that my interest and involvement in the paranormal started from the time I was small. At first, I didn't choose the esoteric so much as it chose me.

As far back as I can remember, I found life a bit loud. I didn't realize at the time, though, that the discomfort I felt wasn't necessarily what everyone felt. Light was often too bright, noises were sometimes too loud, and my skin sometimes felt too sensitive. If I were a little kid today, a psychologist might say I had sensory processing disorder, though I'm only speculating.

I also had a low-grade ache in my muscles, which later on in life I realized was fibromyalgia (something I still have today). Most of all I couldn't tell if the emotions I felt were mine or someone else's. When people would comment on how shy and quiet I was, they didn't always mean it as a compliment. I was a "good little girl" and "extremely mature" for my age. The mixed messages were confusing.

I understood the energy in a room. Especially if people felt distressed and were hiding it. People would feel comfortable telling me everything, and I knew something had changed by the time we'd finished talking. They'd feel lighter, better, and be smiling. It never occurred to me that it was unusual for adults to feel better from talking to a child. Sometimes I'd tell people what their emotions were and surprise them with my accuracy. A few people didn't like that, especially my parents, who didn't give the time of day to the concept that a little kid could read them and know exactly what they were feeling and thinking. Often my observation was given when adults weren't asking for it, but occasionally they'd talked my ear off and asked what I thought. My observations were too woo-woo and what did a kid know anyway?

I also loved spooky things. Movies, TV shows, and books. During my leisure time, I'd write stories and ideas for movies and TV shows (some spooky, some not). I thank the lucky stars my parents had no objection to my interest in any of this, and my mother let me read anything I wanted. And yes, I read The Exorcist when I was eleven years old. I couldn't get enough of reading about ghosts, hauntings, Bigfoot, UFOs...all the things.

When I became a teenager, and later as an adult, people would frequently tell me they felt like a weight had been lifted away from them after they'd chatted with me. My guess is that most people didn't know why. In my work life, despite being an introvert, I did front-line jobs that required a huge amount of phone and in-person people contact. I was excellent at not only coaxing people who didn't understand each other into coming to an agreement but that I could take angry people and calm them down. They'd go away feeling heard, satisfied, and sometimes even smile. Over the years this included some individuals with mental illnesses that had escalated to a high degree. Most of the time, I went away from the situation feeling satisfied the conflict was dissolved, but also physically and mentally depleted. Again, I figured this was normal. I thought, okay so I'm a good negotiator. Yes, I learned only recently that my skill was partly developed because of complex post-traumatic stress. I was a huge magnet for bullies, and the trauma that caused...well, children look for ways to cope, don't they? I learned that many of the skills I'd acquired were a mix of coping and psychic/intuitive abilities.

A person like this must have a ton of paranormal experiences, right? The problem, if you can call it that, is that I didn't always know I was having a paranormal experience. Too often we think we understand what a paranormal situation or event looks like. It's an apparition popping out to scare us. A near-death experience, an EVP on a recorder, an intuition that warns us of danger. All of those things could be classified as paranormal. Yet there's more out there in the world that's subtle and unrecognizable as esoteric until further examination. I spent considerable time ignoring my intuition (to my regret), psychic hits, and other unusual experiences in an attempt to not be seen as a crazy person and in my own mind to be genuinely "scientific" in my approach to life.

As a child, I was drawn to all things Irish and British. I knew my ancestry was British and Irish and often wondered if my ancestors had lived in the places I read about and longed to visit. I used to have a reoccurring dream as a child about being on a high, green hilltop scattered with ruins and a graveyard near the ruins filled with Celtic crosses. There was a woman kneeling next to one of the crosses. I didn't recognize her. In 1983, I was in a college class on Irish literature and the class had an opportunity to take a nine-day trip to Ireland. The whole idea was beyond exciting and scary (introvert, remember) but I took the plunge and signed up. As I looked out of the Aer Lingus 747 window and saw the greenest land I'd ever witnessed, a tremendous sense of recognition passed over me. Once on the ground and outside the airport, I also recognized a certain scent. It was beyond familiar to me. I asked someone what it was. "A peat fire," they said. The thing is, I'd never smelled a peat fire in my entire life. All during my trip my sense of recognition, bone-deep and as if I was home, refused to abate. During one tour we visited the Rock of Cashel in Tipperary. The ruins sit on a high hill. I was taking photographs in the graveyard when I realized a woman was kneeling next to a Celtic cross. Boom! It hit me like a proverbial ton of bricks. My childhood reoccurring dream had come true. I stood there for some time, amazed and shocked.

One of my oddest experiences happened in the 1990s when my husband and I lived in England for three years. I'd always wanted to visit Britain, and when I heard we were to live in England for three years, I was thrilled. I had the same experience in England, Scotland, and Wales as I had in Ireland; I felt as if I'd come home after an interminable time away.

One year we went to Edinburgh, Scotland for their world-famous Hogmanay event. We signed up to take a tour through the South Bridge Vaults. Once there, the tour guide opened the door to the building and took us down a winding staircase illuminated by candles. He'd flipped the electric light switch and it didn't work. Whether it was set up that way to add to the atmosphere, I don't know, but it certainly gave the place a spooky ambiance. He lit candles set on each step as we went down. I am not claustrophobic, and I'm not scared of things underground. I didn't feel particularly spooked, just curious about the history and ghost stories. Everything was peachy...until it wasn't.

We reached a barrel vault room with a somewhat high ceiling, and everything changed for me in the blink of an eye. The air felt too close.

At first, I figured thirty people in relative proximity to each other might be getting to me. I stayed close to my husband. The feeling that I couldn't get a full breath became worse. Much, much worse. Even though it was very cold down there, I started to feel hot, and my hands started to sweat. Dread and apprehension overwhelmed me until I couldn't wait to leave. The idea of running obsessed me. In my head, I could hear, "Let me out, let me out, let me out." I couldn't believe how I felt, and it disturbed me like nothing else I'd ever experienced. I'd never had a panic attack before, but this felt like what people described as a panic attack. Being one who doesn't like to create drama, I managed to keep how I felt from everyone.

I don't recall now how long we stood in that room, but by the time we left, I realized I hadn't heard a word the tour guide said about its ghosts or history. If I thought I'd escape the feeling by leaving that room, I was partially right. When we left the tour sometime later, the relief was enormous. I told my husband about my experience and asked him if he'd felt anything. He hadn't.

Ever the skeptical believer, I thought maybe I'd developed claustrophobia. When we visited the wartime tunnels at Dover Castle, which are also underground, I thought the same thing might happen. It didn't. When I went into dungeons in other castles, I might sense things that happened in the castle and in the dungeon, but I never again felt that strange panic in any underground place. For months afterward, I was eager to learn if anyone else had the same experience as I did in the Edinburgh South Bridge vaults or other underground tours in that city. There wasn't too much on the Internet at that time about experiences in the tunnels, but once we returned to the United States, I located more articles alluding to others who'd felt exactly the same way in the tunnels...and in that particular room where I'd experienced the issue.

Mediums and psychics I've talked to since then have told me that perhaps I'd been "jumped" by a spirit that was trying to make me feel/understand something that happened to them in the vaults. Or perhaps I had picked up on the past experience of someone who'd been in the tunnels, living there many centuries ago. To say this experience made an everlasting impression on me is an understatement. Knowing what I do now, I would welcome a chance to return to Britain (especially Edinburgh) and investigate the paranormal.

A few years after we returned to the United States, I joined a paranormal investigation group. It was something I always wanted to do. During the short time the group was in operation, we investigated private homes and buildings in Bisbee, Arizona including the famous Copper Queen Hotel. When that group dissolved, I was fortunate enough to join another group, and we have investigated properties in Arizona. During my time with these groups, I've noted that most investigations don't generate a lot of fruitful evidence. It isn't like it is on television for most investigators. Many groups don't utilize a medium, and in my first group, I didn't recognize my abilities at that time. The group I belong to now has two mediums, including myself. I believe it is up to each group to use whatever methods they wish to investigate, including whether to include a psychic/medium or not.

In 2018, I took a series of courses from a medium related to increasing intuition and psychic capability. During one of those classes, I discovered that so many of the visions and images I randomly received in my mind's eye were mediumship abilities. It blew me away. Even then I was skeptical. I figured... well, I'm a writer. I imagine a lot of stuff. All the time. How did I know I wasn't making it all up in my imagination? Until it was pointed out to me over and over that I knew things about people, places, situations, and those in spirit that I couldn't know unless I was utilizing mediumship and psychic ability.

I noticed a pattern with my mediumship readings that blew me away. It wasn't something I even imagined would happen in my mediumship journey. Many times, a spirit that had taken its own life would come into my readings. I was surprised this was happening so frequently. I've learned that spirits who passed in this matter will contact mediums they believe understand them and won't judge them. I have also made contact with murder victims.

Since I first learned of my mediumship abilities, I've been building on those skills and attempting a greater understanding of it all. Currently, I offer mediumship, psychic/intuitive, and oracle card readings for individuals. I offer a Dive Deep reading that combines mediumship with an oracle card reading with the idea of expanding a client's understanding of spirit and his/her own life situation. I love bringing people life clarification.

These days I also weave fictional stories as a novelist and screenwriter. I've come full circle for the moment, and there are many other experiences I could relay. The few I've noted above are some of the more notable. I look forward to many more adventures in the paranormal world.

A Lifelong Obsession with the Unknown

Marie D. Jones

I'm not sure when my obsession with all things unknown began, or why. I have recollections of being obsessed with ghosts, aliens, UFOs, and strange creatures since I was about five years of age. This was back in the 1960s, long before the onslaught of paranormal and UFO-related TV, cable, radio shows, and podcasts that people today are exposed to on a daily basis, along with hundreds, if not thousands, of paranormal-themed groups and pages on social media.

Back in the day, we only had broadcast television, regular terrestrial radio, and books (and they were print, not digital!).

I was a storyteller from day one, always making up long, elaborate stories about trivial things like going to shop for shoes. I wrote stories, too, being one of those freaky kids who could read and write from toddlerhood. Writing was who I was, and how I expressed myself. I like to say I came out of the womb with a pad and pen, but I also came out of the womb with this intense connection with the unseen, unknown world, one I knew was just as real as my head and shoulders, knees, and toes.

My early stories were mostly about ghosts and alien creatures. My mom instilled a love of stories into me, reading them at night before bedtime, and telling made-up stories to my siblings and me on a floor mat in front of our kitchen door, which she would call the "magic carpet." I recall telling my mom I saw Bigfoot in the woods right behind our house in Rockland County, New York. Turned out it was just a neighbor walking through the trees, but what on Earth prompted me to think it was Bigfoot at such a young age?

I had vivid dreams of UFOs hovering overhead, of aliens landing and coming towards my house, of cities in the sky, and on one occasion, when I was seven, I dreamt I saw a skull-like face peering at me from our garage window. Later I would see images of alien "greys" and realize that was what I saw. These dreams felt so real, different from my normal dreams, and to this day I can recall every last detail.

At the local library, I would stock up on books about ghosts and aliens, if I could find them, along with books about nature and science. I loved science. My father was a geophysicist and seismologist, so science was a big deal in our household. My mother was creative and imaginative, and no doubt sparked my creative pursuits. I had the best of both worlds and never saw a gap between the known and the imagined, the world we see and the world we cannot see.

When I was seven or eight, I had a defining moment that would set in stone my destiny to become a "digger of truths." My father was telling my brother, who was 18 months younger than me, that at one time our entire area was underwater. My brother loved dinosaurs and was excited about the fact that at one time in history, they roamed the land we now live upon. I listened attentively and decided I needed to go find out if that was true for myself. The next morning, I got a soup spoon from the drawer and went outside to the backyard. I began to dig a hole.

I dug and dug until I decided a spoon was not going to do the trick. I went inside and asked my mom for a much larger spoon. I continued to dig. Then I went into the garage and got a shovel and really got down to business. As was normal for those times, neighborhood kids were outside playing, and a few came into the yard and asked what I was doing. "Looking for dinosaur fossils," I told them. In great Tom Sawyer fashion, I then got a few of them to fetch their own shovels and do the digging for me. I wasn't stupid.

My mom wondered what I was up to and looked out the upper bedroom window to find me standing inside a 4-foot-deep hole in the swing set area, holding up rocks. Those rocks were fossils of seashells. I proved to myself and others my Dad was right. I still have those fossils to this day and after that, my parents were very careful about what they said in my presence.

A second defining moment came around that same time. My father and our neighbor across the street, Mike, were really into UFOs. My dad was the science go-to guy in our small but close neighborhood and one night everyone was outside pointing at a brilliantly bright light in the sky. Was it a UFO? The excitement was palpable. I ran up to our house and got my Dad out of his favorite place, the bathroom. He begrudgingly followed me back outside to where a small crowd gathered, waiting in breathless anticipation. He took one look upward and said, "It's Venus." Then he turned and walked back up to our house and vanished, no doubt back into the bathroom.

You could have cut the disappointment with a knife.

My father often talked about how he couldn't bring up the subject of UFOs in the "halls of academia," but he could on his own time. Mike had given him some classic UFO paperbacks that now belong to me. When *In Search Of* was on, we watched every episode over the years. It was a passion my Dad and I shared. He passed away in late 2011 after we wrote a book together about supervolcanos.

Another defining moment occurred one night when my dad and a few of the scientists he worked with were gathered at our small kitchen table, playing cards and smoking...and talking about UFOs. I sat at my father's feet listening, marveling at how these brilliant men of science were all believers, but could never say so in a formal, professional setting.

That secured for me my love of blending science and the paranormal. My father once told me that science is never settled and is always changing and that there was, indeed, a science behind ghosts and UFOs, even if we didn't yet understand it. I never forgot that. I had many defining moments of my writing destiny, but one in particular blended science, writing, and the paranormal, although it's not one I am proud of.

During the famous moon landing in 1968, we watched with my grandparents on our black and white television in our living room. My grandfather had brought along his big reel-to-reel tape recorder so we could capture history. Years later we played back the tape and there was Neil Armstrong saying his famous words about one small step for mankind...but in the foreground was my voice telling a story about a headless ghost that was haunting a couple in their new house. Yes, I ruined a huge historical documentation with a ghost story. We laughed about it later, and I thought, there you go. That's me. That's who I am.

As a teenager, I wrote and published horror and science fiction stories for small press magazines and read everything I could get my hands on about UFOs. Ufology was my biggest passion in terms of the paranormal. I was into ghosts and cryptids but downright obsessed with UFOs. I could never pinpoint any experience I had that might have led me to believe I had been abducted or had a close encounter. It was just always there. The only time I ever saw what could have been a UFO happened much later when I lived in San Diego and witnessed an object flying in the dusk sky that even with my extensive research could not identify.

Throughout my later years, I had a few paranormal experiences that were intriguing and kept me interested enough to pursue my research and eventually write over a dozen books on various related subjects. I never had a "direct encounter" with a ghost but came close enough. In fact, I seemed to be very sensitive to "otherworldly energies" and able to pick up on changes in the vibrations around me.

When I was a teenager, I had a friend who believed her family was experiencing poltergeist activity. They were terrified and had gone to their local Lutheran church for help but got no support. I never wanted to spend the night there because I was scared it was true, but she convinced me to stay over one night, and nothing happened out of the ordinary until the next morning when we were eating breakfast and watching *Auntie Mame* in the den, and I felt the coldest wave of energy pass through every cell of my body. The windows were closed. Carol leaned over and said, "Did you feel it?" I never stayed over again, and they sold the house. The new owners leveled it to the ground and rebuilt it.

I had other experiences going into rooms where I would almost be repelled backward, only to later find out someone was murdered there. When I lived in New York, we came to California one year for a vacation and went to the Hotel Del Coronado in San Diego, where I experienced that same repulsion, of being pushed backward from a corridor that was marked off for construction. We later found out someone had been murdered down that hallway.

When we later moved to San Diego, I heard about the legend of the Lady In White that haunted the woods in an area called Questhaven. I decided one sunny day to drive into the woods to investigate. It was long before the area was built up a bit more with homes. I drove along and suddenly felt the "walls closing in around me" and my car stopped dead. The skies clouded over, and it began to pour. It had been sunny and clear and now it was pouring rain and my car would not move. I got the engine going but the tires skidded. I was crying and panicking when just as suddenly, it stopped raining and my car lurched forward. I quickly did a U-turn and high-tailed it out of the woods, noticing with some trepidation when I got back to the main road that only my car was wet with raindrops. Everything else was bone dry.

Those kinds of experiences continued. Indirect, but enough to keep me interested and certain there were other realities than this one. I never saw a ghost or a full-bodied apparition. My experiences were what I call "circumstantial evidence," but that was enough for me.

During the late 1980s into the 1990s, I was heavily involved with MUFON, the Mutual UFO Network, as a trained field investigator. I also wrote for CUFOS, the Center of UFO Studies, and other UFO publications. Eventually, I started my own MUFON chapter in North County, San Diego, and had the most chilling experience of my life. This was at the time when alien abductions were just starting to be discussed in the media and we were getting people coming to meetings claiming to have had abduction experiences. Again, because it was a new field of study for most of us, we didn't know what to do so we eventually found some great hypnotherapists to work with these people, who were confused and terrified and, with the exception of a couple of blatant attention-seekers, wanted to know what was happening to them.

During that time, I began to get phone calls on my landline, as this was long before cell phones, from a man who used a voice changer. It has a metallic, robotic sound. Stilted and formal. This man, who I could not identify because there was no caller ID on my landline then, would tell me things about myself that nobody could have ever known. Things I had never told anyone, not even my husband at the time. He also would tell me what I was wearing, what magazine was on my nightstand, or what I was cooking at the stove. I got freaked out and tried to use Star 69 but it would never work. I called the phone company, and they somehow couldn't identify the caller's number!

I didn't tell my husband right away, thinking it was perhaps a prank, but it got more invasive, and the man told me to stop looking into one particular abduction case I was working on, or else...I am a tough Italian New Yorker, but it was so chilling I quit MUFON the next day and never looked back. Turns out the gal who I ran the MUFON meetings with had her house broken into and her husband found strange men on their property. She claimed to have been abducted along with her family and she was so spooked, we both agreed to end the northern San Diego MUFON group. She moved to another state shortly after receiving a death threat about a book she was writing documenting her abduction experiences. I kept my UFO interest closer to the vest from that point on. I would experience strange activity like that years later when writing about mind control, cults, and MKUltra.

Later, I was informed by my friend, UFO researcher and author Nick Redfern, that my experience was a classic Men In Black encounter and he interviewed me for his book on MIBs. To this day, just thinking about it gives me goosebumps.

After that, I poured my interests into my writing and began a long career of writing non-fiction books about everything from quantum physics and the paranormal, Deja vu, unknown anomalies, UFOs, poltergeists, altered states of consciousness, parallel realities, and how resonance might explain the paranormal. I didn't want to be pinpointed into just one area and was fortunate enough to find publishers that let me tackle any subject I pleased, including New Page Books, Hierophant Books, Red Wheel/ Weiser, and Visible Ink Press. I also wrote about metaphysical and science subjects, too. To date, I have over 30 books in print. Of all of my books, *PSIence: How New Discoveries in Quantum Physics and New Science May Explain the Existence of Paranormal Phenomena*, written in 2006, is my favorite not just because it was my first "big" book but because it allowed me to explore the links between science and the paranormal in a way that had not been done much before. The book's reception was amazing, with appearances on radio all over the world, including one on *Coast-to-Coast AM* that for years was one of their top-rated shows. I was also featured on the History Channel's *Nostradamus Effect* and *Ancient Aliens* series. To this day, I've appeared on over 2500 radio shows and written extensively for over two dozen publications, including *New Dawn Magazine, Atlantis Rising, Paranormal Underground, Phenomenon*, and more.

I've done so much radio and had some strange encounters on the air as well. On one show, the two women hosts and I got to talking about an experience I had in the 1990s when I was going to see Carl Sagan speak at the Planetary Society. On the way there, I experienced two hours of missing time. I never suspected anything weird, but on that radio show the two ladies quietly informed me that the location I was in was a hot spot known for abductions and suggested I get hypnotized. I thought about it but haven't yet done so! I think there is a part of me that knows I'd be disappointed if nothing happened, and terrified if something did. Better to keep some mystery about it.

I've written and researched paranormal phenomena for several decades and never truly experienced a direct encounter with a ghost or spirit of a beloved relative. I did hear my grandfather, Poppy, call out my nickname a few times after he passed away, but how easy is it to pass off something like that as my imagination? Maybe I just wanted to hear his voice, to be comforted in my grief? I was a skeptic and never considered that type of experience "paranormal" right off the bat. Surely, there were other common-sense explanations.

Even though I never saw a ghost of a past relative, I may very well have gotten a phone call from one of them after she died. I believe I received a phone call at the moment just after the death of my father's mother, my Nana. Not a phone call before death, or in the hospital bed at the moment of death to say goodbye. I'm talking about the recorded time of death according to hospital records and the death certificate.

The call from the other side came from our family matriarch, a formidable woman who carried a lot of weight in all of our lives, and though we lived all the way across the country, still managed to be a big presence even in her absence. This was over 15 years ago and long before cell phones and caller ID, so when the call came a bit past 11:00 at night, I had no way of knowing who it was. Because only family called that late, and usually if something was wrong, I answered in a panic, only to find static on the other end. I stayed on the line for at least a minute, saying "Hello" over and over again. But to no avail. I hung up and passed it off as a wrong number or a crank call.

About an hour later my sister called to tell me our father had contacted her about Nana's passing. The weird thing was, she, too, got a phone call around the same time. So did my father, who lived in another state and time zone. We later found out that according to the recorded time of death, that's when our phones all rang simultaneously.

Because it only happened once, I passed it off as a weird coincidence, but I did some research and found out that these phone calls from the other side at or around the moment of death are incredibly common, and it seemed that everyone I mentioned it to had an experience of their own to report.

When my father died years later, I had an experience that even defied the phone call from the dead. At the moment of my father's death (which I did not yet know about), a very close friend texted me and asked if I was doing okay. I replied, "Yeah, why?" He said he felt as though something bad had happened. I assured him I was okay, but about an hour later, I got a call from my sister that my father had died while in hospice. We had just been out to visit him, so it was quite a shock. The time of his death? At the same exact moment, my friend had texted asking if I was doing alright. He knew something bad had happened even before I did. When his own father died, I had a similar feeling of something being off, a disturbance in the force, if you will.

Despite my never seeing a full-bodied apparition of my Poppy, my Nana, or my father, these experiences were eerie and surreal enough for me to believe that loved ones can find ways to reach out to us when they want to let us know they will be, and are, okay on the other side.

I did encounter some pushback writing about science and the paranormal from a handful of men, a couple who outright stole my research and tried to plagiarize my writing. Most men welcomed me as a peer, though. As a woman in this field, it sometimes seems as though we are expected to keep a certain "place" and not venture out of those boundaries. Women in the paranormal have so much to offer, as we bring gifts that are much needed to the study arena. We are level-headed yet understand emotion. We have powerful intuition and are often more sensitive to energy fields and fluctuations. We work hard and collaborate well. I have seen so many women in the last ten to fifteen years breaking ground in the fields of ghost investigations, mediumship, ufology, and cryptozoology, as well as research into ancient knowledge and civilizations. Oh, they were probably always there doing their work, but lately, they are really stepping out of the background and into the foreground where they belong, standing alone or alongside the men in the field.

My three biggest influences in terms of my interests in the paranormal were all women. In the 1980s, I was enamored with reading about Shirley MacLaine's deep dives into past lives and mystical experiences. Later, I discovered Linda Moulton Howe. Here was a well-respected investigative reporter with a fabulous reputation digging into the bizarre world of cattle and animal mutilations and possible links to UFO sightings. This, to me, was tough stuff for anyone to research, and Linda was at the top of the game. It didn't matter that she was female. The quality of her work was so good, that nobody cared. She inspired the researcher in me.

My biggest influence bar none was Lynne McTaggart, author of the book, which truly changed my entire perspective on the paranormal and its links to science and physics. When I first heard about *The Field: The*

Quest for the Secret Force of the Universe, it was via another of my favorite authors and people in general, Dr. Wayne Dyer. He wrote about Lynne's book in his own book, *The Power of Intention*. I ran out and got *The Field* and nothing was ever the same for me. It totally changed how I looked at reality and how the unseen and the seen, the unknown and the known, are all linked in the quantum field of possibility. It remains one of a handful of books I have read in my adulthood that most changed my life.

These and many other women were my trailblazers.

Today, more women are researching, investigating, and writing about the paranormal and making their marks through other avenues such as podcasts, haunted tours, and blogs/vlogs. I love it. We need all egos aside and all hands on deck if we ever truly want to reveal the truths we seek.

For me, I never really cared about being a woman. I just did my thing as I had always done. Maybe it goes back to being a tomboy, or a stubborn New York Italian, but I never let anyone define me and I investigated and wrote about the things that interested me in the way I wanted. For those few detractors that tried to derail me, sorry, it didn't work.

But in the last few years, I've felt the winds of change in terms of my purpose and goals.

My love of writing actually began with making up stories, and I longed to return to fiction and screenwriting over the last five years. I recently made the decision when COVID-19 hit to go back to fiction and film on an almost full-time basis, while still leaving the door open for new non-fiction should "the spirit move me." I have found that I can use fiction to also explore my love of all things unseen and unknown and I tend to gravitate towards science fiction, horror, and the paranormal in many of my novels, scripts, and novellas. I sold a couple of screenplays during the COVID-19 years and hope to sell more. I am slowly getting out novels that have been sitting in the drawer and editing them for their debut in the real world.

I cannot ever foresee a time when I won't be obsessed with UFOs or intrigued by the paranormal and the world of unknown anomalies. I want to take my spoon and go dig for the truth. I have no idea if I or anyone else in these fields will ever find it, but we have this inner drive, this obsession, that cannot die. There are times when it quiets down a bit when I'm deeply engaged in some personal aspect of life, but it's always there. I seek out the TV shows (my most recent obsession seems to be women Bigfoot hunters!), the movies, the books, the podcasts. I cannot get enough.

Over my long and extensive career, I have made hundreds of friends and acquaintances, many of them explorers like me, and we always joke about what would happen if all the truths were one day revealed. We'd be bored out of our skulls! Perhaps there is a part of us, a part of me, that hopes they never are all revealed. So much of the joy, the passion, the obsession is the chase itself. The journey to find out more about the world, and our place in it. And any chance I get to combine my two passions - writing and the paranormal- I'll take it!

Although I still wouldn't mind seeing a UFO up close one day, as long as they don't abduct me.

A Lifelong Passion for Exploring the Connection Between Life, Death, and Beyond

Nicole Strickland

Humans are innately curious and attracted to exploring that, which remains on the periphery. Various cultures from all walks of life have showcased an interest in life after death for thousands of years. Most paranormal researchers will tell you about that profound encounter or series of encounters that catapulted them into their committed investigation of the unknown.

In my younger years, I never envisioned myself out in the trenches studying anomalous phenomena, including the connection between life, death, and beyond. Although, from a young age, I always showcased a natural inquisitive attraction to bizarre, ghostly occurrences. In my prepubescent and teen years, I read and watched anything related to ghosts, hauntings, and the preternatural. This eventually led to a life-long passion for exploring the afterlife, paranormal realms, and meta-physical domains.

My first otherworldly experience occurred on a warm summer evening in Las Vegas, Nevada, as my parents and I were drying off after a swim in our backyard pool. I was about four or five years old and remember it like it occurred yesterday. The sun was quietly setting beyond the horizon when all of a sudden, I noticed a cloud of a grey misty-like form morph into a humanoid shape as it floated between the three of us. I motioned toward my mom and dad and said, "Did you see that draft?" My parents were oblivious to what I saw and at such a tender age, I didn't understand why. Having experience and knowledge of paranormal phenomena as an adult, I realize that either they couldn't see this ethereal vapor or it was meant for only me to experience. I have no definitive idea why I used the word "draft" to explain what I witnessed. To this day, it remains a mystery.

There are many succeeding incorporeal happenings that followed, which have all shaped my passion for investigating and researching the afterlife, the paranormal, and beyond. I am forever indebted to my grandmother, Helen LoPinto, as she was the integral family member who opened the window for me to further envelope my love for para-normal study. As a Northern Italian with roots in Boston, Mass-achusetts, Helen used to say that she was born with a veil over her head or a type of en caul birth that is incredibly rare where the baby is born encased in his or her amniotic sac. People born in this manner are said to be natural healers, possess intuitive sensitivities, have the ability to traverse through many worlds, and even see the future. I can recall many times when Helen exhibited her innate perception. For example, she'd call family members up on the phone and ask them, "If they were okay or if there was something wrong." She was accurate almost every single time as she just sensed things. There have been many experiences throughout my life that highly suggest this maternal line of intuition has been passed down to my mom and me.

Yet, the life-changing encounter with Helen's spirit while I was attending the University of Arizona further kindled my limitless quest to explore the frontiers of the unknown as well as the developing self-awareness of my innate intuition. Helen called me in the early evening hours of October 24, 2000. During our brief phone call, she asked if I was okay. At the time, I thought it was a rather odd question. As I reminisce, I realize that she was ensuring that her family was fine before venturing off to the stars. I think she knew she was about to pass on and our phone conversation served as a forewarning. At around the same time the following day, I received a call from my mom, Norma Strickland, Helen's youngest daughter. I instinctively knew by the tone of my mother's voice that something wasn't right. As she echoed the words, "Hi sweetheart, I love you. I'm so sorry but grandma passed away early this morning...," the flood of heartache and grief overcame me. My grandmother passed away on my mom's birthday. There's a deeper meaning here that only the cosmos understands. Off I was to San Diego to spend some quality time with my family and attend Helen's peaceful viewing at Greenwood Mortuary. For reasons unknown, she never wanted a funeral, so we paid our respects to her in other ways.

About a week after my return to Tucson, Arizona, I started to experience odd occurrences in my upstairs apartment that I hadn't encountered before. The knobs on my front and bedroom doors seemed to intermittently rattle by themselves. At first, I dismissed these events and ascribed them to vibration from other units. Yet, I couldn't escape the memory of how Helen, in mortal form, would go around the doors of her house at night to make sure they were all locked. One night as I was studying for my classes, I felt an invisible hand caress my face and knew it came from someone I dearly loved. It was at this instant that I pondered the possibility of my grandmother communicating from the other side. Contemplation turned into confirmation when I saw Helen's serene spirit form near my bedroom closet a couple of days later. With an aura of bright light surrounding her, she looked about ten years younger, adorned in her favorite blue and white, flowered house dress. Although the sighting lasted about a second or two, it seemed to play out in slow motion, allowing me to truly savor the moment.

I initially wondered if this experience was a bereavement hallucination on my part as I was extremely close to Helen. It has also been suggested that a death spirit imitated my grandmother's ethereal form and that it wasn't her. Innate knowing coupled with my experiences as a paranormal researcher has reassured me that Helen appeared in those days following her transition. She came to me knowing that I was able to sense her, and she knew that I would share it with the family. My mom and I reminded her that she was free from the physical realm and able to venture off to her new life beyond the ethers. Since my infancy, I always seemed to be more intuitive than others and I believe this is something Helen knew and allowed me to see through this profound encounter.

For over twenty years, I have been dedicating my free time to researching and communicating with the afterlife and beyond. My journey into paranormal discovery was never planned, but it has certainly been a calling. It came to fruition as it was synchronously meant to. Initially, I worked with various Southern California paranormal groups to learn the fundamental basics of ghost research and paranormal study. In 2009, I founded the well-respected San Diego Paranormal Research Society (SDPRS) and have served as its case manager and director. Serving mainly in Southern California, the team specializes in the study of the afterlife and ghost research, including ghosts/spirits, haunted locations, and spirit communication.

After years of dedicated commitment, SDPRS has earned itself a reputation as one of San Diego's go-to groups. The team conducts paranormal investigations and case studies of private residences, businesses, and historical abodes. We've investigated many of San Diego's notable historical locations as well as theaters, prisons, abandoned hospitals, ships, battlefields, and numerous historical sites. The team also provides mentorship and an educational platform for those to further learn about supernatural field study via books, classes, and presentations. Additionally, SDPRS had tenure at Vista's Rancho Buena Vista Adobe for nearly ten years, hosting the monthly "Spirits of the Adobe" fundraising tours, where attendees learned about the site's rich history and notable ghostly occurrences. If you'd like to learn more, I invite you to read my book, *Spirits of Rancho Buena Vista Adobe*, published by Haunted America.

Here's where I'd like to mention an important notion highlighted in my book, *The Afterlife Chronicles: Exploring the Connection between*

Life, Death, and Beyond. Studying the afterlife and unknown dimensions has not only taught me a lot about myself but has granted me opportunities to become further united with my passion for history and those who walked the land before us. Even though I have always enjoyed history, I have gained a deeper appreciation for and knowledge of historical events through my work as a paranormal researcher. Quantum mechanics suggests that the past, present, and future may be more interconnected than we think.

Fifteen years ago, I had the fortunate opportunity to meet Dale Kaczmarek, president of the Ghost Research Society (GRS) at a conference in Northern California. Dale is one of the field's esteemed paranormal researchers and it has been an honor to be mentored by him. Since 2008, I have served as the GRS's Southern California Area Research Director and California Coordinator. One of my most memorable experiences was participating in a 2009 overnight investigation of Louisville, Kentucky's Waverly Hills Sanatorium and Decatur, Illinois' Lincoln Theater. I look forward to future outings with GRS at some of America's most historic locales, such as Gettysburg, Pennsylvania.

Tuberculosis or the "White Death" seeped into America during the 1800s and early 1900s. There was no cure for this insidious and tremendously contagious plague as it ravaged families and townships. In 1900, the one city in America with the highest tuberculosis death rate was Louisville, Kentucky. Waverly Hills Sanatorium, the structure we're familiar with today, opened its doors in 1926 and was known for being the most skilled in the United States for treating and hopefully combating the "White Death" plague. All in all, 63,000 plus souls perished on these grounds, and this is one of the prevailing theories that can possibly explain the paranormal activity circulating throughout and around the monstrous building.

Investigating Waverly Hills Sanatorium was an eye-opening experience, allowing me to almost simultaneously sense the history, sizeable human loss, and ghostly occurrences as if they all became one. This was one of the top-ten locations on my bucket list and I did not take it lightly. I paid my respects to the thousands who passed away from Tuberculosis, often without their loved ones nearby. Lisa Krick, Nicole Tito, and I joined forces and conducted several audio and laser grid experiments, with the latter highlighting the famous shadow figure sightings many witness morphing into and out of the walls. I remember standing still in the middle of the hallways as I glared at the dark, misty forms attempting to take on humanoid shapes. Could these forms be the imprints and memories of the patients and medical staff from long ago? One day soon, I hope to revisit these hallowed grounds.

On that same trip in 2009, GRS also attended Troy Taylor's Haunted America Conference in Decatur, Illinois. This little town is known for the iconic Lincoln Theater, a historically rich and very haunted abode that I was fortunate to investigate. According to Taylor, the theater opened in 1916 with a tremendous seating capacity, a massive stage, and many ghost stories. You see, the Lincoln Theater was not the original structure to stand in its place in downtown Decatur. The first documented building on the grounds was the Priest Hotel, constructed in 1860. It endured proprietor and name changes over the years; on April 21, 1915, a catastrophic fire erupted, killing two people and damaging various surrounding structures.

Lisa Krick, Nicole Tito, and I grouped together and mainly conducted audio experimentation during the night's paranormal investigation of the Lincoln Theater. Interestingly, we captured a Class A EVP in the dressing room area; however, the EVP was captured by only Nicole Tito and me. Since Lisa had her recorder on voice-activation mode, we theorize that is the reason why the vocalization wasn't documented on her device.

"What are you going to perform tonight?" I asked.

A seemingly intelligent response of "Magic" occurred right after, unheard by the naked ear at the time, but of course, captured on digital recorders. I then proceeded to ask, "What are you getting ready for?" and no response was heard or documented.

The three of us did not hear this captivating response in real-time, thus classifying it as an EVP. It must be noted that the famed magician, Harry Blackstone Sr., returned to perform at the Lincoln Theater in September 1942. It's highly possible that it was his spirit voice we captured in the dressing rooms based on how his voice and intonation sounded.

The RMS *Queen Mary* is my second home, another location that has captured my heart. Since 2005, I have researched the iconic ocean liner's rich historical tapestry and legendary paranormal happenings. None of this was ever planned; but somehow, some way, I've become internationally known for my knowledge of the *Queen Mary.* The ship has this uncanny way of connecting with people and choosing those who can feel her living soul and purpose. Many of her current and former crew, WWII veterans, war brides, and recurring visitors share this heartfelt sentiment, including myself. In my strong personal opinion, I also believe that the ship is quite sentient, which permits a duality between her and her resident ethereal energies. I have had many profound spiritual experiences aboard her decks as well as a vault of captured phenomena in the form of audio, photographs, and video. Whether it be through my books, presentations, and/or interviews, I will continue to share the legendary story of the *Queen Mary,* the greatest ocean liner ever built.

Writing has always been a pastime that I've enjoyed. People gratify their souls when they write about something they're passionate about. In 2009, I achieved my dream of authoring my first book, *Field Guide to Southern California Hauntings.* Other books followed, including *The Haunted Queen of the Seas: The Living Legend of the* RMS *Queen Mary, Spirited Queen Mary: Her Haunted Legend,* RMS *Queen Mary: Voices from Her Voyages, San Diego's Most Haunted: The Historical Legacy and Paranormal Marvels of America's Finest City* and *Spirits of Rancho Buena Vista Adobe,* among others. I'm proud to say that all three of my books about the legendary RMS *Queen Mary* are popular sellers aboard the ship. It's an honor to share the *Queen Mary's* incredible narrative with people from all over the world.

Although I've been traditionally published, I've had an enduring desire to unveil my own self-publishing imprint, which has several future titles in the works relating to the afterlife, paranormal, and beyond. In November 2022, that vision came to fruition with the creation of Kayli Max Books, a meaningful ode to my beloved cats who crossed over the Rainbow Bridge. The first two manuscripts to be issued under this imprint include *Max and Kayli: Two Remarkable Felines Forever Imprinted on My Heart* and *The Afterlife Chronicles: Exploring the Connection between Life, Death, and Beyond,* which hit the #1 new release in six categories on Amazon. It's been an honor to be one of *Paranormal Underground Magazine's* writers and correspondents; to date, several of my articles have been published. The magazine is one of the leading authorities on perspectives relating to all areas of the paranormal and fringe topics.

Public speaking is another one of my side hustles. As with writing, talking about something that's valuable to people ignites a spark in one's creative muse. It's something that my soul yearns to do. I offer various types of presentations, including "The Afterlife Chronicles: Exploring the Connection Between Life, Death and Beyond," "Children and the Paranormal: Psychic Kids," "Ghostology," "History of Spiritualism," "Trends in Paranormal Research and Investigation," "Tulpas and Thought Projections: Implications in Paranormal Research," and others. To date, I have presented at many conferences as well as at business events, libraries, and universities. These events are always eye-opening as they give people the chance to meet like-minded individuals and learn from others.

It's been enjoyable to talk about my work as a paranormal researcher and experiencer in local and national television programming, documentary films, newspapers, magazines, and hundreds of radio shows/podcasts. My appearances include BIO's *My Ghost Story: Caught on Camera,* Travel Channel's *Ghost Stories* and *Famously Afraid, Paranormal Journeys, Good Morning San Diego, San Diego Living, KPBS Evening Edition, Channel 8 News Evening Edition,* and the groundbreaking documentary *All Around Us: Inside the Life of Psychic Medium Seth Michael.*

Although I have been interviewed in a myriad of media outlets, that is by no means a motivating factor for why I investigate the unknown. It's one of those aspects that can come with the territory, but it shouldn't be the main impetus for why someone researches the paranormal. If it is for some people, then they should take a hard look at themselves. This is a whole other discussion, but I firmly believe that the media/entertainment industry often exploits the spirit realm and otherworldly domains as if they are here mainly for our amusement. I hope that the future of paranormal inquiry can realign more with an academic approach as opposed to catering to the dramatic and sensational.

Or at least accommodate a healthy blend of education and entertainment.

My main motivation for studying the unknown is to learn the intricacies of our world and the universes around us. Perhaps, we're not meant to understand all the secrets of the universe and galaxies beyond, but that shouldn't stop us from trying to seek out their wonders. Being able to impart my knowledge of and experiences in the afterlife and paranormal research to those with a thirst to learn more about the vast field of the unknown is another motivating factor for me. The positive feedback from my audience inspires me in so many limitless ways. One of my most memorable experiences occurred after I finished one of my Escondido Public Library presentations on exploring the connection between life, death, and beyond. With a few tears in her eyes, a woman hugged and thanked me for opening up her awareness of life after death. She shared that one of her beloved family members had recently passed. There's a cosmic shift happening, allowing the living and spirit realms to connect more than ever before. I think this is one of the reasons why we're seeing an influx of those willing to talk about and commune with loved ones and pets who've crossed the veil.

I've loved connecting the world to the paranormal through radio shows and podcasts. Hosting a program like this enables us to associate with and learn from others. Over the years, I've been interviewed on numerous terrestrial and Internet-based programs throughout America and abroad. Hosted by WLTK-db station owner, Todd Bates, *Haunted Voices Radio* was one of the longest-running shows on the paranormal. It's currently on hiatus. In 2020, Todd invited me to co-host and executive produce this show. I somewhat knew that I would eventually come out with my own program and that came to fruition on October 8, 2020, when I debuted the *Afterlife Chronicles* on the same network. I was completely overjoyed when *Feedspot* selected my show as one of the top 25 programs on the afterlife. It's been enlightening to interview others who've had similar experiences with anomalous phenomena and have shared unique outlooks regarding the paranormal. After all, learning about the fringes of our universe is a collective endeavor.

It's been an honor to talk to an array of accomplished individuals, including doctors, medical personnel, near-death experiencers, psychic mediums, authors, and fellow paranormal researchers. I decided to go on my own and revamp my show to reach a wider audience. In addition to interests in ghosts, Bigfoot, Ufology, and other fringe topics, humanity is also craving goodness and positivity, characteristics that provided the main idea for my newly refurbished live show and podcast, *The Life Inspiration Project.* It's a unique platform that aims to spread encouragement, awareness, and inspiration through a variety of different subjects and disciplines, including afterlife/paranormal experiencers and researchers. As a result, the *Afterlife Chronicles* is not lost in the shuffle; instead, it has become intertwined with the larger scope of *The Life Inspiration Project*, set to debut in early 2024.

As a meticulous and no-nonsense paranormal researcher, I don't prefer to always utilize a cookie-cutter set-up on all my investigations and/or case studies. Of course, preliminary work consisting of adjunct research, client interviews, and environmental monitoring will occur across the board. I tend to select certain methodological practices that correlate with eyewitness reports and certain claims of anomalous activity. For example, if people have mostly encountered disembodied vocalizations as opposed to other types of phenomena, then it makes sense to initially center on audio experimentation and so forth. Depending on what's captured and documented, the team may move on to a more detailed investigative analysis or case study down the road.

Although I am well-versed in various paranormal research methodologies, I have a strong passion for audio experimentation, including Electronic Voice Phenomena and Instrumental Trans Communication. In addition to utilizing standard approaches and a discussion-based style, I often use what I call the "telepathic audio method." This entails intuitively/telepathically asking questions as opposed to voicing them out loud since there seems to be a telekinetic component to spiritual communication. As you're conducting the session, make sure you accurately note the questions/statements you telepathically ask/state and the times at which you do so. The team has collected some intriguing responses using this practice.

Over many years, I have amassed a large collection of spirit vocalizations from various recording devices. I approach my investigative work with a healthy blend of intuition, metaphysics, and science. In my humble opinion, one cannot give paranormal research justice without paying attention to the human body's senses and innate intuitive modalities. I examine the various influences of otherworldly occurrences and how they affect the overall activity and people's reactions to and perceptions of it. I often look at how the living world may cause and/or affect ghostly events. I carefully examine how psychokinesis (PK), infrasound, quantum theories of consciousness, tulpas/thought projections, and various aspects of our environment, etc., play into the formula of paranormal activity. Humans are more intertwined within our world and the worlds around us than we think.

Thoughtful researchers often look outside the box and critically think about the inner gears of anomalous phenomena. It's important to decipher how bias, suggestibility, and religious/familial backgrounds fit into the equation of exploring ghostly happenings. Furthermore, discovering how various scientific fields (physics, chemistry, physiology, psychology, etc.) affect spiritual occurrences should be a hallmark of paranormal study.

There is something bigger than just acquiring objective evidence from a paranormal investigation or case study. After reviewing various data from a project, I am now left with many questions: "What do we do, now?" "What can we offer the spiritual energies?" "Are they seeking our help and if so, how should we approach assisting them?" "Are they communicating with us to give a solid message or to help further our understanding of their existence?" I am now aware of the fact that there is a duty among all paranormal researchers besides just data collection and historical research, for example. It involves spending more time on the reasons behind our specific personal encounters with the afterlife and beyond. What truly matters is the rapport we build with these energies, in addition to the teachings and messages exchanged between the living and spirit worlds.

To be human is to not be without ego. It can be both beneficial and a hindrance to our everyday living. In my humble opinion, the ego needs to be placed on the shelf when conducting any type of work with the spiritual realms. Experiencing and/or studying the afterlife and beyond is best served when approached from a place of humility and understanding. Pretentious attitudes don't help advance field study, nor do they offer the respect this field deserves. Therefore, I consistently strive to approach my work with the Golden Rule in mind. During an investigation, you don't necessarily know whether you're encountering someone's deceased friend, pet, or relative. Treating them with dignity should be a hallmark trait of all fringe investigators. Of course, this appropriate conduct should carry over to clients and their properties, teammates, and the field of study at large.

I'm not convinced that the mortal realm is permitted to know the exact makeup and intricacies of the afterlife and beyond. Nonetheless, people are having beautiful, life-changing experiences with loved ones who've transitioned or they've come upon a being from another dimension that they want to learn more about. Researchers of the unknown are applying theories and experimenting with various methods to communicate with the spirit realm and other worlds. When you think about the concept of collective consciousness, sharing our experiences and findings only amplifies individual and communal awareness, insight, and understanding.

Many people, including myself, have found that their innate intuitive powers have strengthened as a result of exploring the paranormal. Every person has embedded intuition and psychic aptitudes. Some are just more mindful and open to them than others. Women are invaluable assets to the paranormal investigation process as they tend to be more attentive to their emotions and instincts. Through my fieldwork and profound personal experiences with deceased loved ones, my sentient abilities have interconnected with my everyday life. All I can say to others is that you'll know when this happens. It's a beautiful realization that will provide endless opportunities for everyday life and further learning about fringe territory and spiritual domains. In addition to utilizing these inherent gifts in regular life and paranormal study, I've also been able to intuitively assist law enforcement with accurate results on some missing person cases, specifically those involving young females.

For some reason, remote viewing comes to me very easily and I've been able to recall the exact locations and circumstances of missing, deceased persons. On more than one occasion, I would instantly get this all-knowing sense that a body was found only to look online and confirm my epiphany. The most recent occurred in 2022 when I was eating Lo Mein noodles. All of a sudden, I felt this rush sensation and said to myself, "They found her body." I then looked online and nothing had broken in. About an hour later, I decided to check on Google once again, and sure enough, news broke that the remains of this individual were found at exactly the same time I felt it. Maybe the art of remote viewing is accomplished by being one with the universe and each other, allowing us to tap into the collective truth.

Two of the most spiritual moments in my life occurred when I had to physically say goodbye to my beautiful cats, Max and Kayli. Max transitioned in 2016 and his sister, Kayli, did so in 2021. The eternal bond that the three of us shared (and still share) transcends beyond words. I have had magnificent encounters with their ethereal forms numerous times all of which have taught me more about what awaits us when it's our turn to join the afterlife. Perhaps, my passion for studying life after death has provided the ultimate foundation for why I'm able to have such significant interactions with those who've passed on.

Two days after Kayli's passing, I was able to slightly astral project in a dream state to connect with her. As of this writing, this phenomenon has occurred 22 times. When this happens, I can hold, see, and talk to her. It's difficult to find the right words to explain this, but these occurrences are not pure dreams, they are pure spiritual encounters. These dream visitations originate in my bedroom, and on my bed and the ambiance is an exact match to how my room looks when I go to sleep. The only difference is that I astrally project slightly out of my body to meet Kayli. I have never been able to do this with any other pet, beloved friend, or family member who's passed on. This is an exceptional gift that I've been granted; perhaps, Kayli is the one who assists me in achieving these extraordinary moments. If you're interested, you can read more about some of these experiences in my Amazon e-book, *Max and Kayli: Two Extraordinary Felines Forever Imprinted on My Heart*. As you can glean, I've become highly intrigued with the concept of astral projection and continue to research the topic. I'm somewhat convinced that it can serve as one of the gateways to connect with the afterlife and spirit worlds.

Delving into the fringe territories, studying otherworldly phenomena, and connecting with the spirit realms are all forms of celestial art. I believe that there is a nexus between various spiritual energies, cryptids, extraterrestrials, interdimensional beings, etc. As paranormal investigators, it's important to link the connections between objective and subjective experiences. It's imperative that we share our findings and theories relating to anomalous occurrences. We're finding that paranormal experiences often fall into a middle category, an area that blends scientific disciplines, metaphysics, intuition, and cosmic obscurities. As mortal beings, we may never find the "how" and "why" of ghostly happenings; perhaps, we're allowed to unlock the secrets of the universe once we transition to the ethereal kingdom. That, which motivates us to try and connect the dots between paranormal encounters and commune with those who have passed on from the mortal realm, remains one of the common denominators as to why we explore the unknown. This is a path that I'll explore well into eternity.

CHAPTER 2

WOMEN AND THE PARANORMAL

Are women at an advantage or disadvantage when it comes to this kind of research and field work? There are a plethora of articles discussing the differences between genders when it comes to things like belief, sensitivity, methodology, and processing of emotions, and no doubt women do have certain aspects of their behavior and physiology, as discussed in this chapter, that lend themselves to these fields of inquiry, but ultimately no matter the gender of the investigator or researcher, the goal is to get to the truth. The following articles examine the close links between women and the paranormal.

Why More Women Believe in the Paranormal Than Men

Marie D. Jones

There is widespread belief in the paranormal today, but according to Scott A. McGreal, MSc, women are more likely to be believers. In his article titled "Why Women Are More Likely to Believe in the Supernatural" for the March 23, 2022 *Psychology Today,* McGreal reports that women are more likely than men to believe in things like ghosts, psychic phenomena, and even astrology. He believes it has something to do with their greater levels of intuitive thinking and points to studies that back that up, but also that women tend to believe more in the hidden, unseen, or invisible things such as ghosts, while men believe more in physical things like Bigfoot and extraterrestrials.

He pointed to a study by Silva and Woody done in 2022 that notes "that gender differences mainly concerned phenomena related to spiritual or non-material forces rather than concrete material entities like Bigfoot or Extraterrestrials. Women also seemed more likely to believe in things like advanced ancient civilizations such as Atlantis, perhaps because of the spiritual associations. Men focused their beliefs more on material things. This same differentiation applies to how men are more likely to prefer rational, analytical thinking to women's more intuitive, empathetic thinking processes.

Outside of the United States, belief in the supernatural is more even

between the genders in places such as Canada, the United Kingdom, Finland, and Austria. Empathy made a difference in how genders cognitively processed the paranormal, with women having a greater propensity for empathizing and compassion for "reading" and understanding the mental states of others, which could give them the distinct edge when it comes to psychic abilities, mediumship, and communicating with spirits and the deceased.

Women and the Fear Response

"Doesn't this stuff scare you?"

It's a question we've all been asked at some point in our paranormal pursuit of the truth. Researching and investigating the unknown involves some aspects of fear by the very fact that it is the unknown we are dealing with, and we may or may not have any built-in perceptions or perspectives to use as reference points. This is subjective and experiential, with no "how-to" manual filled with die-hard facts to tell us what might happen and how to respond.

Yet all the women in these fields don't let fear stop them from truly desiring to understand unknown anomalies, whether it be ghosts or UFOs, psi abilities, or cryptids. Fear acts as a master motivator but also as a reminder to be awake and aware of one's surroundings during an investigation and to be mentally and intellectually ready and open to anything and everything when engaged in research.

Do women handle fear and stress, often a precursor to fear, differently than men? If so, how might this benefit their investigative pursuits?

In "Fear: Men vs. Women" for the May 25, 2018, *Fearless Psychology*, we are told that there are two main ways we humans deal with fear. Fight or flight or tend-and-befriend. "Until recently it was assumed that when faced with fearful situations, both men and women react the same way," the article states, citing that the tried-and-true process has always been fight or flight, which is triggered by any perception of a threat and causes a number of physiological effects in the body such as faster heart and breathing rates, muscle tension, and a rise in blood pressure. All of these get the body pumped and ready to either fight the source of danger or flee from it.

But researcher Shelley E. Taylor and her colleagues at UCLA proposed that women display another behavioral tendency – that of tend-and-befriend. This behavior is no doubt related to the inherent instinct of women to protect themselves and their children and relates to attachment, caregiving, and a rise in oxytocin and reproductive hormones associated with nurturing and strengthening social connections. "Tending involves nurturant activities designed to protect the self and offspring that promote safety and reduce distress; befriending is the creation and maintenance of social networks that may aid in this process," Taylor stated in "Why Men and Women Handle Stress Differently" for WebMD's *Women's Health Guide*.

This might explain why, when stressed out, men like to be left alone and women often seek the company of friends or give more attention to their children. Men also prefer to seek out escape activities or some kind of relaxing diversion when stressed, whereas women seek support or a way to process their emotional experiences and come up with ways to do something about it. While the fear and stress responses in both genders are similar, these differences can account for the slightly different ways men and women approach the paranormal worlds they research and investigate.

When it comes to doing paranormal research, many women tend to be more open, collaborative, and receptive enough to overcome their fears because their primitive ancestors had to be when dealing with challenges to themselves or the safety of their children. Women also tend to display more intuition and psychic abilities, which are receptive qualities, and appear to be better at embracing their surroundings and situations by looking for ways to lessen the fear factors that exist and feel safer where they are. Men can be, as well, but are more reactive than intuitive and usually respond with more active, dominant, and even aggressive behaviors.

To protect their families from a threat, each gender has its own way of dealing with a perceived fear and both are necessary and complimentary to keep the family unit safe. Yet feminine receptivity is a benefit for dealing with a mystery or something unknown that is being confronted because it allows for inner insight, wisdom, and knowledge to be a part of the response mechanism, rather than just left-brain, physical action.

Mothers who have that inbred protectiveness of their children can attest to using "mommy intuition" throughout the course of their day, and whether a woman is a mother or not, that talent exists.

Women may also be more perceptive to subtle energy shifts and changes than men because of their more developed sensitivities to their surroundings. That may allow women an edge in not only perceiving paranormal anomalies but in sensing how to respond to them.

Surprisingly, studies have shown that women actually display more fear responses than men towards all kinds of situational things such as fear of flying, darkness, heights, or enclosed spaces, and also things they find to be repulsive, gross, and disgusting, such as spiders, snakes, insects, and rats. Yet women are just as brave at entering a potentially haunted location that is dark, closed off, claustrophobic, and possibly riddled with rats and cockroaches. In general, neither gender necessarily loves rats and enclosed spaces, but we often stereotype women specifically as weak, easily scared, and meek, especially when there's a spider or rat involved.

It's been said many times that women are more compassionate and understanding toward the living and this compassion and empathy may translate to how they approach the spirits of the dead or any unknown anomalous presence, and perhaps it's that befriending spirit in women, pun intended, that helps them feel more comfortable and at home around the unknown. When researching ghosts, cryptids, and aliens, maybe women have the uncanny ability to create some level of connectivity to these other living things, even if they cannot communicate with them in a more literal sense. Not saying that men don't do this, too, but the art of connection is a right-brain art perfected by the female gender and could inspire more trust and openness on both sides of the paranormal equation.

Many people may think that women are not as brave as men when it comes to paranormal adventures. Some women who participate in paranormal fields find other women less supportive than men. While this is not across the board, we can't fail to note that other women sometimes cringe at the very thought of venturing down the road of investigating hauntings, Bigfoot, UFOs, and any other number of unusual subjects in that realm and find it strange or off-putting if other women do enjoy exploring these things; which makes women who participate in the "fringe" individuals who possess a lot of courage to go against societal expectations about what is "correct" for a woman to participate in or enjoy as a hobby or profession. The belief that women are expected to avoid spooky or dangerous things is interesting, considering there are studies that consistently show women faring better in situations that are dire, including famine, disaster, and disease. It is built into women to take on "all the things" even if society may ignore this factor.

We often forget that women are just as strong, capable, and bold as men are, and that applies even when it comes to spooky things like investigating a UFO abduction or talking with a terrified poltergeist victim. Men bring so much of their own gifts to the table, but women may be more able to get witnesses and experiencers to feel comfortable and open up, simply because they are more social, empathetic, and nurturing. They bring a host of their own inherent gifts to the same table even when confronted with something that, at first appearance, seems frightening or uncertain. They don't back away or go off running and screaming (most of the time!), but rather seek to "tend" to the issue at hand and often with a nurturing touch, and possibly even find a way to connect or "befriend" it.

Then again, maybe they just like to "feel the fear and do it anyway."

Are Women More Intuitive & Sensitive To The Paranormal Than Men?

Denise A. Agnew

Women's intuition.

Whenever the term is used, it is often with a roll of the eyes and a hint of snideness or disbelief.

It's often portrayed in movies, television, and books as a veiled slight. Some men use the term women's intuition as a convenient way to brush off a woman's beliefs and insult female intelligence. Women will even use the term to explain to others why they decided to do something they can't quantify with "logic" or explain in scientific terms.

Yet women's intuition is really only a segment of a bigger overall question.

Are women more intuitive and perhaps more sensitive to the paranormal?

Many times, in families, when a paranormal investigation team is called in, the wife and/or daughter is the one having experiences while the men in the household don't have anomalous encounters or don't acknowledge what they are experiencing could be paranormal.

Despite varying obstacles and belief systems, women continue to report paranormal occurrences more frequently than men. Is it purely a talent women have? Are women's brains that different? There are numerous factors to consider when asking this question.

Some women will denigrate another woman's intuition or paranormal experiences because it avoids the controversy altogether. If the woman is a skeptic overall, she might ignore her own abilities or another woman's intuitive, psychic, or otherwise paranormal encounters. If a woman is a skeptical believer, she might acknowledge that the paranormal and intuition exist but remain open to the idea that not everything that can't be explained has paranormal origins.

Cultural belief systems have a big influence on what people believe or don't believe and what they will acknowledge out loud. In some religious circles, it is forbidden to report paranormal experiences and/or abilities or acknowledge their existence.

Yet there is one cultural influence that is so huge it can't be ignored. The last ten to fifteen years of reality television paranormal shows have gone a long way toward opening minds and making anything paranormal more open and acceptable to more people. People may have unrealistic expectations of what paranormal investigations are like if all they've seen or experienced is a reality television version. Women who join or have founded paranormal investigation teams sometimes approach investigations differently than a team comprised of all or mostly men. Women are more likely to acknowledge and utilize the abilities of psychics and mediums on their team. (I am a member of an all-women team where two of us are mediums and the other is definitely psychic. We still consider ourselves skeptical believers.)

This isn't to say that all women who utilize their intuition believe in the paranormal. After all, they can label the experience any way they wish. Women's intuition is often considered harmless whereas the paranormal breeds complications, especially if the woman isn't supported by family or friends when she tells them about her experiences. Whether she will suppress her intuition or paranormal encounters regardless of people's opinions and approval relies entirely on her individual personality. Deciding to emerge as a believer in the paranormal is a risk some will take, and others won't.

Fear is a huge motivator on whether people might acknowledge and act on their intuition and paranormal beliefs. Life, they believe, is simpler without the complications. They think if they ignore the esoteric it will go away. Sometimes it does. Sometimes it refuses to be ignored.

For some people, the unknown isn't always scary. They are willing to say, "I don't know" and leave it at that without fear or maybe even a desire to find out the answer. For some the unknown is exciting and they will go to great lengths to find the answers. They may or may not be comfortable with never finding the answers, but they trudge on, nonetheless. The journey is just as important as the end.

Women often prefer and utilize intuition to make decisions even if they don't realize that is what they are using to make the decisions. Even if society doesn't say it out loud, women are expected to utilize their empathic abilities to understand situations and people with greater depth and that expectation alone gives them more freedom to utilize it if they choose. Men are often socialized in that it is more acceptable to think with an analytical process, and even if they use their intuition to great advantage, they are less likely to acknowledge or even understand if they are using it. Women are more likely to believe that intuitive and paranormal experiences are far more complicated than any one single psychological factor or belief system.

Ask many cops (who even at the time of this publication are mostly men) if their intuition has saved their bacon and they will say, "Yes." Many of them will say they believe that during the full moon, crazy things happen on the streets.

What does science have to say about how men and women differ in their beliefs about intuition and the paranormal? Well, it's complicated. It depends on who you talk to. The general consensus seems to be that science doesn't fully understand why women generally believe in intuition and the paranormal more than men or why women might be more intuitively inclined. They have theories, though.

The Association For Psychological Science suggested in January 2011 that you should trust your gut, but only sometimes. Their study said, "Hunch decisions can either be an ally or lead to costly and dangerous mistakes." According to them the viability of the advice people receive from their gut telling them what to do could come from being aware of their body's response. In their study, people were monitored for their heart rates during a card game. Some people's "gut feelings" offered them great hunches while other people's bodies told them the wrong thing. The study found a link between gut feelings and utilizing accurate decision-making that came down to people who were in tune with their heartbeat. Those who could learn to listen to their heartbeat/heart rate were more likely to win card games. Others didn't pay attention to how their heart reacted and therefore tended to lose more often. The study postulated that physiology has more to do with intuition than people think.

While I found the idea of this study interesting, I can only say that if that's the way my intuition works, it certainly isn't a conscious effort on my part to pay attention to my heartbeat and act on a clue it might give me.

Could there be something physiologically with women that makes it more likely they would note and then act on their intuition?

Scientists in Spain from the University of Granada asserted that hormones in the womb have something to do with it. A lower dose of testosterone before birth could cause someone to be more intuitive in adulthood. They showed in the study that women who were exposed to higher levels of testosterone tended to be less intuitive and may rely more on what is called reflexive rational analysis. Researchers gave volunteers a cognitive reflection test, which is supposed to reveal whether you're more intuitive or analytical. In this study, they say those who got incorrect answers tended to rely more on intuition and less on analysis. This study was published in the journal *Psychoneuroendocrinology* in May 2014.

In my personal opinion, I don't think this is one hundred percent correct that people who use intuition are always consistently "wrong." I spent a lot of my life ignoring my instincts about people and situations (especially when I was a kid), and then boom...later I'd find out I should've gone with my first instinct because the first instinct was spot on. As an adult, I've learned to rely more on my intuition to get the "right" answer.

I have a perfect example of when I "guessed" based on intuition and got two math problems right that I shouldn't have. As a kid, I struggled constantly with math. The teachers didn't understand it, and they didn't know how to help me. This was way before anyone realized there is a learning disability (dyscalculia) that causes varying degrees of difficulty with math/number ability and sometimes other aspects of a person's life.

I did very well in all of my classes as long as they had nothing to do with math or numbers of any kind. For example, I disliked my chemistry class with a passion but loved my English literature. I barely passed chemistry...it was the math within the class. Something that should've given me trouble, but I seemed to understand enough to get a B in class was Algebra. Go figure!

When I was fourteen the school gave me a test trying to decipher my problem. This test consisted of a huge variety of questions, including subjects I hadn't taken in school. The last two questions they asked dealt with trigonometry and calculus, neither of which I had taken. I told them I didn't know the answers. They asked me to guess. I was frustrated at that point, so I just flipped out the answers to both questions immediately after they asked them once more. They were astonished. I'd answered both questions correctly.

They told my mother that she had a very smart daughter but I was an enigma. I was, they said, college-level comprehension of English, vocabulary, comprehension, and many other subjects. When it came to math, I was fourth-grade level or below with the exception of the trigonometry and calculus questions I shouldn't have comprehended at all. I think, just perhaps, that intuition gave me the answers to the calculus and trig questions.

Women's intuitive ability might even go back to the cave. Women have traditionally been primary caregivers for children, and the powerful drive to first survive and then protect those children could have created an extraordinary depth of instincts and intuition. Because humans are animals, we're hardwired with instincts that hopefully help us survive (hence the fight, flight, freeze, fawn response). At the same time, some of these responses can be learned from life experiences, especially at the time we are children, and what we learn during those experiences assists us in "surviving" a situation in the future.

Taking survival in mind, women are socialized from birth to be afraid of the male animal. This isn't a myth, but it's also something women learn, to various degrees, from the time they are children. Keep an eye peeled, pay attention to your surroundings, and use your instincts to beware of danger. Many times, utilizing instinct and intuition along with socialization has saved a woman's life.

I realized only a year ago that my number one go-to survival instinct is to fawn. When I look at childhood trauma it makes perfect sense. Does that make me more intuitive as a woman? Very possibly, but I'm guessing there is many a man who does the same thing I do to survive and relies on his intuition as a part of it. Survival instincts are more than how to escape a bear or a person wielding a knife. They're how we survive social/personal interactions and sometimes even fuel a personal desire to help others.

Many years ago, I worked at two different universities back-to-back. In each of those jobs I was a front-line person who interacted with dozens of people every day by telephone, walk-ins, and later by appointment as an admissions advisor. Many times, I assisted people experiencing intense emotions, not all of them good. Some people were angry, some were dealing with extreme upset of various kinds, i.e., crying, yelling, you name it. And in a few cases, they were suffering from schizophrenia, paranoia, or other mental illness. I was very good at devising comfort, ideas, solutions, and resolutions to a high number of these people's issues. Over time I became skilled at knowing how, what, and where to say and do just the right thing to bring about good outcomes. In the case of one student with paranoid schizophrenia, I was able to talk him down in a situation that was fraught with all sorts of possibilities, some of them very unpleasant. I could say that intuition had a part in it.

These days I also utilize my intuition heavily. As a creativity coach, I tap into what is going on with that particular client. They might have writer's block, but not everyone's writer's block is caused by the same thing. It's up to me to intuit and discover the truth, some of it hidden in the creative individual's psyche. It's like a mental archaeological expedition.

As an intuitive/oracle card reader, I've discovered I'm able to understand, with very little interaction with a person, their thoughts, feelings, needs, beliefs, and problems. The accuracy can be astounding to me and the person receiving the reading. As a medium, I have been able to contact those in spirit and relay information to the client that I could not have known any other way. This includes contacting a large number of those in spirit who committed suicide or were murdered.

Always learning something new broadens the brain's ability to stay cognitively healthy. The same goes for intuition. Women who utilize their intuition regularly are exercising their ability to harness it to their benefit, and the more often they "train" themselves to use this intuition, the better results they will achieve. Men who take the plunge and trust their intuition often see equal success with their hunches even if they choose not to acknowledge it out loud. Intuition, whether for men or women, is sometimes a matter of practice making perfect. As with all abilities, some people will charge out of the gate with more talent in it, but this ability is something that anyone can expand given his or her willingness to do so.

More recent conjecture could lead one to believe that it is just that simple...belief is a huge factor in whether intuition works for someone, regardless of whether they are a man or woman. After all, you are far more likely to succeed at something if you believe you can. If you believe you can't succeed, the chances that you won't are more likely.

As we can see, the question of whether women are more intuitive and more sensitive to the paranormal isn't cut and dried.

There's an episode of one of my favorite shows, *The X-Files*, that I vibe with when it comes to intuition and psychic abilities. In the episode called, "Clyde Bruckman's Final Repose," Mulder relentlessly asks reluctant psychic Bruckman how he knows what he knows. The conversation goes like this:

MULDER: How are you receiving this information about the body's location?

CLYDE BRUCKMAN: How should I know?

MULDER: I mean, are you seeing it in a vision or is it a... sensation? How do you know where to go?

CLYDE BRUCKMAN: I just know.

MULDER: But how do you know?

CLYDE BRUCKMAN: I don't know!

Let's just say I've had similar conversations before.

What have these experiences taught me? Intuition and the paranormal are like the vastness of space, which we may never understand. Or, perhaps in the afterlife, all the answers lie there. I'll find out when I arrive there, and so will everyone else. In the meantime, it's wise to keep searching for answers, use your intuition, keep exploring, and never give up.

How Women's Grief & Loss Influence Their Approaches To Paranormal Research

Nicole Strickland

Many people are introduced to the paranormal after they've endured an NDE (near-death experience) or the loss of a loved one. Or maybe they had a profound encounter with another ghost or spirit, which influenced their desire to delve into the fringe territories. These people become more interested in the age-old question of what happens to us when we die and transition from this plane to the next. They become more in tune with their natural intuitive talents and desire to use them to communicate with deceased loved ones or other beings. In a sense, dealing with the grief and loss process from a recent death can commence a lifelong desire to investigate and research paranormal phenomena.

The grieving process is universal; no matter your religion, culture, or demographic, every single person has experienced the anguish of losing a loved one or treasured pet. Those delving into paranormal research, as well as caregivers, nurses, doctors, and first responders, have been given a front-row seat to the dying process. The stories that they share regarding NDEs and deathbed visitations as well as witnessing one's last mortal breath add to the collective interest in how life continues after physical death.

There are various stages of grief, with no exact order as to how one experiences them; however, it's typical to encounter them in sequence. They help us come to terms with what we are feeling after someone close to us passes away. Women tend to manage grief and loss differently than men, which can influence how they investigate anomalous phenomena and further connect with the spirit realms.

It's not surprising that females are more apt to share their emotions and openly express the feelings they're enduring after losing someone. As such, women will acquire support whether it be through group or individual sessions with therapists. This, in turn, allows them to effectively process the stages of grief as opposed to bottling them inside and causing ensuing emotional distress.

Many women automatically utilize their innate intuition and channeling techniques when communicating with spiritual beings. Although less concrete, the results from this type of humanistic approach can be more convincing as they impact our emotions. Since some individuals only rely on tangible, scientific data of anomalous phenomena, we know that this can be a disadvantage for many female researchers who mainly utilize intrinsic psychic and sensitive abilities.

Women need to openly share their sentient aptitudes and profound encounters with spirit as a way to break through this roadblock and create a seamless pathway to understanding and accepting metaphysical approaches. After all, research and experience combined highly suggest the telepathic link between our mortal world, the afterlife, and other dimensions. Not only that but the telepathic link women have with other paranormal investigators. Intelligent ethereal energies will naturally gravitate to communing with female researchers who are openly intuitive. Of course, this rapport can also provide a better understanding of a location's historical tapestry and paranormal activity.

Women tend to be similar in how they grieve the loss of a loved one; as such, they often share the sadness and dejection they face as a result of losing someone close to them, creating even more of a union between other females. This bond can influence how women approach their work as paranormal researchers in many ways. It can also lead to bias and the power of suggestion where they sense a fellow researcher's emotional grief, which can conflict with the energy they sense from the spirit world. Authentic encounters with the afterlife and beyond are often achieved from the heart. Female investigators will typically empathize with a fellow teammate who's endured the heartache from loss; thus, providing a natural foundation for communing with ethereal beings.

Whether it's a private residence, business, or notable historical location, it's important to know that we may come across and communicate with someone's father, mother, brother, sister, son, daughter, etc. Paranormal researchers should always keep the Golden Rule at the forefront and be respectful and reverent to the spiritual energies they come across. Since women are able to tap into their emotional compass, they are capable of sympathizing with and understanding a spiritual being's situation. For example, let's say that an earthbound (ghost) passed away after a traumatic death and doesn't know that he or she has passed away. Those, including women, who are able to emotionally identify with an entity's predicament can be better equipped to help facilitate his or her healing.

Being open to their sixth sense and inherent sensitivity may permit women and men to get in touch with the ethereal kingdom through bereavement hallucinations, dream visitations, and synchronicity. A griever, via a hallucinatory condition, sees, feels, or hears the individual(s) who've passed on. When this happens, the mourner may sense these energies and learn key information about them. This type of pathological grief has been recommended as a new classification in psychiatry's DSM-5 diagnostic handbook. Neuroscientists have explored the underlying brain compositions and operations that may shed light on the reasons for these grief hallucinations.

Typically, these encounters are comforting and make the living feel as though they haven't endured any loss. These experiences are more common with those we personally knew and loved but can also extend to the ethereal energies we meet during paranormal investigations or case studies. What's interesting to consider is whether these hallucinations have any paranormal and/or spiritual origin. Do living individuals produce these hallucinations out of intense grief, or do the spirits of our dearly departed sense our sadness and, as a result, manifest to our senses? It may be a combination, and it is definitely a topic that warrants further research.

Examined by Carl Jung, synchronicity includes a simultaneous series of events that are extensively related without having a recognizable underlying connection. They are thought to be meaningful coincidences in that they occur with no fundamental relationship while at the same time holding some sort of significance. Synchronicity occurs at precise moments when we need to hear spiritual messages being imparted to us. It can also help allay one's sadness during the grieving process.

When discussing paranormal phenomena, Jung emphasized that this notion directly paralleled concepts such as the relativity theory and quantum mechanics. He further asserted that synchronicity serves the role of helping people shift from egocentric thinking toward higher consciousness or wholeness – the doorway to authentically connecting with the spiritual domains. With a natural aptitude for accessing intuition and channeling skills, women are often the frontrunners in experiencing synchronistic events further leading to a connection with the other side.

Almost everyone has dreamed of a departed loved one or beloved pet. In fact, it's very common to receive messages from the spirit world during this unconscious state as our inhibitions and preoccupations are reduced. The veil between the living realm and the afterlife is at its thinnest when we sleep. Both men and women can have spirit encounters during sleep; however, it may be more common in women since they are more in touch with their emotions, feelings, and intuitive psyches. Many female paranormal investigators have reported dream encounters with ethereal energies they've come across during investigations or case studies of haunted locations.

Dream visitations are some of the most influential methods a spiritual being can use when communicating with the living. The Society for Psychical Research (SPR) began the scientific study of these telepathic dreams; in 1886, it published *Phantasms of the Living*, which highlighted and analyzed numerous unique cases of documented extrasensory dream encounters. The authors found that both the agent and recipient were somehow interconnected.

Louisa Rhine, wife, and associate of modern experimental parapsychologist Joseph Banks Rhine amassed more than 10,000 spontaneous events of possible psi experiences (psychic phenomena), which became the subjects of many articles and books. In her conclusive review, Rhine deduced that 65% of all extrasensory perception (ESP) encounters occurred within dreams, a statistic that's been approved by various smaller-scale inquiries (Strickland 2023, 33-34).

Being in touch with one's emotions and innate sentient abilities provides a healthy curiosity and desire to explore paranormal phenomena – and of course, to further connect with those who've walked the land before us. Perhaps, blending both metaphysics with scientific inquiries can provide a conduit to an intricate understanding of life after death and anomalous phenomena. Women are not to be underestimated in the field of exploring the peripheries of unexplainable occurrences. Individually, and as a team, they will continue to provide insight into and shed light on the mysteries of the unknown.

Women and the History of Spiritualism

Nicole Strickland

The belief in life after death goes back thousands of years. Some individuals hold that a person's soul reincarnates with no prior memory of his or her previous life. Certain creeds feel that the deceased may travel to a certain place of existence, one that God decides based on how that person lived his or her life. While there are differing views on exactly what the afterlife entails, one aspect among many cultures remains consistent: the universal belief in eternal life.

The Bible holds hundreds of mentions of angelic communication with living people. Individuals from around the globe contemplate what happens to the soul after physical death. The idea of the hereafter was alluded to in well-known written works of Descartes, Homer, Plato, and many others; this was the basis for Dante Alighieri's *The Divine Comedy,* an Italian long-narrative poem written in 1320. Many of the world's most influential artists and writers have been inspired by what happens to us when we pass on.

One cannot explore modern-day paranormal research without reading, or at least, hearing about the influential era of Spiritualism, where approximately four million to eleven million people identified as Spiritualists in the late 19th century. The once-trendy fad commenced in the 1840s in upstate New York, home to preceding religious movements that sprouted during the Second Great Awakening where secular refurbishment took place. Those who embraced Spiritualism felt that they had control of their own salvation. Communicating with spirits provided a foundation of awareness for an individual soul's destiny.

By the 1840s, the views and practices of 18th-century Australian healer, Franz Anton Mesmer, infiltrated the United States. Mesmer proposed that all things in the universe were controlled by a "magnetic fluid" that could become ill if it experienced any imbalance. To combat this problem, Mesmer waved his hands over a patient's body, thereby initiating a spellbinding, hypnotic state, which permitted him to harmonize the magnetic energy and reestablish desired health.

18th-century Swedish philosopher, Emanuel Swedenborg, was another influencer of the times. He believed in an afterlife having three heavens, three hells, and a domain of spirits, a provisional place that everyone traveled to upon physical death. In his book *Heaven and Hell*, he asserts that he was allowed to endure death and awaken in spirit, with angels accompanying him in the process. It was after this poignant encounter that he was able to perceive the spiritual world and understand what happens to the soul after death, in many cases convincing people of his ability to communicate with the dead.

With an arsenal of appeal, Spiritualism influenced credulous folks all the way to those possessing philosophical, and scientific aptitudes. As its main claim to fame, Spiritualism deemed that spirits were more advanced than humans and that contacting them was feasible. Alongside the advancement of science and technology during the Victorian period, people were also susceptible to supernatural occurrences and occult practices.

The movement enticed some of the greatest thinkers of the time, such as physicists Marie and Pierre Curie, evolutionary biologist Alfred Russel Wallace, *Sherlock Holmes* creator Arthur Conan Doyle, and chemist and fellow physicist William Crookes, to name a few. These great minds adhered to the notion that scientific methods were the keys to proving spiritual existence. The afterlife, according to those who followed this practice, was seen, not as an end to one's reality but as one where spiritual beings could evolve. Skeptics and believers alike shared the compelling obsession to delve deep within its vaults.

Those following Spiritualist creeds connect with the deceased mainly through the use of a psychic medium, an individual believed to possess the skills to contact the afterlife. Some chose to work in a trance-like state, whereas others claimed to be the means whereby psychokinetic (PK) energy was created by the human mind. Spiritualists declare that it's highly feasible for the living to communicate with the spirits of deceased people. They also feel that spirit channelers are innately gifted to facilitate such interaction, even though anyone can learn to do so with practice and exposure. Followers felt that astral beings were capable of perfection as they moved through higher planes in the hereafter. Those residing in the celestial domain can offer advice and knowledge on moral and ethical issues.

Many feminists of that era were attracted to Spiritualism as it gave them a public voice in the area of communicating with spiritual beings. According to Barbara Weisberg in her book *Talking to the Dead: Kate and Maggie Fox and the Rise of Spiritualism,* female psychic mediums reigned over the eerie spiritual manifestations in the parlor while men typically showcased more of a philosophic tendency on paper. Women were seen more as woo-woo dreamers and men were depicted as logical, conscious lecturers (2004, 146). As we know, these are traits still seen in today's arena of metaphysical and paranormal practices.

Spiritualism enabled women to take up new social roles as psychic mediums and public speakers. By embracing their spiritual desires, they were able to be somewhat independent and feel comfortable articulating their viewpoints. Many women found the premise of Spiritualism to be quite therapeutic as it provided a conduit, through which they could communicate with departed family members and children. Additionally, the movement also had a direct effect on women's suffrage and advocating for the equality of sexes.

Discussion on women's rights to vote had origins dating back to the early 1800s. During the blossoming of the Spiritualist movement, Seneca Falls held the first women's rights convention advocating for the social, civil, and religious rights of adult females. In a statewide California election on October 10, 1911, about 250,000 men voted on the suffrage for women amendment to the State constitution and it was approved by just over 3,500 votes. The Golden State became the sixth state in the United States to concede this right to women. This accomplishment was in part due to the influence Spiritualism had on women as recognizable members of society.

The séance was the preferred choice of those wishing to communicate with the deceased during the Spiritualist movement. During a séance, a psychic medium acted as a spirit channeler while the rest of the sitters surrounded a table. Typically held in a darkened space, the session commenced with a hymn as a way to set a peaceful atmosphere. The medium would then receive and translate spirit messages and distribute them to members of the audience. For those who desired more concrete proof of ethereal contact, channelers would turn to apported items or those allegedly sent from the afterlife. Some of these objects included jewelry, trinkets, flowers, or handkerchiefs.

Audiences accepted women in their trance-like states while conducting group séances. Female psychic mediums of this era were able to travel and appear on lecture circuits discussing topics related to spirituality. Some of the notable female Spiritualists included Cora L. V. Scott, Ascha W. Sprague, Frances Ann Conant, Nettie Colburn Maynard, Charlotte Beebe Wilbour, Emma Hardinge Britten, Amanda Britt Spence, Eliza W. Farnham, Mrs. Laura Cuppy Smith, Laura de Force Gordon, and Elizabeth Lowe Watson.

Famous women of the time who followed the Spiritualist doctrine included Queen Victoria and Mary Todd Lincoln. Grieving over the 1861 demise of her husband, Prince Albert, Queen Victoria became intrigued with the movement. She often wore all-black clothing and adorned mourning jewelry housing photos of Albert and strands of his hair. She also tried to get in touch with his spirit; 13-year-old psychic medium Robert James Lees believed that Albert had a message for his wife. Thus, Victoria asked for a séance with the teenager where he revealed private information that only she knew. Mary Todd Lincoln dipped her toes in Spiritualism after her son Willie passed away from typhoid fever. In addition to trying to communicate with her departed husband, President Abraham Lincoln, she held and then hosted her own séances.

Female psychic mediums during the Victorian period were usually young, single, Caucasian, and of the Protestant religion. Hailing from

New York and New England, they maintained broad-minded views on various civil rights topics. While Spiritualism afforded women opportunities to become influential members of society, they were often vilified and deemed dishonest and fraudulent. The movement was instrumental in exposing deceitful behavior, whether it be fake ectoplasm, falsified photographs of the dead, or other types of trickery used in séances.

The idea of Ectoplasm became a hot topic of discussion and oftentimes, swayed people into believing that they contacted a spirit; that is, until debunkers exposed its deceptive origins. It was Nobel laureate and French physiologist Charles Richet who initially invented the term, which has made its rounds in popular films such as *Ghostbusters*. It was considered to be a glutinous material that materialized from a psychic medium's body, typically from the ears only to come to rest in fat coils on the shoulders. An even more macabre manifestation occurred when this viscous substance was said to produce embryonic limbs and heads that would resemble a spiritual stillbirth from a woman's genital area. Ectoplasm was usually fashioned out of cheesecloth, gauze, or other textiles.

As Spiritualism reached its height in popularity, psychic mediums' aptitudes continued to diversify and progress. Some women were purportedly able to move objects whereas others preferred to channel energy through a living being or spiritual entity. In the late 1880s, some channelers allegedly produced full-body apparitions who supposedly conversed with the audience. The authenticity of psychic mediums declined as these manifestations became more ostentatious in nature. Well-known scientists and groups of debunkers began to scrutinize the séances and often found evidence of fraud.

Although Spiritualism appealed to both men and women, its origins began with the latter on March 31, 1848, in the town of Hydesville, New York. Sisters, fourteen-year-old Margaretta "Maggie" Fox along with eleven-year-old Catherine persuaded some of their neighbors that the eerie knocking and tapping sounds in their home emanated from the afterlife. They allegedly communicated with the spirit of a peddler who was killed in their farmhouse five years prior. Residents searched the family's cellar and found hair strands and possible bone fragments. Not long after, this little area bordering the south shore of Lake Ontario became fixated on the alleged paranormal phenomena.

Seemingly, each night as bedtime approached, the Fox sisters claimed that they heard a succession of these noises on the walls and furniture. With the presence of a skeptical neighbor, the girls sat together on their bed while their mother, Margaret, commenced the exposition.

"Now count five," Margaret demanded as five thuds were heard.

"Count fifteen," she said right after.

Thirty-three rapping sounds occurred after she asked the entity to relay the neighbor's age. She continued to say, "If you are an injured spirit, manifest it by three raps." And it apparently responded.

After some time, Kate and Margaret were sent to live in Rochester, New York with their older sister, Leah Fox Fish. That area buzzed with religious reform as Mormonism and Millerism sprouted in New York State's Finger Lakes region. Community spear headers Isaac and Amy Post were influenced by the Fox sisters' account and the fact that Leah was also known as a psychic medium. Isaac and Amy invited the sisters to their home to see if they could entice the spirits to communicate. Soon after, 400 people came to see the siblings in a banquet room the Posts rented. In a private chamber, Kate and Margaret were disrobed and inspected by a group of skeptics, who found no concrete evidence of fakery.

Combining the ideologies of both Mesmer and Swedenborg, 19th-century clairvoyant Andrew Jackson Davis, invited Kate and Margaret to his residence in New York City to experience their psychic medium aptitudes. The Fox sisters soon embarked on a professional tour to showcase their mediumship abilities, thus securing a spot as three of Spiritualism's most influential people. They rented a suite at Manhattan's Barnum's Hotel on the corner of Broadway and Maiden Lane. For the price of one dollar, they performed their séances in the establishment's parlor at 10 a.m., 5 p.m., and 8 p.m., with as many as thirty attendees, gathered around a large table. Notable members of the New York Society attended these sittings. While Leah sojourned in New York, Kate and Maggie traveled to other cities, including Cleveland, Cincinnati, Columbus, St. Louis, Washington D.C., and Philadelphia.

Maggie ended up dating and subsequently marrying explorer Elisha Kent Kane. He convinced her to retire from conducting séances and enroll in school at his request. After his passing in 1857, she converted to Catholicism and while mourning his untimely death, she became an alcoholic and promised to abandon Spiritualism. Kate wed a devout Spiritualist and continually advanced her psychic medium abilities. Her business flourished both during and subsequent to the Civil War when it not only brought two million new followers to Spiritualism but permitted surviving family members to find comfort while grieving the loss of their loved one(s). She transcribed messages from the afterlife in extraordinary ways, such as relaying two synchronous communications at the same time or writing one while saying the other. The notoriety and expectations placed upon her eventually took their toll and she, too, took to the bottle just like her sister Maggie.

In light of her appearance at the New York Academy of Music on October 21, 1888, the *New York World* published an interview with Margaret Fox where she publicly condemned the notion of Spiritualism. Receiving a substantial sum of $1,500, she was angered at her older sister Leah and other foremost Spiritualists who overtly reprimanded Kate's alcoholism and alleged inability to take care of her two young children.

"My sister Katie and myself were very young children when this horrible deception began," Maggie said.

"At night when we went to bed, we used to tie an apple on a string and move the string up and down, causing the apple to bump on the floor, or we would drop the apple on the floor, making a strange noise every time it would rebound," she continued to relay.

"A great many people when they hear the rapping imagine at once that the spirits are touching them," she said. "It is a very common delusion. Some very wealthy people came to see me some years ago when I lived on 42nd Street and I did some rapping for them. I made the spirit rap on the chair and one of the ladies cried out, 'I feel the spirit tapping me on the shoulder.' Of course, that was pure imagination" (Abbott, 2012).

Right before she left the stage, Margaret thanked God that she was able to denounce and further expose the fraud. According to the press, this occasion proved to be "a death blow" to Spiritualism causing its followers to fervently take sides. While some came to her defense, others asserted that Margaret's decision to abandon the movement was avaricious in nature since she was unable to be financially profitable as a psychic medium.

Regardless of the motive, Margaret recanted her confession just twelve months later, claiming that her spirit guides implored her to do so. This only confounded the situation, provoking more repugnance from staunch Spiritualists. Under the alias of Mrs. Spencer, Margaret disclosed various illusions that psychic mediums utilized, such as how they used their teeth or feet to inscribe messages on blank slates. Sadly, she never reunited with Leah who passed away in 1890. Alcohol abuse eventually claimed Kate's life two years later with Margaret joining her sisters in the afterlife in March 1893. It was that year when Spiritualists unveiled the National Spiritualist Association, known today as the National Spiritualist Association of Churches.

The Fox sisters were gauged by many qualified scientists and skeptics alike after claiming they could communicate with spirits. Physician E.P. Longworthy appraised Kate and Margaret and took note of how the knockings or raps usually came from under their feet or when their dresses touched the table. He, therefore, determined that they caused the sounds. Reverend John M. Austin later asserted that the noises could be triggered by cracking joints in the toes, with Reverend D. Potts demonstrating this to an inquisitive audience.

However, between 1871 and 1874, noted physicist William Crookes determined an authentic origin of the rapping noises even though some mediums he examined were exposed as frauds. The smoking gun came to fruition in 1851 as Mrs. Norman Culver, a relative of the Fox family, openly disclosed via a signed affidavit that she had helped Kate and Margaret during their sittings by touching them to signify when to cause the rapping sounds. Additionally, she also admitted that the sisters told her how they made the sounds: by cracking their toes while using their ankles and knees.

There is no doubt that the Fox sisters initiated the main force that drove Spiritualism to new heights; thus, establishing it as a social phenomenon. Those succeeding in their path, many of them female, influenced women's positions in society and new viewpoints related to spiritual existence. People throughout the United States and Europe held séances and supported methods of automatic writing and spirit photography as a way to speak to the departed. With a palpable allure for nearly 40 years, Spiritualism comprised a contradictory mix of truth and fraud and arguably inspired the framework whereby paranormal research is practiced today. Spiritualist churches still exist, especially in Canada, the United Kingdom, and the United States.

The Spiritualist movement created the need for science-based paranormal research and investigation. Its claims of life after death virtually crafted the desire to scientifically study what goes on after the human body ceases to function. As many people during the Victorian era were cited for fraudulence, the movement caused those to objectively look at the practices of Spiritualists and develop a gold standard for honest, constructive examination of paranormal events. This led to the birth of the Society for Psychical Research in 1882, the premiere organization formed to scientifically study claims of psychic phenomena and paranormal occurrences, including telepathy, intuition, apparitions, and hauntings. Modern-day researchers utilize the methodical framework initiated by the society's numerous intellectuals and scientists.

Even though Spiritualism led to the unearthing of many fraudulent mediums, it further perpetuated a curiosity about the paranormal and life after death. Perhaps those who possess a desire to learn about and communicate with the spirit realm in modern times had ancestors who were also interested in the subject. Even with its undesirable events, Spiritualism has demonstrated the viable notion that life goes on after physical death. Furthermore, it goes to show that death does not free a person from mortal world consequences; as in the hereafter, the soul continues to evolve and make amends with life's outcomes.

CHAPTER 3

MEET THE WOMEN ON THE FRINGE

Our wonderful women are presented here in alphabetical order to make things easier for you, the reader, to look up specific names in the table of contents. Some have written their own personal narratives, and others asked to be formally interviewed with specific questions. All have so much wisdom, insight, and experience to share. Many of these women are not widely known in the fields they work in, but many are. They all have incredible stories to tell about how they came into the world of the paranormal and deserve to be honored and acknowledged. Allow us, without further ado, to introduce you to...the women on the fringe.

Mary Becker

Ghost Excavator, Researcher, Author, Actor, Tour Guide

My experiences with the uncanny began in early childhood and continues to this day. My interest intensified while growing up in a house with a residual haunting of some "thing" that walked up and down the stairwell that was located off the kitchen and occurred particularly when the house was quiet. As a very young child, I would also "see" my grandmother's ghost on several occasions soon after she passed away in addition to other sightings of ghosts. I was further perplexed that sometimes "I just knew things" about places, events, or people, and this knowledge was considered "abnormal behavior" by others.

My curiosity about ghosts and hauntings deepened after listening to stories told by my brothers, my Irish aunts, and cousins, and watching movies, especially those related to haunted houses. Subsequently, my research and investigation of ghosts and hauntings accelerated after meeting John Sabol. John is an archaeologist, anthropologist, actor, and author who uses his academic/theatrical background along with ethnographic research and historical documentation in applying these disciplines to what he has coined a "Ghost Excavation™." John has published his research and documentation in his many books, university peer-reviewed articles, lectures, and on social media platforms.

My background is diversified as I have many years of experience as an executive and administrative assistant, a teacher, an actor, a model, a dancer, along with being a history enthusiast. This training and experience work favorably in performing scenarios on a Ghost Excavation as well as using my administrative side in organizing and preparing field investigations.

John and I met after he sent me a friend request on Facebook, and I accepted only because we had mutual friends. A few weeks after becoming "friends," we planned our first meeting at the burial site of Edgar Allen Poe in Baltimore, Maryland – a fitting place for us! Due to our similar likes, interests, and backgrounds, a partnership with John evolved. It is not only a working partnership that includes a mutual goal in striving to legitimize ghost research, but also a loving one.

What is a Ghost Excavation and What is Involved?

A Ghost Excavation is, most importantly, about the ghost's memories, situations, events, and habitual acts. A Ghost Excavation is an educational, creative process using particular methods and theories to stimulate not only a surface area but the layered history and memories of the people related to that area, in order to manifest any interactive presences, exploring if any remain attached to particular spaces at a location or in a landscape setting, especially one in ruin and/or abandoned. The use of scenarios creates an atmosphere of what might have happened in that space, while keeping to historical facts, respecting the experience of those who once occupied the space and place, plus appreciating and validating the ghost's past by honoring its culture and social values. Immersing yourself into particular memories is meant to identify as one of them. It is a respectful and insightful way to allow the interactive ghost(s) to feel comfortable in responding or talking about themselves. It is very effective, and I will give personal examples later.

These are the disciplinary approaches used in every Ghost Excavation:

- Cultural Anthropology - cultural behavior and beliefs of a particular time;

- Archaeology – dig into, or concentrate, on a specific layer of memory and experience;
- Performance and Dramaturgy (theory and practice of dramatic arrangement) – use culturally targeted scenarios targeted toward past presences and their environs in order to bring about those emerging presences that may still remain.
- E.O.C.s – Ethnography of Communication. Used by anthropologists in the field for determining cultural context. Not to be confused with EVPs (electronic voice phenomena), EOCs involve all the sensory modalities that may emerge during a performance excavation.
- P.O.P. Methodology – <u>P</u>erform (to the ghost); <u>O</u>bserve (watch the performance and the space to record and inform the performers and their interactions with surfacing phenomena); <u>P</u>articipate (once an entity manifests, continue to perform until activity ceases). P.O.P. was devised by John Sabol.

Unlike many paranormal investigations I have been part of, a Ghost Excavation does not use "para-history," nor does it base the investigation on ghost legends (legend tripping), nor unnecessary contemporary equipment (that was not part of past experience and memory) placed in a room and left remaining in the area without enacting a scenario that could generate a manifestation. A Ghost Excavation plays to specific past socio-cultural environments at alleged haunted locations, specifically to any still attached interactive presences.

Unlike many ghost hunts, a Ghost Excavation does not use commands or demands unless it is contextual to a particular layer of past memory. In this way, we relate directly to the attached entities, their history, and their knowledge, and evoke their memories. We perform scenarios similar to role-playing, but it is context-specific to particular past tasks in specific spaces, a resonating approach that is relevant to the time, place, and people who once occupied the location.

Even though during an investigation we concentrate on a particular era, an interactive ghost from another time, other than the scenario enacted, may emerge. When this occurs, we immediately perform to that particular manifestation and modify the scenario that is enacted.

There is no "waiting for something to occur" during a Ghost Excavation. Unlike many ghost hunts, there is no sitting or standing in a darkened room, asking general questions. Often, I hear absurd demands and command questions such as "Show us a sign of your presence!" "Is anyone here with us tonight?" "Shut that door!" "Do you know you are dead?" "Move the lights on this meter!" "Turn the flashlight on or off!" I call these statements, "Victorian parlor tricks." After all, it is disrespectful to speak to one another in this tone in our present-day life and certainly, we should not speak in this manner to past presences as that type of behavior was probably not part of their culture. I find it incredible that some ghost investigators demand a ghost to move meter lights or to turn a flashlight on and off, especially when those particular items were not part of their memory or technology. Oftentimes, the ghost must be thinking, "What is a flashlight?!" or "What is a meter?!"

During Ghost Excavations, we have found that using modern-day terminologies, tech equipment, and commands and demands oftentimes creates a negative effect and a negative environment resulting in little to no response by an interactive ghost(s). I have often had ghost investigators say to me that an ethereal voice will tell them to "GET OUT!" Is this because the ghost investigator is not relating to or immersing themselves in the ghosts' culture and time period? Never in a Ghost Excavation has the team reported to me the words "Get out!" during an investigation. It is my belief that we respect, listen, and respond to the interactive presences accordingly, and on their terms.

Rarely is there inactivity during a scenario, however; whenever there is no response, we stop and continue on to the next scenario. Actually, by performing several scenarios, we create a more resonant environment and rapport with any attached ghost(s). When a scenario works, they can sometimes last up to an hour or more. The investigative performers in these settings oftentimes are not able to see or hear what the observers are recording or hearing through video and audio means. A common direction cue from John to me while doing a scenario is "Keep going, Mary! Keep going!" This is a "high" for me as I know I have connected with a presence and it is responding to me, contextually.

For documentation during scenarios, we use a "piggyback" or layered approach. It consists of those enacting the scenario. Various types of cameras and audio are pointed at those individuals but the equipment is set off to the side. Then, observers, with additional cameras and audio, are watching and recording the observers. This "piggybacking" works quite effectively in documenting the mise en scène (the arrangement of scenery and stage properties) of a haunted space. John is the director of these scenarios and is very good at inspiring the team.

There are more details in the implementation of a Ghost Excavation as to the team's roles, the size of the team, what is expected of each team member in documenting the scene, the clothing to be worn, investigative behavior, tech equipment (audio/video/cameras) and their placement in the scene, and prior research, but it would be too long and involved to explain it here. I recommend that one reads books and articles written by John Sabol and myself on Amazon.com and utk.academia.edu/JohnSabol, a free access website.

Personal Experiences and Examples During Ghost Excavations

My most interesting and productive responses during scenarios are ones that I have performed while interacting with the ghosts of children. I have played various roles including a visiting teacher and a nanny. Here are a couple of examples and personal experiences:

Knickerbocker Hotel, Linesville, Pennsylvania

At the Knickerbocker Hotel, there are many historical layers beginning from when it was built to the present, with each room decorated in a style typical of a particular period in the hotel's history. The original builders and owners of the hotel, according to deeds and documents, resided there with their young children during the 1880s. The hotel is no longer operational but now serves as a ghost research center and events venue. The hotel was located near a now-defunct train station that was used by many heading westward as well as an overnight stopping point. We investigated the hotel several times. At the last excavation there, we stayed for eight consecutive days.

For this scenario, with my hair pulled into a bun, I dressed in a skirt and shirtwaist blouse reminiscent of the time period we were targeting – the 1880s. This mode of dress creates an approachable effect for any children who may remain attached there, as you immerse yourself in that scene. The team served as observers and had set up audio and video equipment, which were set off to the side and out of range of the scenario setting, to make it less intimidating to any lingering entities. John served as the director of this particular mise en scène.

The scenario setting was located on the second floor's large landing area at the top of the stairwell. It is an area known to be where many of the boarders' and owners' children played. My first scenario involved playing "hide and seek" with the children. I began to count while covering my eyes with my hands while the children hid. (While performing scenarios, it is best to speak slowly and then pause as this method seems to work best in hearing and receiving responses.) I counted, "One, two, three..." up until the number ten. Observers with audio equipment and observers watching a live feed reported hearing a child counting along with me.

When we replayed the audio, we could hear the child's voice not only counting with me, but the child saying the number ten before I did. There is also another audio response with a child's voice who repeatedly said the number "five," while I was "seeking" the children. I tried counting a few more times but the responses ceased. Did these responses stop because it was getting late and it was the child's bedtime? More investigative work seems to be the answer. Some of these recordings can be heard on our website Ghost Excavation: EOCs (EVPs) – The Knickerbocker Experience and Expanding the Ordinary - C.A.S.P.E.R.

Brunswick Railroad Museum, Brunswick, Maryland

The Brunswick Railroad Museum, built in 1904, served multiple functions over the years including one used by the Fraternal Order of

Redman, and, for my area of interest, as a temporary schoolhouse until the school in town was rebuilt after it burned down in 1928. The scenario took place on the 2nd floor of the building in front of a large cardboard photo of schoolchildren, almost life-size, from around the 1920s. The team of observers and equipment were placed out of sight of the scenario. In my teacher's garb, I wore a plain button-down white blouse and black skirt with my hair pulled back in a bun. I decided that I would be a visiting teacher at the school. When I introduced myself to the students, I referred to myself as Miss Mary. Contextual audio recordings included a young child answering "Rodney" when I did a roster calling out students' names. Other contextual responses included, "We will watch Miss Mary", "I don't like Miss Mary" and "I'm sorry." Other than hurt feelings over "I don't like Miss Mary," I took it in stride all in the name of ghost research!

These examples I presented are why I continue to pursue Ghost Excavation methodologies and theories. With its oftentimes immediate responses, I argue that it is due largely to the in-depth research, the following of particular disciplinary approaches, and the dedication of the team. Even though a Ghost Excavation is an involved process, it is very rewarding. I further argue the benefit of speaking and presenting Ghost Excavation data at paranormal, pop culture, and science conferences plus other venues in the United States and internationally. Additionally, publishing articles and books gives credence, legitimacy, and respect to ghost research. It is also another tool for ghost researchers and investigators to implement.

In conclusion, if ghosts react to memories of situations, events, and habitual acts, then Ghost Excavations, I propose, are context-specific to past layers of memories that remain attached or embedded at the site in specific layered spaces.

Bio: *Mary Becker is a Ghost Excavator, Researcher, Author, Actor, Tour Guide, and Co-organizer of I.P.E. Research Center. She is originally from the Washington, DC area and now resides in Bedford, Pennsylvania with John Sabol and a host of ghosts in their home. Mary is the researcher, marketer, organizer, and administrative assistant for C.A.S.P.E.R. (Center for the Archaeological Studies of Presence Through Ethnographic Resonance) as well as co-chair of I.P.E (Interpretive Performance Excavation) Research Center with John Sabol. She has performed in several television pilots, sizzles, and a guest on several radio and Internet talk shows plus spoken at various conferences in the USA and abroad. She also has a background in modeling, dancing, acting, and musicals.*

With John Sabol, Mary produced, edited, and performed in the documentary "Ghost Excavation at Burnside Bridge: Going Home After Seeing the Elephant" showcasing John Sabol's P.O.P theory (Perform-Observe-Participate). She is also the editor and publisher of Ghost Excavation Books, Inc. ™©

Together with John Sabol, Mary is the co-founder of "Haunted History Tours" at Omni Bedford Springs Resort & Spa, Bedford, Pennsylvania.

Email: marybecker62@yahoo.com

Website: ghostexcavation.com

Books and eBooks by author or co-authored, available through Amazon.com and other online bookstores:

Hauntings, History, and Fieldwork: A Sensitive's Journey (2020)
Following in the Dusty Footsteps of Dracula's Shadow: A Media Archaeological Excavation (2021)
The Archaeological Eerie (2021)
The Feminine Macabre: A Woman's Journal of All Things Strange and Unusual, Volume 1 (2021)

Mary Bethune

Paranormal Investigator, Co-Founder Team O.P.P.S., Instrumental Trans-Communication Researcher & Practitioner

I have led a life believing and experiencing the unknown. Consequently, I always have felt out of place in mainstream society. Growing up, it was difficult to find like-minded people to talk about the paranormal, ghostly encounters, the afterlife, or field investigations.

As a young child, I saw and heard spirits and had prophetic dreams. Being raised in a Puerto Rican, Catholic family was difficult. I was told not to speak of it and left alone to deal with whatever happened. I knew I was different from other people. My experiences as a young girl from age six onward, fueled my passion for the paranormal.

The family was leaving out of state to visit my ailing grandmother. Moments before the phone rang, I went to my mother and told her we didn't have to go as grandma was dead. The phone rang and my mother was told that indeed, "gramma" had just passed. Months prior to that, I had repetitive dreams about a funeral. The day of the funeral was exactly like my dream.

Since that time, I have read every book, watched every show, and searched for others like me.

My husband's crossing over in 2007 was the incident that got me into paranormal research. I have always believed in the afterlife. Doug was dying of cancer. We had frequently talked of the afterlife, but he wasn't 100% convinced. He wanted his dog Nikki to cross him over. I told him to call for her when he was ready. On the day of his crossing, Doug was in a coma and on oxygen. Prior to this, he kept saying "440, 515." I finally figured out he was trying to choose what time to leave. At exactly 4:40 a.m., he sat up, took off his oxygen mask, and began calling Nikki. "Come on girl, let's go!" Then a bright light came into the room for a few seconds and then faded away. Doug had transitioned.

Years later, I went on to have an ADC (after-death communication) with Rochelle Wright, MSW. She created a form of grief therapy that induces ADC through EMDR and binaural beat music. This changed my life, and I knew this was my calling. I needed to get the word out that we do not die and by doing so, especially helps those who are grieving. I was fortunate to be trained by Rochelle in this method.

In 2008, I joined a group of like-minded people. We formed a paranormal team called ParaWa. From there, I and others went on to form the Olympic Peninsula Paranormal Society or OPPS. We are still going strong at 14 years. OPPS team members are interested in the truth, whether it is paranormal or not. We have become an organized, compassionate team through trial and error, learning from our research, each other, and other teams. The group uses the same investigation protocols with each investigation.

We developed these to help us stay focused and make sure we are all collecting evidence the same way.

I have a science background, schooled in nursing and medicine. I was taught the scientific method and critical thinking. As a paranormal investigator, I use this in every investigation. My role as a team lead and investigator is to educate the public and be available for private, business, and historical investigations, as well as help those with grief, through ADC, referrals, and personal experiences.

I am also an avid ITC researcher, pushing the envelope and the team by introducing the ghost box, Estes sessions, doing video feedback loop, direct voice radio communication, and water ITC. I am part of the North American Spirit Contact station on the other side. There are a number of us working with them to help build a bridge to the living from the afterlife. Our hope is to awaken everyone to the survival of life after death and teach afterlife communication.

I have been so fortunate to investigate many locations. My favorites are the USS *Turner Joy* in Bremerton, Washington, the Washoe Club in Virginia City, Nevada, and the Walker Ames House in Port Gamble, Washington.

There are a few cases that stand out. We investigated a home where a family had a young child cross over. During our evidence review, we caught a music box playing a beautiful tune. As we were playing the EVP for the family, we were told that this tune was played on his music box every night before he went to sleep. There wasn't a dry eye at the table.

Another case was the USS *Turner Joy*. I call one of the ghosts there, "The pervert in the bathroom." The women on the team all felt nervous using the only bathroom on the ship. We all felt we were being watched. After a thorough search, we found nothing. Later, I decided to keep my recorder running as I went to the bathroom. During the evidence review, I caught a very enthusiastic "Yeah" as I was on the toilet!

Having researched and investigated for over a decade, I've noticed changes in this field. Investigators are pushing for more scientific research and validation. Unfortunately, there seems to be a bit too much intolerance for other differing methods and not enough sharing of evidence and methodologies. That's what I'd like to see change. We won't advance as a serious field unless this happens.

My search for validation of the afterlife has led me on some amazing journeys. There are so many great pioneers, researchers, and futurists in this field.

Here are a few of my favorites:

Hans Holzer: parapsychologist, author, paranormal researcher, and field investigator during the 1960s through the 1990s. He was out there before others were, relying on historical research, witness interviews and working with psychics at locations before any team was ever formed.

Marc Macy: founder of INIT (International Network for Instrumental Trans-Communication) in the 1970s. He had contact with the other side through TV, phones, radios, and computers.

Marcello Bacci: Starting in 1949, he held sessions in his home with his vacuum tube radio for grieving family members by bringing messages from their departed loved ones.

Sarah Estep: She was a 1970s ITC and EVP pioneer and the founder of the American Association of Electronic Voice Phenomena and the EVP classification system.

Sonia Rinaldi: She's a Brazilian researcher helping people connect to the other side with audio, video, and photography of people living in the afterlife.

Rochelle Wright: She's a licensed mental health and EMDR therapist specializing in trauma and grief. She developed a method of psychotherapy called, Guided Afterlife Connections that enables people to contact those that have crossed over.

Frank Sumption and Bruce Halliday: Frank was the founder of the Ghost Box in 2002. Bruce Halliday is a Ghost Box pioneer and my mentor.

Team OPPS: The group has inspired me to grow, believe, and encourage my outside-the-box thinking!

Inspiration is helping you open your mind to all possibilities, think outside the box, not fear what others think of you, stand firm in your beliefs, and be dedicated to them.

Each and every one on this list has done that for me. I never thought I would help start a paranormal team, present at conferences, teach classes, have a medical professional magazine write about my interest in the paranormal, and be on TV and the radio. They inspired me and gave me the knowledge and courage for this. I am so fortunate.

I'd like to close by telling you two things about my mantras. Known phenomena do not constitute the whole of reality and love lasts longer than life. (It's what I call a "dazzle" shot that I received from my husband, Doug, who transitioned 16 years ago.)

Bio: *Mary has been for the last 14 years a local paranormal investigator, co-founder, past case manager, and current co-team leader for OPPS. She is an avid Instrumental Trans-Communication researcher and practitioner, specializing in the Ghost Box and Direct Voice Radio communication. From a young age, Mary has had prophetic dreams and has seen and heard spirits. She is also an afterlife researcher, hoping to teach and help everyone realize that life goes on after death. She is actively involved with the spirit contact team at the North American station and was trained by Rochelle Wright, MS, LMHC, CDP in repair and reattachment grief therapy, which opens up communication with those on the other side. She has been a medical practitioner for 47 years and lives in Bremerton, WA.*

Constance Victoria Briggs

Author, Researcher, Galactic Historian, Public Speaker

Please tell us a little about you and what your field of study/expertise is.

I am an author, researcher, galactic historian, and public speaker specializing in the mysteries of the universe and how they are connected to Earth. It is my job to disseminate information in this area. Specifically, I investigate the topics of extraterrestrials (who they are and why they are here), UFOs (their history with Earth, who is controlling them and why they are here), ancient astronauts (extraterrestrials that visited and interacted with humanity in the distant past), and strange moon phenomena (the mysterious lunar phenomena and what it means). I believe that there is more to our universe than we have been taught and that we need to look deeper and search further if we want to know the truth of who we are, where we come from, and what lies beyond.

In my work these days, I am actively researching humanity's galactic connections by looking for evidence of extraterrestrials and UFOs from the ancient world through today. Some of the topics that I explore include whether the Earth was terraformed by extraterrestrials; the theory that Earth was seeded with life by other-worldly beings; and the possible extraterrestrial involvement in the creation of humans. I seek out evidence that humanity was and still is being visited by beings from other worlds and explore the idea that there was and maybe still is a battle for Earth. I also research any signs, signals, and messages, showing evidence that extraterrestrials are trying to communicate with humanity. I investigate the possibility that extraterrestrials may have a physical presence on Earth. It is my hope to discover who they are, and what their goals may be when it comes to Earth and humanity. I keep up to date on the current research into the phenomena of Unidentified Flying Objects (UFOs), as well as Unidentified Submerged Objects (USOs). I am also researching the possibility of there being authoritative hierarchies within our galaxy that may include other-worldly federations and councils that are responsible for order within the galaxy and the potential galactic community.

My books on cosmic topics thus far include *Earth's Galactic History and Its Extraterrestrial Connection*; *The Moon's Galactic History: A Look at the Moon's Extraterrestrial Past and Its Connection to Earth*; *The Encyclopedia of Moon Mysteries: Secrets*, and *Conspiracy Theories, Anomalies, Extraterrestrials and More*. My other books include *Encyclopedia of the Unseen World*: *The Ultimate Guide to Apparitions, Death Bed Visions, Mediums, Shadow People, Wandering Spirits, and Much, Much More*; *Encyclopedia of God: An A-Z Guide to Thoughts, Ideas, and Beliefs about God*; and *The Encyclopedia of Angels: An A-Z Guide with Nearly 4,000 Entries*.

How did you first get involved in this field?

Ever since I was a child, I have wondered if we are alone in the universe. The idea of outer space, space travel, beings from other worlds, and life on other planets always resonated with me. It excited me. I was very much attracted to science fiction shows. As a child, I felt as though I was being propelled into different worlds when watching them. I was very much drawn to such shows as *Lost in Space* and *Star Trek*. I was like a sponge taking in all that I was seeing and learning in such shows and movies. I wanted to be a part of it all. I still do. Needless to say, I was no ordinary kid. I was a dreamer of other places, other worlds, other realms, and how I was connected to it all. This led me on a journey into religious studies and later metaphysics. I amassed a great deal of knowledge along the way about our ancient past, life after death, and the unseen world, which ultimately led to my studies about the cosmos, other worlds, extraterrestrials, and our place in the universe. It has been an amazing life of learning and a fascinating journey for me. Today, I see the world differently than the average person. When I look at the world, I see more than others with an understanding that there is more to our world than we know and more to the universe than we have been taught.

Was there an experience you had that compelled you to further study?

I have had paranormal experiences in my life. I realized that as a child I had seen a UFO. At the time, I did not know what I was looking at. It was dark, and I was in the car with my mother who was driving. I was in the back seat when I saw colorful lights in the sky. I knew it wasn't a plane, it wasn't a helicopter, and it wasn't a blimp, which was all we saw in the skies back then. It was just hovering there with its lights flashing. I have returned to that memory several times, and all I can say is that it was a UFO. I was around nine years old at the time. I have also had some of what I believe were "angelic" experiences. Also, when I was 14 years old, I saw a humanoid being that I now believe was extraterrestrial in origin. Also, both of my parents have passed away, and both have reached out from the other side to help me understand that they are still alive and doing well in another realm. I have also had many fascinating out-of-body experiences where I have traveled to other places.

As an adult, I pursued my love of the cosmos through my research and writing. I had always had a desire to be involved in the research and studies of the UFO phenomenon and learn about the extraterrestrials, and most especially the more advanced spiritual extraterrestrials. These, I believe are working in Earth's vicinity and are here to help. I knew that I would have to hold off on sharing my research in the form of writing until after my children were grown, which I did. My first two books in the area of cosmic mysteries were two books on the moon. The first was *The Encyclopedia of Moon Mysteries: Secrets, Conspiracy Theories, Anom-*

alies, Extraterrestrials, and More. The second is *The Moon's Galactic History: A Look at the Moon's Extraterrestrial Past and Its Connection to Earth*. There are a lot of strange phenomena going on with the moon. In my opinion, it is very likely that there is a civilization up there. If not a civilization, then quite possibly there is a lunar base with extraterrestrials working there in some capacity. I was very excited to learn these things and thought it was important for others to have this information as well. My third book on the area of humanity's cosmic connection is *Earth's Galactic History and Its Extraterrestrial Connection*. In humanity's evolving journey in learning about life in outer space, I wanted to relay Earth's history with extraterrestrials. We have a long intricate history with extraterrestrials that most people are not yet aware of. It takes a lot of digging and research to understand what happened in the past and how it affects us today. The purpose of *Earth's Galactic History and Its Extraterrestrial Connection* is to help people understand that this is not a new phenomenon, but something that we have been living with all along. It has taken us time as a young race of beings to finally grow and understand this. We had to move from being a new primitive race to a more sophisticated, knowledgeable worldwide community. Today, more people are seeking answers to our connection with the stars and how it has affected humanity. More people are waking up. *Earth's Galactic History and Its Extraterrestrial Connection* is a beginning to understanding that journey.

How has your journey progressed into writing and speaking on your research findings?

I wanted to share my research with others to help them understand that we are not alone in the universe. I also wanted to help those who have had "unusual" experiences to know that there are things on Earth and in the cosmos that we have not been taught about and that if they see something "strange" they are not alone, and they are not "crazy." I wanted to help people understand the mysteries of the universe and the true reality that we are living in. Our world is changing, people have the right to know that things are not as they seem. But this takes time. As a world society and as a species, we are waking up. People are now questioning who we are, where we came from, and how we arrived here. Many are moving away from some of the old belief systems that held us trapped for so long and hindered open-mindedness and independent thinking. Many people are questioning and looking for answers. I am hoping to help people to find those answers. We are all on this journey of discovery together.

What is the most fascinating thing you've come across in your own research?

In the area of cosmic research, it fascinates me that we have been visited by beings from other worlds since the beginning of our history. UFOs coming to Earth is not new. This has been going on since the beginning. Earth has always been visited by people from other worlds, and I don't mean little gray beings only, as are seen everywhere in the media. There are a variety of extraterrestrials that have visited Earth down through the ages. There have been benevolent extraterrestrials that came here to help humanity to thrive. In some cases, they have given us updated science and technology, but only to a point, and from what I understand, very discreetly. I believe today, given the terrible state that the world is in, some are here again to help humanity. However, there have been malevolent beings that have come here as well. There is definitely a polarity in the universe, and it appears that on Earth we have experienced both sides of this.

Do you feel women have special gifts and talents that they bring to the table in your field of study?

In the early days of the UFO phenomenon, let's say the 1940s through the 1970s, there were mostly men performing research in this area. Men were the go-to people for questions when it came to UFOs and potential alien life in outer space. This is no longer the case. Today, there are many women involved in this research and are speaking out in this area. It's refreshing to see. As a woman, it is wonderful to be a part of it all and to be taken seriously.

Has being a woman helped or hurt you along your journey, and can you give an example of how?

Being a woman in this field today is not a hindrance as it may have been let's say, in the 1940s to 1970s as I mentioned before. I feel that there is an acceptance of all in this field of study. People want and need information. They are no longer interested in who is providing the information; they want answers no matter who is presenting them. It is no longer a man's field only.

Do you think the time is coming when "fringe" studies are simply going to be accepted as normal fields of scientific research? Do you think the world is coming to realize that reality is so much more than what people can see/feel/hear/think/touch with their five senses?

I think the time is here. I think this field of study is becoming more normalized. People are beginning to take it seriously, especially with all the sources of information today and with cameras everywhere. People are startled to find so many strange phenomena going on out there. More people are seeing and experiencing things they have never seen or heard of before and they want explanations. They want to understand what is happening. People no longer want to be in the dark about these things. They are beginning to see that our world is not what they thought. Our reality is not what they thought. People want knowledge. They want to be armed so to speak, so that if they do encounter or experience something strange or different then they can better understand what they are dealing with. So yes, I think there will be more areas of study in our future when it comes to the paranormal. To quote Mark Twain, "Truth is stranger than fiction." That is an understatement.

What would you most like people to know about what you do and why you feel so passionate about it?

I would like them to know that we have evidence today that we are not alone in the universe. We have entered a time when information about

Earth's cosmic and extraterrestrial connection is coming out very fast. In our everyday lives, more people are seeing evidence of it. The evidence suggests that we are not alone, and we never have been. There is proof that shows that we have been visited by extraterrestrials from the beginning of human history and that Earth is being visited today. The question is whether humanity will accept this reality. I believe that we are on the verge of the next step in moving into a more futuristic worldwide society and eventually making direct contact with people from the stars. If we are to enter a time when we will evolve to be greater than we are now, then we need to learn about our extraterrestrial origins. Only then will we be able to move forward into a time when we can join what I believe is a "galactic community." Therefore, it behooves us to examine as much information from our past on the subject, as well as explore the theories and possibilities of how we are connected to the stars.

The timing is apropos because the topic of Earth's cosmic origins and the fact that there are extraterrestrials out there is being closely scrutinized today. In fact, more information than ever before on the topic is becoming available. Even some governments are declassifying documents on their findings and experiences with extraterrestrials. I feel that humanity needed to reach a level of development before this information could be widely disseminated. I believe that as a world society, we need to understand that there are advanced civilizations out there that are far ahead of us in terms of science, technology, and peaceful ways of existence.

This is important for us to know. This knowledge could help us to grow as a worldwide community. I believe this is important for us to move forward. Without this knowledge, without accepting the fact that there is more out there than we know, we are not complete. We will remain in the dark existing in a false reality. I don't want a false reality to be the future of my children and grandchildren. I had an acquaintance tell me recently that they have, "no interest," in the subjects of extraterrestrials and UFOs. Not having an interest does not make this go away. It only keeps us ignorant. Knowledge is power. We do not know what position we may find ourselves in one day when it comes to people from other worlds.

I believe that for the most part, we have reached a point in human history where we are ready to accept the reality that we are not alone in the universe and that we are a piece of a whole. I mean that we are a part of something big, something bigger than ourselves, bigger than this world. We are a part of a universe filled with life, a part of a galactic community, and we need to wake up to this reality. It is my thinking and my passion that we are now ready for that spacefaring, *Star Trek* future that so many have been anticipating. We just may find that learning where we are headed in relation to the cosmos, and the fact that we are not alone, may move us into a better way of living, a better state of being, and improve life on our planet. If we want to grow and improve life on Earth, if we want to save the Earth and prepare for a better future for all of us, then we need the full story of who we are, where we came from, and what and who is out there. Knowing this may be the difference between us having a spacefaring future, an apocalyptic one, or no future at all. I feel that this knowledge and information is important to all people, in all corners of the world. Disseminating this information to people to help them better understand our place in the cosmos is my passion.

Bio: *Constance Victoria Briggs is an author, researcher, and public speaker specializing in cosmic mysteries including, galactic and moon mysteries, ancient astronauts, extraterrestrials, and the unseen world. She is the author of Earth's Galactic History and Its Extraterrestrial Connection; The Moon's Galactic History: A Look at the Moon's Extraterrestrial Past and Its Connection to Earth; The Encyclopedia of Moon Mysteries: Secrets, Conspiracy Theories, Anomalies, Extraterrestrials and More; Encyclopedia of the Unseen World: The Ultimate Guide to Apparitions,*

Death Bed Visions, Mediums, Shadow People, Wandering Spirits, and Much, Much More; Encyclopedia of God: An A-Z Guide to Thoughts, Ideas, and Beliefs about God; The Encyclopedia of Angels: An A-Z Guide with Nearly 4,000 Entries. Constance is a regularly invited guest speaker on numerous radio shows, podcasts and YouTube shows discussing such topics as extraterrestrials, ancient aliens, life after death, after-death communication, out-of-body experiences, moon mysteries, and more. Some of the prominent shows that Briggs has been featured on include Coast to Coast AM with George Noory, Midnight Society, The Leak Project, The Kingdom of Nye, Earth Ancients, Paranormal Soup, The Paranormal and the Sacred, Broadcast Team Alpha, Forbidden Knowledge, Quantum Guides, Behind the Obsidian Curtain, Spaced Out Radio, and Raised by Giants. Briggs has also been featured in Shadows of Your Mind Magazine and UNX Magazine. Briggs was a presenter at the 2021 Total Disclosure, Inner Truth Summit, and the 2022 Watchers Talk Humanity Unplugged Conference. It is Constance's goal to investigate the mysteries of the universe and how they connect to humanity. Constance and her family make their home in Southern California.

Email*:*
cvb@constancevictoriabriggs.com
Facebook*:*
Constance Victoria Briggs
Moon Mysteries.
Website*:*
constancevictoriabriggs.com.
Instagram*:*
constancevbriggs22
TikTok*:*
@constancevbriggs

Teresa Carol

Intuitive Counselor, Ordained
Minister, Certified B.E.A.T.
Practitioner, Author

In 1983, I was a student at the Psychic Energy Center in Tacoma, Washington exploring the sudden emergence of my psychic abilities when an extremely distressed man came in to report paranormal activity in his home. He claimed that once weekly, he would hear someone walking on his roof and shortly after a fire would break out somewhere within the neighborhood. He had reports that proved a high occurrence of fires within his housing area and also police reports of domestic violence and excessive incidences of alcohol-related felonies. No one knew how to help him. However, as I was seeing spirits, it was decided I should go out with a team of psychics and take a look. The results were amazing! Not only was this the beginning of my 40-year career as a full-time professional psychic and paranormal investigator, but we were able to clear the spirits and within weeks the entire area began to shift from a rundown neighborhood to a community of individuals that unexpectedly took pride in their homes. The reports of fires and alcohol-related incidents dropped to less than 1 percent.

My role as a paranormal researcher has been three-fold: I am a professional psychic who specializes in resolving paranormal activity and a paranormal educator and writer.

Over the years I have used my psychic sensitivity to determine what's what; sometimes there is a loose pipe, a tree rubbing against the building, and the occasional hoax. But when there is a ghost, an elemental, a vortex, or other paranormal phenomena, I find a solution and resolve it. I complete all my investigations with a comprehensive written report. Because I can see and communicate with spirits and other paranormal entities, I have been called, "Ambassador to the Subtle Realms," by the *Tacoma News Tribune* and "Speaker for the Dead" by various Native American communities.

In addition, I have used many of my paranormal investigations to train and educate others who are interested in developing their psychic skills and desire to understand paranormal phenomena. I teach classes, participate in ghost conferences, as well as take students to participate in hands-on paranormal events. I also write articles and books on the paranormal. *All Spooked Up* is a book that contains the story of how I use a ghost in my house as an educational experience for my students; *How to Spook Yourself Up: A Manual for Paranormal Investigation*, is a comprehensive guide on how to investigate the paranormal.

There are several things I feel could greatly contribute to paranormal research: Firstly, as I frequently am able to validate my findings, it would be helpful to have a scientific team that could set a standard of methodology and terminology for the collection and research of data. I feel this would go far to establish credibility in the paranormal research field. Additionally, this would create an established vocabulary so that all researchers would be concise in the reporting of information.

The terms that describe ghosts, spirits, entities, demons, specters, apparitions, spooks, and souls are all currently used interchangeably. These refer to a variety of phenomena and create confusion and misunderstanding when used without an established definition. Secondly, I feel it would be a great benefit to have access to a cadaver dog as I am frequently shown where the bodies are buried, but I have no proof, and thus a trained dog would offer substantial credibility to present to the police. Thirdly, it would be of great advantage to have access to historians and genealogy researchers at a reasonable cost, as I am often given information such as events, previous buildings, and names during an investigation. Once while investigating a famous home in Puyallup, Washington, a ghost informed me that he was a representative of the

Oregon territories, which later became the Washington territories. He gave me detailed information about President James Buchannan and the Pig Wars of 1859. He spoke passionately about the Washington area not becoming part of the British kingdom. I had no previous knowledge about this history and was excited when a local librarian was able to confirm the information.

My investigations begin with a walk-through, viewing the building, the property, and the surrounding area. I prefer to go out with a team and I write my impressions down on a clipboard. Once the entire location has been viewed, the team and I discuss our findings and report to the owners. After a decision is made, I participate in the clearing and resetting of the energies. Whenever possible I include the clients in releasing the ghost, placating the elementals, screening the vortex, or whatever needs to be attended to. Often the client or a family member has intuitive abilities and I offer education and referrals to assist them in developing their gifts. Afterward, I go home and do a few astral visitations to be sure that the phenomena have been dealt with and then write a detailed report.

My favorite investigation was of a tree spirit, which inhabited a custom-built cedar home. The owner had pictures of the home's interior when the house was first built. Almost twenty years later, all of the woodwork was riddled with knot holes that resembled eyes, few of which appeared in the original photographs. Even more interesting was that the silhouette of a small man appeared on the back of the bathroom door. Lithen was a forest guardian who had been driven out of an old-growth forest when it was destroyed to create a housing development. Having lost his natural habitat, he moved into a cedar home, the only available wooden structure. He had literally grown up with the children and referred to the lady of the house as "Momma." It was an amazing experience to discover this earth elemental. He continues to live in his cedar home, but a new cedar tree has been planted in his honor so that he can eventually live outside.

There is an area near Shelton, Washington that fascinates me. I have seen several creatures known as Breka. They have the form of a man with horns and goats' legs much like a satyr. They claim to be "protectors of the land." They appear whenever the land is being razed or contaminated. They jump onto roofs and vehicles and leave hoof prints. They sabotage logging equipment and block access to waterways that are being polluted. Their tracks often lead to an area where they abruptly stop as if they have passed through an invisible doorway. I have been unable to gain any information other than my experiences and the reports of those who have been attacked by them.

Prior to 2015, I had not been part of a paranormal team. In 1983, when I began my career as a paranormal investigator and psychic, I was in high demand because there was no one else in the local area, so I took on students and literally trained them on the job. During this time, I developed a professional training manual, *How To Spook Yourself Up*, which was published in 2018. Over the following years, many of my students and fellow practitioners began to explore the field and build teams on which I served as a consultant. In 2015, I joined my first team, Conscious Paranormal Research and Investigations, or CPRI, which has since been dissolved. I'm currently a member of the Olympic Peninsula Paranormal Society (OPPS) out of Washington State. It's great to be part of a professional team with high integrity. I spent so many years of my paranormal career alone, learning from experience and occasionally consulting with another psychic. Having a team that helps with the work, the insights, and the resolve is a delightful experience that reframes everything into a more playful adventure.

There are so many remarkable individuals in the paranormal field that it is impossible to narrow it down. Two of my favorites are Rocky Smith, host of the annual Oregon Ghost Conference, and Pete Orbea, organizer of the Port Gamble Ghost Conference. I admire the years they have put into developing high-integrity conferences, which allow paranormal practitioners to meet, share information, and educate the public. Both of these men have created professional venues that feature the best psychics, metaphysicians, and paranormal investigators in the field.

When I first started my career in 1985, I was ridiculed and often openly humiliated as the public was very superstitious and prejudiced concerning psychics. Today, I am happy to report that people are more open-minded and willing to entertain the idea of a metaphysical reality. My life has been a journey into the paranormal and psychic realms. I am happy to share my experiences and understandings with others and hope that one day it becomes an established area of scientific study.

Bio: *Teresa Carol is an intuitive counselor, an ordained minister, a certified B.E.S.T. Practitioner, a retired Washington State counselor, and the author of All Spooked Up and How to Spook Yourself Up: A Manual for Paranormal Investigation. She holds a degree in psychology. Since 1985, Teresa has worked as a professional life coach and teacher of metaphysics, spiritual awakening, and psychic development. Having traveled to over 30 countries, Teresa has studied healing, Shamanism, and spirituality directly from indigenous people. Featured in Evening Magazine, and listed in Who's Who of Extraordinary People, she has been a guest on countless television and radio programs, as well as interviewed in newspapers and magazines. Teresa believes people have their own answers; they just need the opportunity and the skills to bring it all together. Working and teaching full-time as a life coach and an intuitive, she lives an extraordinary life and offers to share her insights to empower others. Currently, Teresa is writing a series of children's books designed to help with psychic and spiritual emergence. Her focus is "helping individuals help themselves."*

Her specialties include paranormal investigation, psychic readings, mediumship, medical intuition, animal communication, numerology, tarot, palm, Shamanism, tea leaf and aura readings, healing, B.E.S.T., and life coach work. www.teresacarol.com

MARIE DUMONT

PARANORMAL INVESTIGATOR, BIGFOOT & SKUNK APE RESEARCHER

My name is Marie Dumont and I am the founder of the Mid Florida Bigfoot Research Group on Facebook and YouTube. I am also the founder of the Mid Florida Bigfoot Research Team and my team consists of myself, Mike Aguilar, Ruby Jo Brew, and Chris Hensley. The intent of my group is to provide a safe place where Florida researchers and group members can collaborate and share their research findings and knowledge with each other, without being bullied or ridiculed. I monitor my group very closely to make sure everyone is always respectful and stays on topic.

My fascination with Florida Bigfoot and Skunk Apes basically started back in 2019 when some of my friends and I went on a tour of the Ocala National Forest and saw some strange large structures that we couldn't explain. Months later, I witnessed a loud and very lengthy vocalization in the Ocala National Forest during a campout with friends on the coldest night of the year. It happened at about 1:30 in the morning and it could be described as a typical classic Ohio Bigfoot howl. It was absolutely incredible and sounded like it came from about a quarter of a mile or so away and the direction it seemed to come from is an area where two lakes are next to each other. Since then, I have been hooked and am bound and determined to be the one to prove that Bigfoot and Skunk Apes are real and that they do exist in Florida!

My Mid Florida Bigfoot Research Team takes researching the Florida Skunk Ape and Bigfoot phenomena very seriously and we are out in the swamps and woods conducting research every single weekend. We have become good friends and we work very well together because we have the same common goal, which is to find as much evidence as we can to raise awareness and to prove that Bigfoot and Skunk Apes do exist in our state. We investigate "squatchy" looking areas like the Green Swamp, Colt Creek State Park, the Ocala National Forest, Myakka State Park, Myakka State Forest, Goethe State Forest, Apalachicola National Forest, various remote areas in Hillsborough, Pasco, and Polk Counties, and of course the infamous Florida Everglades.

Each researcher on my team brings something different to the table. For instance, I am a creative and artistic person, so I am very good at locating structures, prints, and out-of-the-ordinary things in nature, as though they are a type of artwork or forest language. Mike Aguilar has a knack for finding good research areas for our team and locating structures and footprints. Ruby Jo Brew has a vast knowledge of Florida plants and wildlife and is good at finding structures, breaks, and oddities. Chris Hensley is our technology expert and has an open-minded scientific approach to the great unknowns of our world, which include Bigfoot and Skunk Apes.

My research team has captured a lot of potential Bigfoot or Skunk Ape evidence like footprints, possible nests or shelters, X structures, teepee, lean-to and asterisk-type structures, strange arrangements of bones, sticks, and branches, along with mysterious hairs that we cannot identify under a microscope. We have heard tree knocks, tree falls, growls, whistles, and strange gibberish talking sounds while out in the field. We have also had objects thrown at us, captured mysterious whispers on our audio equipment (EVPs), and have had our cell phones and research equipment malfunction many times (captured on video), which we just can't explain. As researchers, we carefully analyze all of our potential evidence with healthy skepticism in order to seek out the truth.

My research team does not claim our findings were caused by a Bigfoot or Skunk Ape because no one knows for sure and we can only speculate. But we do share the interesting things we find out in the field on my Facebook group page for our fellow Florida researchers and members to ponder and discuss. We are all in this together and it is our goal as Bigfoot and Skunk Ape researchers to share our knowledge with others to help prove that these elusive creatures do exist.

As you can imagine, it can be extremely challenging to research Bigfoot and Skunk Apes in Florida. It is a very taboo subject here and no one dares to speak openly about them or report their sightings, for fear of ridicule. Most people in Florida still think that Bigfoot only exists in the Pacific Northwest, which is absolutely not true because they have been seen throughout the country. According to the BFRO (Bigfoot Field Researchers Organization), Florida is ranked #3 for the most reported Bigfoot sightings in the United States, which is quite impressive for our state. A lot of people are seeing these elusive bipedal creatures throughout Florida and there is no way that everyone can be lying about their experiences.

The biggest challenges I believe we face in Florida are the extreme heat, humidity, and terrain, which varies dramatically from region to region. We have 17 million acres of forest land in our state consisting of deep swamps, flat woods, pines, scrub oaks, subtropical hammocks, dry prairies, saw palmettos, wet sawgrass marshes, and floodplain forests. So basically, the types of evidence that a Bigfoot researcher would find in the Pacific Northwest would be completely different from what they would find here in Florida. Most places in Florida are extremely dense, swampy, and dangerous to maneuver through and since we don't have the large, lush trees like what is found in the Pacific Northwest, the structures that are found here in Florida are usually much smaller in size and harder to spot since they are typically being made with smaller building materials like palmetto fronds, brittle scrawny oak branches, cypress or pine tree saplings, sticks and twigs.

The Skunk Ape mostly resides in the remote tropical areas of South Florida. It is viewed as a smaller cousin of Bigfoot that typically inhabits swamps, is very lean in stature, less hairy, and has been reported to be only around 5 to 7 feet tall. The name "Skunk Ape" was derived from an early sighting of a smaller-sized Bigfoot, which had a white stripe running down the back of his head like a skunk. But most people believe the name came from the reported nasty smell of the creature, and they typically only have four toes instead of five. Four-toed footprints have been cast by various researchers, including the Skunk Ape expert himself, David Shealy, and by cryptozoologist Dr. Bill Hewitt. David has had four personal sightings of the creature throughout his life in the Everglades and some of the local residents, Native Americans, and public officials in the Big Cypress Preserve area have also seen them. The Miccosukee and Seminole Native American tribes that live in the Everglades also state they have encountered Skunk Apes in the woods and swamps there for hundreds of years and respectfully treat them as their own tribe. In the Central and North Florida areas, the typical 6- to 9-foot-tall Bigfoot creatures with five toes have been seen and reported. Most eyewitnesses report them as being mostly reddish/brown in color or sometimes black.

I personally enjoy going out on research investigations and being out in nature. There is something about it that is very calming and good for the soul to connect with nature in this busy world. It's exciting to be out in the woods and swamps and for me, it's like going on a treasure hunt because you never know what you will find or experience. Even if I only get to see wildflowers or purple mushrooms sprouting in the swamp, it's still exciting because it's all beautiful and Mother Nature at its finest.

Being a female in this field of study has been challenging. The Bigfoot community in general is predominately male, so there are times when females are not taken as seriously as men. Even though I have spent more time in the woods and swamps and have seen and experienced more things than most men have, it continues to be a challenge to prove that I am a serious Bigfoot researcher. Because of that, I felt the need to start my Mid Florida Bigfoot Research Group on Facebook and I put together a great dedicated research team, which I believe is gaining respect in the Bigfoot community. Generally, I believe that women by nature, have a sharper eye for details than most men do and I believe that's why I'm so successful at finding structures, footprints, and strange things in nature that seem unnatural or out of place.

Technology has definitely improved over the years for Bigfoot researchers but it's still not where it needs to be. Good research equipment can be very expensive and most people cannot afford to spend thousands of dollars to buy the kind of equipment that is used on all the Bigfoot TV shows. We can all speculate but no one really knows exactly what we are dealing without there and what techniques or special abilities Bigfoot and Skunk Apes may possibly have and use for their survival. So, it's difficult to develop research equipment to provide indisputable evidence for the existence of something that is still unknown.

The David Shealy Sighting Research Study

On May 3, 2023, I released a new research study documentary film called *The David Shealy Skunk Ape Sighting Research Study* on my Mid Florida Bigfoot Research Group YouTube channel. The documentary is about the infamous Skunk Ape sighting that Skunk Ape expert, David Shealy, filmed back on July 8, 2000, in the Everglades at the Big Cypress Preserve. A full two-minute clip of the original David Shealy video of a Skunk Ape running through a sawgrass marsh (Dave Shealy's 2000 Skunk Ape Footage) can be found on YouTube on the *Smithsonian Magazine* channel.

Over the past 23 years, David Shealy has been the subject of ridicule from critics around the world who claim that his Skunk Ape sighting was a hoax (a man wearing a suit). However, none of those critics have seriously tried to research the subject in detail to determine if the sighting was real or not. Assumptions were just made without knowing any of the facts behind his Skunk Ape sighting.

During a discussion with David Shealy, we learned that no one has ever tried to conduct any kind of serious investigation of that sighting in the past 23 years. It was then that we decided to be the first research team to ever go out to the location of his sighting to conduct a three-month research study in order to search for the truth.

Our research study began in December 2022, when I went to the Skunk Ape Research Headquarters in Ochopee, Florida to meet up with David Shealy. David took me out on an ATV to the actual location of his sighting, which is approximately 1.5 miles behind the campground. The dry season in the Everglades runs from December through April, and due to the amount of water still out in the sawgrass marsh at that time, taking an ATV out there was the most effective way to get to the site. We rode around the area together and David retold his Skunk Ape sighting story and pointed out specific landmarks along the way where things in his video were located.

In February 2023, my Mid Florida Bigfoot Research Team and I traveled down to the Everglades to conduct our first reenactment research study of the infamous Skunk Ape sighting and invited guest Bigfoot researchers, Mike Familant (*The Shadow of Big Red Eye*) and Wiley Biro (*Sussex County Bigfoot*) to join us. Once there, Mike Aguilar and Chris Hensley attempted to run the same general course that the Skunk Ape had traveled in the video, while Mike Familant, Ruby Jo Brew, and I filmed them. Due to the terrain, the heat, the holes in the ground, the deep mud, the thickness and depth of the sawgrass, watching for gators and snakes, and trying to keep from tripping and falling, it was virtually impossible for them to run the course so they could mostly only walk it. They were both overheated and exhausted from the experience.

In March 2023, we traveled back down to the Everglades again to conduct a second reenactment research study and invited special guest Thomas Brandon to join us. Thomas is 6'3 inches tall and is a long-distance trail runner with experience running in various terrains, which made him the perfect candidate to attempt our second reenactment. We asked Thomas to swing his arms while he was attempting to run the general course and Mike Aguilar also attempted the reenactment again with him. Thomas was able to run at times but forgot to swing his arms consistently because he was more focused on what he was trying to run through. He ended up encountering the same issues and obstacles that the other team members had the first time, which was battling the heat, avoiding deep holes in the ground, the mud, and the thickness, height, and depth of the sawgrass. He had difficulty moving his legs through the thick sawgrass without tripping and falling and also couldn't run in a straight line because he was looking for the path of least resistance in the sawgrass (the easiest place to take his next step) as he couldn't see through it. At times during the reenactment, the team members filming

Thomas could not see him because of the height of the sawgrass. Afterward, Thomas stated that the thick sawgrass was much harder than he had expected to try to run through and he was also overheated and exhausted from the experience.

After the reenactments, I then conducted hours of research online to try and find out what the weather and climate conditions were 23 years ago on that day. I was able to collect some data from various Everglades Water Management and Weather websites, which provided me with the average climate at the time (some rain in the area), the average temperature (90 degrees F), the average percentage of humidity (75%), the "feel like" temperature at the time (109.5 degrees F) and the total amount of rainfall (29.02 inches).

In conclusion, we believe that it is unlikely that this was a person wearing a costume running quickly through the sawgrass marsh in one to two feet of water, in the extremely hot and humid weather at that time in the Everglades. Our research and personal observations also confirm this as well. My research team and I will continue to conduct ongoing investigations in the Everglades, as well as other parts of South Florida to search for the truth about Skunk Apes.

My advice for new or future researchers would be to keep an open mind about all things paranormal, including Bigfoot and the Skunk Ape. There are so many exciting and mysterious things out there in the world, especially in the woods and swamps of Florida. Just because you may not have ever seen or experienced something before or it sounds totally unbelievable to you, doesn't mean that it doesn't exist or it can't happen. As researchers, we need to look at all the evidence, no matter how strange it may or may not be. Otherwise, we are just directing the outcome of what we think is true about Bigfoot and not finding out the actual possible weird truth about them. There are still many species of animals, insects, etc., on earth that are still yet to be discovered, so anything is possible out there. Once you go out exploring, you will begin to discover things that are completely unexplainable. So, get off the couch, go out in the woods, and search for the truth about Bigfoot and Skunk Apes!

Bio: *Marie Dumont is a native Floridian and has been a paranormal investigator for over 30 years. She has always been interested and fascinated with all things paranormal and has had many paranormal experiences of all kinds throughout her life. Her popular Mid Florida Bigfoot Research Group can be found on both Facebook and YouTube. She has also launched a website for her research team that you can check out at www.midfloridabigfoot.com which provides information about the team, team member bios, helpful research blogs, a list of media appearances, and an impressive research photo gallery of some of their most compelling findings they have found while out in the field.*

Margaret "Maggie" Florio

Paranormal Investigator/Researcher, Member of TRIPRG

I was first motivated to become a paranormal investigator/researcher after experiencing an event I couldn't explain and later contacting The Rhode Island Paranormal Research Group (TRIPRG) to verify what I witnessed. After communicating with the director of the group via email for about three months, he invited me to become a member of TRIPRG.

We met at a local library for an interview, and he asked me to attend a group meeting where the members were able to interview me as well. That was in March 2003 and I became a probationary member following the meeting. Six months later, I became a full member. I was the group secretary for many years and was the assistant director for about five years before becoming the director in October 2013.

The paranormal has always held a certain fascination for me since a very young age. I loved ghost stories and in 1966, a TV show called *Dark Shadows* premiered. *Dark Shadows* was a daily soap opera that incorporated elements of the supernatural (ghosts, a vampire, a were-wolf, time travel, monsters, etc.). Like many fans, I would run home from my bus stop after school so I wouldn't miss one second of the show. When I was eight years old, I saw my first apparition. Up until that point, I believed that ghosts (and other supernatural beings) were make-believe, only found in books and on TV.

It was a sultry Saturday night, and I was in my bed when I woke up to see a lady standing at my window. We didn't have air conditioners and my bedroom was on the second floor, so the window was wide open with the shade up and curtains open. During the warm months, my bed would be next to the window with just enough room between the outside wall and my bed to make the bed in the morning.

The lady was facing me, about four feet away and the light from the streetlight was shining on her so I could clearly see her from the neck to just below her knees. Her face and feet were in the shadows, but she was not transparent and looked like a living person. Her hand was holding the curtain back and it was very delicate looking, small with thin fingers. It wasn't wrinkled or bony like an old lady and looked like it belonged to a young lady in her 20s or 30s. She had on a long dress with long sleeves and a high neck. The material was dark and had a pattern on it like small flowers or a calico print. I remember thinking, "How can she stand being dressed like that?" All I had on was a pair of underpants and a sheet over me, and I was very warm. I decided I must be dreaming, so I closed my left eye, then my right eye, then both eyes and every time I opened them, she was still there.

All this happened in a matter of minutes. The lady didn't move and really didn't even seem aware of my presence. I didn't want her to notice me, so I lay there quietly watching her until I fell asleep. The next morning, I went downstairs to the kitchen and my dad was standing with his back to me at the stove, making breakfast. My mother and sister were sitting at the kitchen table reading the Sunday paper. I asked my mother and sister if they had been in my room the night before and they both said no. Then I told them what I had seen, and my mother insisted I had been dreaming. After I explained the lady remained after I had closed my eyes and reopened them a few times, my dad turned around and said, "It must have been a ghost!" It was at that moment I knew that ghosts were real, and I had to learn more about them. Thus began my passion for the unknown and I would ride my bike to the local library to eventually read every book they had on the subject of the supernatural.

My dear father was a history buff and could remember names and dates of historic events like he had a repository in his head. He also was a voracious reader of historical literature. I suppose my love of history and reading comes from him, but I don't have the memory for it that he had. The search for answers in the paranormal is often found in history, whether it be in historical documents, legends, or historic structures. The paranormal brings history alive and people who attend ghost-hunting events or investigations find themselves getting a history lesson as well. I like to learn about a location before visiting, whether it be on an investigation or as a casual tourist. Usually, I will search for information online because it is readily available. Speaking to people who are familiar with the site is also very helpful as is looking up historical records at the local library or city hall. Other paranormal researchers can also be very helpful if they have visited the site and have research to share.

I try to use many different methods for investigating/researching the paranormal. Dowsing is a method I often use when in very old locations as a means of finding out about any spirits that may be present. While using dowsing rods or a pendulum while asking "yes" or "no" questions, I can get information about sex, age, cause of death, year of death, name, and how many spirits may be in a location. This method is more friendly to spirits in older locations who may mistake the more modern tools for weapons or who are afraid of the noises and lights they produce.

A paranormal investigator doesn't have to spend a fortune on gadgets and gizmos. A camera, voice recorder, compass, flashlight, notebook, and pen are all you really need. The most important tool is an open mind as it is crucial to find out what is really happening in a location. Things are not usually what they seem! When I first began investigating the paranormal with TRIPRG, our group was one of a handful in our state. There were just a few locations that had ghost tours that charged admission. Now, there are many paranormal groups in our small state with new ones starting up all the time. It is difficult to find historic places to investigate that do not charge admission. It seems that the paranormal has become commercialized. This may be due to the proliferation of TV shows on the paranormal or the number of people entering the field because of those shows. Some investigators are in the field to become famous or experience a haunting rather than helping a client or contributing something significant to this field of study. I really hope that people who are thinking of entering the paranormal field take it seriously.

When I am contacted by someone who wants his or her property investigated, I first conduct a telephone interview. Research is then done on the property with the owner's permission. A small investigation team of two to four people is then assembled, and a daytime preliminary investigation is scheduled with the client. During the preliminary investigation, baseline EMF and atmospheric readings are taken and noted, photos and video are captured, EVP sessions are recorded, and all paperwork is filled out for client permission and confidentiality. The preliminary investigation usually takes an hour or two. If we have unexplained activity while we are there, it may last longer.

All data collected during the investigation is reviewed by the team and if there is possible evidence of the paranormal, we will schedule a full investigation. The full investigation takes place at night and can last from three hours to overnight. There may be more investigators, depending on the size of the property and more equipment is used to collect data. Depending on the activity and evidence collected, several visits may be necessary in order to come to a conclusion. In the paranormal field, we are often left with more questions than answers. We meet with the clients to go over our findings and provide them with an investigation report. A case file is created for all reports, photos, EVP, and other data, which is kept in the group archive.

Our group has investigated hundreds of cases over the years, most of which were private cases. The majority of those private cases are confidential. The case for which our group received the most publicity was our investigation of the *Charles W. Morgan* whaling ship in Mystic, Connecticut during the summer of 2006. We had received e-mails from three unrelated people describing strange experiences while touring the vessel. When we contacted the publicity director for the Mystic Seaport, where the ship is docked, he expressed interest in having us investigate it. We then met with him and toured the ship. The publicity director agreed to allow us access to an investigation for one night by ourselves. Subsequent investigations would be accompanied by members of various media. We agreed to these terms and the night of our group investigation was certainly one for the ages. The following investigations involving the media coverage were also productive and we gained an appreciation for the groups that have television shows, dealing with sound and camera crews on a regular basis.

My favorite location to investigate is Fort Adams in Newport, RI. Our group conducted paranormal investigations and ghost tours there for five years. During that time, we became familiar with the spirits we encountered, and they became familiar with us. The organization that runs the fort, The Fort Adams Trust, is constantly renovating different areas of the fort and opening them up for us to investigate. I captured what I consider to be my best photograph of an apparition in one of the powder magazines.

We also captured EVP of children playing in the officer's quarters when there were no children present. Our group no longer conducts the ghost tours at Fort Adams, but we still go back there occasionally for investigations and often bring other paranormal groups along as our guests.

The Rhode Island Paranormal Research Group and Society was founded on September 11, 1984, by Raymond Leferrier, Amanda Reynolds, Tammy Aldrich, and Andrew Laird. We are one of the oldest, continuously operating paranormal groups in New England. Currently, we have eight members and are based in Coventry, RI. Investigations are conducted free of charge and our client's privacy is of utmost importance. TRIPRG is dedicated to educating the public about paranormal phenomena and members are often sought out for presentations. We have a Facebook page and a website at www.rhodeislandparanormal.com. We have contributed to several books such as *The Everything Ghost Hunting Book, Ghosts of Newport,* and *True Tales of Life and Death at Fort Adams.*

I truly admire Maria Pons-Schmidt, also known as Geister Maria Schmidt. She is the founder of Haunted Journeys as well as the founder and chief experience organizer at Mysterious Adventures Tours. Maria may be better known for her work on National Ghost Hunting Day and the World's Largest Ghost Hunt. She and her husband Bob are former owners of the Seven Sisters Bed and Breakfast. I recently found out firsthand that Maria is a talented medium who uses automatic writing while communicating with spirit. She is a tireless traveler who makes sure that members of her tour groups have the best and spookiest experiences possible. Maria is a warm, caring, empathic, intelligent, and energetic individual who has earned my deepest respect in the field of the paranormal.

Bio: *Maggie has had an interest in the supernatural since she was a child and saw her first ghost at the age of eight. Maggie joined TRIPRG in March of 2003 after contacting the group about an experience she had while attending a party at the Aldrich Mansion. She graduated from Rhode Island College where she majored in Music Performance and Education. Maggie became Director of TRIPRG in 2013 after serving as group secretary and assistant director for several years.*

Mallie Fox

Owner of "Paranormal Girl" Lifestyle Brand, Podcast Host, Seen on Strange Evidence on Discovery Plus

When I was a kid, around eight or nine, I would lie in bed and think about death. And to be honest, it would freak me out. I had so much fear about dying, I would cry myself to sleep. Thoughts would race through my mind about what happens when we die. I had so many questions. Do I close my eyes, and like a switch, everything goes black and that's it...life no longer exists. Or is it similar to what we're taught in Sunday school? If we are good, we go to Heaven where we can watch over our loved ones and continue to have some type of existence. Or Lord forbid, if we don't go to Heaven, do we become ghosts and forever roam the earth? Or, what about the possibility of reincarnation? To me, the thought of reincarnation gave me the most comfort. At least my soul would continue on, even if it was in a different body, and experiencing a new life.

So, what made me interested in the paranormal? It wasn't because I grew up in a haunted house, had a visitation from a loved one, or experienced something I couldn't explain. It was actually my strong fear of death and wanting to know if there is some kind of existence after we die.

My first paranormal experience that supported the idea of existence after death happened in my apartment. I lived in a very old building and strange things would happen such as the water faucet turning on by itself, appliances turning on and off, disembodied voices, and objects moving. The good news is that I wasn't going crazy as others had experienced it as well when visiting my apartment. The strange activity didn't bother me. As a matter of fact, it was kind of exciting. But then something happened, unfortunately, more than once, that made me feel uneasy and hesitant to sleep in my own bedroom.

Late at night, I would hear what sounded like movement in my closet. I would hear the glass doorknob jiggle and squeak as it turned. The door would open, followed by footsteps on the wooden floor. You could hear the footsteps walk along the edge of the bed and then stop, right in front of me. I could feel a presence as if something was standing over me, waiting for my eyes to open. When I finally mustered up the courage to open my eyes, nothing was there.

After that experience, I wanted to learn more about the paranormal. I read every book I could get my hands on, watched documentaries on the subject, and toured places that were known to be haunted just so I could say I'd been there. But that wasn't enough. I wanted to go on an actual investigation of a haunted location. I wanted to use technology to communicate with the other side and capture enough evidence to prove that ghosts do exist. Unfortunately, at that time, it was difficult to get access to a location to investigate if you were not associated with a paranormal investigation team. Not a lot of paranormal teams existed and if they did, they were not accepting new members.

However, that all began to change with the increasing number of paranormal television shows. Suddenly, the paranormal field was becoming popular, and paranormal teams were popping up everywhere. In 2006, the Twin Cities Paranormal Society was formed, and they were looking for members. I joined the team and took on the position of researcher.

The researcher's job was to find any information regarding the people and buildings associated with an upcoming investigation. This was perfect for me! I enjoyed learning about people, wondering about what kind of personality they had, what it was like for them to live in that time period, and what kind of secrets they kept...those sorts of questions. And then, who doesn't love old buildings? The craftsmanship, the beautiful details, and the stories within their walls. Being a researcher gave me the opportunity to combine my passion for history and old architecture with my desire to find answers regarding the afterlife.

I visited libraries, government buildings, and historical societies to find photos, news articles, abstracts, and any other kind of documents that might be important for our upcoming investigation(s). Uncovering information regarding the property's history gave the team insight as to why the place could be haunted and possibly support any evidence that was captured during the investigation.

Even though my time was short with the Twin Cities Paranormal Society, I learned a lot during that period. And little did I know, my experience with TCPS would be the jumping-off point for my paranormal journey. My interests expanded into the realm of ufology, cryptids, the occult, conspiracy theories, and other phenomena. I was given opportunities in radio and television. I had the chance to meet people in the paranormal field whom I've admired for a long time including Rosemary Ellen Guiley and Linda Godfrey, both successful authors and leading experts in the paranormal field. I traveled to different countries and investigated some of the most haunted places in the world.

Some of my favorite investigations were at the Lady Victoria Colliery, the National Mining Museum in Scotland, basically the whole town of Virginia City, Nevada, and the Grant House Hotel in Rush City, Minnesota. All three locations did not disappoint with paranormal activity ranging from full-body apparitions, objects being thrown across the room, and disembodied voices to footsteps, doors slamming shut, and physical touch.

When I first started investigating, I was so serious. I would haul around a gigantic bag filled with every gadget you could think of. I found myself focusing too much on the equipment and not enough on my surroundings. I came to that conclusion when I took part in an EVP session. Everyone stared at the voice recorder and listened intently for any kind of response, completely unaware of what was going on around them. I'm not sure what made me look up, but I did and that's when I saw a full-bodied apparition. It was just standing there, in front of the window, watching us. And before I knew it, he was gone. Had I not looked up, I would have missed out on an incredible experience.

After that, I took on a more enjoyable, laid-back approach. I started using my equipment less and less and began to use my senses more. Now on investigations, I typically bring a flashlight, a voice recorder, and maybe one or two other items and that's it.

Not everyone will agree with my technique and that's okay because I believe there is no right or wrong way to investigate. However, in our field of paranormal research, there needs to be mutual respect. We need to respect each other's thoughts and opinions because we're all on the same level, searching for answers to the universe's greatest unsolved mysteries.

Bio: Mallie Fox is the owner of "Paranormal Girl," a lifestyle brand where women inspire and encourage each other in the paranormal field. She is currently the host of On the Rox with Mallie Fox podcast. She can be seen on Strange Evidence on Discovery Plus Channel (2018 to present) and was a cast member of Ghost Bait on Biography Channel (2013). She was

also a co-host on Darkness Radio, a paranormal talk radio show in the Twin Cities (2009 to 2015). When she's not investigating the strange and unusual, you can find her in Detroit, visiting antique and salvage shops for her 140-year-old home.

BECKY MCKIDDY-GYDESEN

OWNER OF TUCSON GHOST COMPANY, FOUNDER & LEAD INVESTIGATOR OF TUCSON GHOST SOCIETY

What motivated me to research the paranormal was the fact that I basically had experiences my entire life. In Toledo, Ohio, I lived in a haunted apartment and grew up in an 1800s haunted house. It seemed that I had paranormal experiences any time I went anywhere there were spirits around. My curiosity grew to find out more information about spirits, such as why they haunt, who they are and how they get their energy. I always had a deep respect for the unknown. I was the weird kid who would apologize for stepping on someone's grave or talk to the energies while I'd walk past their burial site.

I have had several paranormal experiences that fueled my interest in the paranormal. Growing up in the haunted house in Toledo, there were always areas I refused to go into after dark because they would creep me out (basically the upstairs and basement). I always felt as if I was being watched in that house. My first major experience however, was in my apartment in Toledo. I hated being alone in that apartment with just my 1-year-old daughter. Every room but the small extra bedroom would make me feel uneasy (the bathroom was the worst!). One night while watching TV, I heard a loud crash and I first thought that my kitten had knocked something off a shelf and broke it. I circled the apartment and found nothing until I entered the living room. There was glass on the floor and a picture out of its frame. However, the frame, although flipped over, was still on the wall. How does a picture flip itself over on a wall? This encounter is what sparked my curiosity about the unknown. There have been many other occurrences too, such as hearing phantom sounds, footsteps, voices, and music, to feeling watched or knowing I wasn't alone, and being touched by unseen forces.

I now own Tucson Ghost Company and am also the founder and lead investigator of a paranormal team called Tucson Ghost Society. As a paranormal team, we never charge for an investigation and we always try to debunk first before labeling things as paranormal. We also research and try to find possible causes as to why the place(s) could be haunted. Research is very important to the paranormal field. History, a lot of times, plays a huge role.

As investigators, we tend to refer to ourselves as open-minded skeptics. As I mentioned before, we want to try to debunk before we call anything paranormal. It's not always a ghost, as we have typically found that exposed or old wiring, rodents in the house, or even medication a person is on can be the main root of the issue. It's so important to cover all the grounds before jumping to conclusions. Using equipment can help tremendously as long as you research and learn about it. Every gadget has a downfall and something besides a ghost can set it off. For example, KII meters are overly sensitive to electrical signals, so not only will they detect spiritual activity but they can also show you where high electrical sources are that are in need of updates.

I would love to see this field taken more seriously as many people are entering it for either fame or to thrill-seek. So many individuals are jumping to conclusions to phenomena being demons or something negative due to the way it's presented in Hollywood. We need to show that paranormal activity is not what Hollywood presents it to be. We need to show respect to the spirits; highlight the paranormal in a more positive light, and to showcase real investigators more, especially women in the field who tend to really get overlooked.

As I mentioned before, we approach each case as skeptics. When we take on a new case, we do not go in assuming a place is haunted. We go in assuming we will be able to find common answers to the alleged haunting (bad wiring, rodents, etc.). Any time something happens, we try to first debunk. If we see a shadow, we try to recreate it to make sure it's not us. If we hear a voice, we make sure no one is around (for example, check outside, etc.). Our team shows great respect to any spirits we may be interacting with and tries to make them comfortable and even laugh. We notice that the more relaxed we are, the more interaction we get. So even though we do ask a normal line of questions (who we are talking to, etc.), our methods of communication tend to be more focused on being silly; such as everyday conversations you have with a friend that focus on different time periods.

So, let's say that we're at a former mining location. Our group would maybe tell a joke and concentrate on questions, such as,

- "How was their day?"
- "Did they find any gold?"
- "What did they have for supper?"

This technique tends to get more interaction than always asking the same old questions of who they are, why they are there, etc. We feel that talking to them like they are a human being and trying to laugh with them is always a good thing.

I have so many favorite locations and have had some very interesting cases. One time, I helped a family to try and get rid of a shadow figure or the "bad shadow man" as the family's little girl called it. This entity made everyone uncomfortable and they hoped we could help. While on the case, I started to feel very sick in the area where it was spotted. I asked, "What is making me sick?" An EVP of, "Maybe it's allergies" occurred. I'll never forget that response. Earlier that night, I told the client that I wasn't sick as my allergies were acting up, so I apologized for sneezing. Luckily, I was able to help the family, stood up to the shadow man, and told him he wasn't allowed to make anyone feel sick or uncomfortable. This family said they never had any issues after that and continues to keep in contact with me to this day.

I also had a business case once that dealt with a suicide spirit that was still holding on and staying at that location. This was a tough one because the spirit attached to me. His name was Carl and he started to make me feel depressed and disconnected. I had asked my co-lead if she could think of any reason as to why I felt this way all of a sudden. This is when her research came in handy and we looked more into Carl. I conducted an EVP session in my home once we had more facts. I asked if it was Carl and what he needed me to do for him. He asked me to pray for him and as soon as I did, the air seemed to get lighter. I felt like myself once again.

My husband encouraged me to do what I enjoy; thus, I formed the Tucson Ghost Society. It is a wonderful team and if it wasn't for its research and dedication, I wouldn't be able to do what I do. We have always been more of a female team, with women in command. Even my daughters are involved and learning the ropes. We do have men on the team too, along with a male team lead. We are all like a family and do things outside of the paranormal together. The entire group goes through a training process, where we teach people the ins and outs of everything we do. To make this a team effort, each person investigates, researches, and reviews information.

In the early days of investigating, I admired the people on the show *Ghost Hunters*, including Grant, Jason, Steve, Dave, Dustin, Kris, Amy, Adam and so on. They were always respectful and didn't make it sound scary to the audience. I based some of my early investigations on how they would conduct their cases. Now however, I truly respect the people who are in this field for the truth as well as those who are truly in it for the right reasons, including teams that don't call everything paranormal and groups that research. I truly admire my family and my team for always trying to find the truth behind every haunting and devoting their time and effort into all of this and not even getting paid a dime.

I became involved in the historical research of the paranormal and started conducting paranormal tours out of my curiosity after having my own experiences. After stumbling across the show *Ghost Hunters*, I learned that people are interested in the paranormal and host tours and ghost hunts. I went on a search to find one so I could go and see what it was about. I went on a tour and one thing led to another; the next thing I knew I bought a ghost tour company. I was then able to expand my company and do hunts and special events. I also became a part of a paranormal team by chance and ended up starting my own when they disbanded. I also ended up with an offer to do a podcast and after a couple weeks that became my own. I switched it up from *Mysteries Explained* to *Everything Under the Moon* and have been doing that for years now. To be quite honest, everything fell into my lap all because of my curiosity.

My tours and ghost hunts are here for education and entertainment. We focus on the history and truth of hauntings. We entertain guests, but we don't add in jump scares or make anything up. We use the time to also explain how it's not all evil and mostly just people like us who have passed on. We teach people to show respect, not to be fearful of the unknown, and to see that it's not what Hollywood makes it out to be.

We just use the normal methods for research, including Internet options for searching old newspapers and interviewing people. History is so important to the paranormal field because so many times it ties into the haunting(s). For example, paranormal activity at a location with a previous fire can include the energy of 100-plus individuals who perished in it. In order to understand the origins of a haunting, it is important to know a location's history and information about that particular building, its area, and people. It can help in so many ways to bring light to the cause(s) of a haunting. Without the history, you would be simply clueless on the how, why, when, who, etc. History can help piece together all the missing links.

My podcast can be found on many podcast networks such as iHeart-Radio, Amazon, Spotify, Spreaker, and more. It talks about hauntings, UFOs, Bigfoot, witchcraft, psychics, tours, Disney, and life in general... basically everything under the moon. By having a podcast, I benefit from connecting with so many others in the paranormal field, learning from and listening to them with an open mind.

Also, it's a way for me to be able to teach people about the paranormal and to allow others to learn from me. It's a great resource for teaching and spreading the word about the spiritual world.

Podcasting is a great medium and resource for the paranormal field right now. People can tune in while doing various activities, such as driving or doing homework. Having an open mind and a passion for the paranormal provides a solid foundation for a good podcast on the subject.

The main message I want to convey to people is that the paranormal isn't super scary nor does it consist of all demons or evil. Spirits are basically people just like you and me.

Bio: *Becky Mckiddy-Gydesen is the owner of the Tucson Ghost Company (established in 2013) and the founder and lead investigator of the Tucson Ghost Society. She is also the host of the Everything Under the Moon podcast where she discusses the paranormal, UFOs, Bigfoot, witchcraft, psychics, tours, Disney, and more. She, along with her team, enjoys teaching people about the paranormal and learning from other investigators.*

Jill Hanson

Certified Hypnotherapist (CHt), Master NLP Practitioner, Independent Researcher, Writer, Former Radio Host

Every woman comes into this world with a unique blueprint that informs her gifts and the work she is to do with her time on this earth. For some women, comfort, and sense-making are found in the nuts and bolts of the world, and they are gifted a playbook from birth simply found within the embrace of the current paradigm. For other women, the map to be followed is more occult-based, a scaffolding veiled in mystery, only found beneath layers of consciousness and perception and along her path as she walks it. I consider myself blessed to be the latter.

Glancing in the rearview, it was apparent very early on that I was fueled by curiosity above all else. I have vivid memories of myself around the age of 7, and the hours I spent sitting cross-legged on the low-pile carpet of my public library, one hour turning into four, utterly consumed by the stories told between the plastic-protected covers of books in the *Mysteries and Unexplained* aisle. Subjects like spontaneous human combustion, UFOs, ghosts, poltergeists, haunted houses, possession, astral projection, mediums, reincarnation, and remote viewing drew me into a world ruled by mysterious universal laws and science that others seemed disinterested in at best, and dismissive of at worst, but described what was to me a familiar aspect of experience. My deep curiosity for the subjects and equally profound confusion at the world's response to them added up to a mystery with irresistible allure, and I was hooked. I explicitly articulated for myself at that young age that this would be what I did when I grew up.

So, at 7, I discovered the transformative solace and sympathetic mirror that was paranormal non-fiction. When I was around the age of 8, I had my first opportunity to put theory into practice. At that age, the family often took road trips through the Colorado desert, and I snatched up the opportunity to stretch out flat on my back in the rear-facing seat of our Oldsmobile Custom Cruiser station wagon, watching the deep field of space for anything luminous that moved. Just as in my experience of the library, hours would flow by as if they were minutes as I immersed myself in possibility and the unknown. The soundtrack to those midnight drives through the desert was always the tinny resonance of Art Bell's voice as *Coast-to-Coast AM* drifted from the glowing radio in the dash.

It was also around this age that I harnessed the ability to "wake" in my dreams, which I had discovered to be lucid dreaming, through my habitual library book binge sessions. Equally as profound and exciting was that on an occasional night, I would find my most essential self spontaneously dispatching from my sleeping body to travel to my elementary school playground to play unhindered and unburdened by my human substance.

Adding to my unique sense of reality and further widening the gap between the average human experience and my own, I observed distinctly humanlike shadow people who crossed my bedroom door each night as they transited the hallway from my parent's bedroom to the spare bedroom. There were also haunting nightmares and sleep paralysis, both were a near nightly affair (interestingly enough both disappeared on nights when I slept outside my family home, though that wasn't a connection I would make until I was much older), as well as my ability to see color on black and white TVs, which faded when I was around 11 years old. This is by no means an exhaustive list of the oddities in my supernormal experience of the reality of my youth, but enough of a brush stroke to paint a picture.

By the time adulthood found me, I was well-versed in a spectrum of anomalous phenomena and the fringe science that helped explain them.

My normal included an ever-present undercurrent of anomalous experiences that followed me as I moved through my days; however, my first years of adulthood were quite customary on the surface: I attended college and studied astrophysics, anthropology, and art. I started an ordinary career in banking and finance. I had the normal human experiences of finding and losing a soulmate, the spice of a few twists and turns, and finally landing in the all-too-common role of a single mother of two young sons. All very normal things, but I realized that after settling for normal for so many years, I had become disconnected from who I truly was. I recognized the necessity of a course correction out of my detour into the weeds if I was to approach anywhere near my God-given potential in this life.

The beautiful thing about finding yourself lost and torn down to your chassis is that you are presented with the brilliant albeit excruciatingly uncomfortable and painful opportunity to rebuild yourself, and that's just what I did. Healing began with a pause, a breath, and two simple questions: "Who do I want to *be*, and what do I want to *do*?" My higher self, dropped in to answer without a second to waste: "I will reclaim my most authentic self, and the mysteries I'm innately and passionately curious about are to be my work." Finally reconnected to my adult path, 8-year-old me rejoiced from another timeline, and I was reborn into a life dedicated to interdisciplinary research in Nonlocal Consciousness Studies.

In that moment of lucidity, I vowed to architect my path forward using my intuition as my compass, following it without question as my own higher wisdom even when my pursuits went against the grain and couldn't make sense to others. *This is the greatest epiphany I've ever had, and the wisest thing I've ever done.* It took over 30 years of trying to fit the normal mold and failing to internalize that *my path was meant to look different.*

My first task in search of myself was to get my academic and scholarly groove back, so I returned to school. The year prior, I had applied and been accepted to a university in North Dakota for a program in human resources, which made a hell of a lot of financial sense for a woman in my position with two young sons to care for, but that first day of class rolled around *and I just couldn't.* I hadn't known the why of it then; I had the nagging knowing that it was the wrong move. So, all logical reasoning aside, all "normie," discouraging self-talk silenced, I tuned into my compass and completed my undergraduate degree in interdisciplinary studies at a university that called to me, then hopped right into a master's degree in Consciousness and Transformative Studies.

The moment I started using my inner voice to guide me, my alignment with what was supposed to be was unmistakable, and magical things started happening in my life. I'd barely taken a breath after my bachelor's degree when I went all-in on my next crazy, soul-sanctioned challenge: I would create an organization as a virtual base camp for my independent consciousness research, writing, and speaking engagements. I took to sharing my work on social media, and within three months, I received an unexpected invitation to bring visibility to my work as a guest on a digital radio station, KGRA-db. After I paused to quell the terror of my inner recovering social phobic, I breathed into the guidance of my inner compass again, and connected with an absolute *knowing* that this opportunity was the universe saying, "It's time to step up, sis...you *are* ready." So, putting the cart before the cart as I've always called it, I accepted the invitation and scheduled my first radio appearance for Thanksgiving even though at that moment, I was scared to within inches of my life at the mere thought of that moment arriving.

Needless to say, I overcame my phobia to face and survive speaking in front of an audience of 30,000+ humans on live radio. *Game changer.* Early the next year the station director invited me back as a guest on several shows, and by May, he approached me about bringing my research to KGRA-db as a host of my own weekly show. Putting the cart before the horse again, I committed, and I did just that from September 2014 to January 2020. During this time, I dedicated the equivalent of a full-time job - forty hours per week, give or take - to my research and preparation for my guests on *The Q.PSIENCE Project.* It was bliss. I was on my path, facing challenges and evolving. I was making my passion my life's work, and in having done so, I had inadvertently prioritized my health and happiness. Gratitude became a primary emotion, and my wildest dreams were bubbling up to occupy waking life.

In November 2015, *Midnight in the Desert* (MITD) producer, Heather Wade, reached out to test my interest in being a guest on Art Bell's radio program. After a very brief but necessary pause purely for the purpose of re-integrating my soul and my body, I was on the MITD calendar for a conversation with Art in January. If nothing else ever came of my journey, I had reached the pinnacle of my childhood vision for myself. Though Art stepped away from radio in early December due to very unfortunate circumstances, a mere month before I was scheduled to speak with him about my impassioned research, I wasn't so disappointed that I couldn't still appreciate a priceless full-circle, soul-level, "#1 on my bucket list" moment, and *that* is as golden as golden gets.

In 2020, after seven years of amazing conversations on talk radio, I reached a point of recognition that while I had personally evolved through the work and that was a great thing, the work itself needed to evolve in order to remain in alignment with my soul's trajectory. It was time to leave my cozy home at KGRA-db to pursue the next leg of my journey, and even though at that time I didn't yet know what that looked like, I took the leap knowing there would be a net to catch me and created space of the next adventure to find me.

Upon signing off for the last time, I reflected on the body of work I'd created, all of the amazing conversations I'd had, the friendships I'd forged, and the community of support I'd built through my listenership. I was moving on with immeasurable immaterial assets that would inform my next challenge, whatever that looked like, and so, I closed that virtual door quietly behind me with a smile and a heart bursting with love for my work, my journey, and my people.

My best work lies ahead, my most exciting discoveries await me, and the greatest questions I will ever ask, have yet to form on my tongue. My next big adventure will take me through the brambles of dismantling an outdated paradigm of biology to architect a new holistic model of life science, which integrates modeling that supports the many incorporeal, extraphysical life forms, entities, and non-human intelligence that are purported to exist, occupying directly imperceptible, intangible, and interdimensional environments and domains. I have plenty of personal experience to draw from in this arena and a world of individual souls who each hold a unique piece of the puzzle just a conversation away.

Science is beautiful. Facts change with new evidence to evolve knowledge, and over time, knowledge deepens to become understanding, and new understanding is the powerful force that shifts paradigms and opens the door to new frontiers. The paranormal is the last great frontier of human exploration and as far as I can tell, the universe has hand-picked only one immutable truth that will help us navigate it: *qualitative data matters* and the women who occupy the fringes, whose curiosity, passion, and hunger for truth pulls them like gravity to the fringes of future knowledge, will be those on the forefront of humanity's critical consciousness evolution.

***Bio:** Jill Hanson is a Certified Hypnotherapist (CHt) and Master NLP practitioner, independent researcher, writer, and former talk radio host of THE Q.PSIENCE PROJECT on KGRA-db. She received her B.A. from California Institute of Integral Studies (CIIS) in San Francisco, CA, with a focus on Quantum Consciousness and Neurodiversity, and is completing a master's degree emphasizing the foundation of a holistic "theory of everything" model of life science that prioritizes an openness to future-paradigm biological discovery, inclusive and expectant of a potential basis for incorporeal, extraphysical lifeforms, entities, and intelligence that occupy directly imperceptible, intangible, and interdimensional environments and domains.*

Through her private practice, Jill combines hypnotic and energetic modalities with coaching tools and techniques to help clients access their purpose and potential, and revels in the opportunity to work with clients around their purported interactions with extraterrestrial, ultraterrestrial/cryptoterrestrial intelligence.

In 2014, Jill was a scheduled presenter at the University of Arizona's Science of Consciousness Conference and has been a featured guest on The Richard Dolan Show, Midnight In the Desert, FATE Magazine Radio, and other popular talk radio shows.

Kiersten Parsons Hathcock

Intuitive Medium, Author, Speaker

I couldn't stop thinking about the tiny voice I heard in the garage that day: "Mom!" rang out sharp and clear from the corner of the workshop but no one was there. As the sound of the familiar call-out faded into the background, goosebumps raced up and down my body. Hearing "Mom" called to me was an everyday experience, but that day, those who regularly called me Mom were still at school.

It was the first time in thirty-six years on Earth that I questioned my sanity. Maybe the polyurethane fumes were making me hear voices. Maybe it was the pressure I was under getting ready for my appearance on the TV show *Shark Tank*. Whatever it was, somewhere deep down, I knew it was real. Unbeknownst to me at the time, this was just the beginning.

Unlike most psychic mediums, I didn't have a near-death experience, and I don't remember talking to spirits from a young age. I was just a normal, middle-aged mom who spent her days running her business and her kids to and from school.

That is until I started channeling the spirits of kids who were murdered by predators. To be clear, I wasn't looking for those little souls, they simply found me. From 2010-2013, I channeled messages from many children in spirit while keeping my undercover medium life under wraps. Some of the children asked me to reach out to their parents and law enforcement. And I did. A few asked me to hang onto their messages, saying that their parents would find me. And they did.

It wasn't until I started having visions of myself as a child that I realized why the kids—many of them killed by sexual predators—were coming to me. I, too, had been sexually abused as a kid, but the memories didn't surface until three years after my intuitive awakening when I was 40.

It's hard to imagine what life would be like right now had I not chosen to walk through the spirit world door. I would have dismissed the repressed memories of abuse and never given myself a chance to heal or learn to trust my inner knowing. In short, I wouldn't have the outlook on life that I do now.

Trusting those intuitive nudges (and then later, full-on spirit experiences) was no easy task in the beginning. Naturally, I turned to what I'd always trusted: Google. After all, I taught myself furniture design by searching Google for instructions. Turns out, you can also search for all things intuitive, too. And I'm not just talking about someone's opinion of intuition. I relied on empirical research data related to metaphysics and quantum physics. I devoured many scientific studies. "If I just had enough data," I thought, I'd start to better understand how talking to those on the other side is even possible.

Aside from random sightings of apparitions, voices that manifested out of thin air, and objects that moved on their own, I didn't start to channel full messages until I turned 37. I will never forget the day the first child in spirit, Nate Pannell, visited me. He was a 13-year-old boy who died from a brain bleed caused by an AVM (arteriovenous malformation) in Defiance, Ohio, the town I grew up in. It was 2010, four years after his death, and Nate's parents shared photos of the four-year anniversary memorial they'd just held in honor of their son. I knew Nate's parents well enough to be connected to them on Facebook, but I wouldn't call them friends back then. I hadn't even realized their son had passed. That's how well we didn't know one another.

The minute I laid eyes on Nate's photo, I could see him in my mind's eye, and he began speaking with me. He shared messages with me that were evidential in nature—private things that only his parents would know. And then he pled with me to share them with his mom and dad.

I mustered the courage to reach out to them shortly after receiving Nate's messages. Thankfully, his parents didn't shut the door on me. In fact, they welcomed me into their hearts and home. For the past 12 years, I've had the pleasure of being a telephone line of sorts between Nate and his parents. Not only am I able to share meaningful messages that help Nate's family cope with his loss, but they also unknowingly gave me the gift of faith and belief.

They validated that what I was experiencing was real, and they helped strengthen my belief that our loved ones do live on in spirit. These gifts were life-changing, considering that up until that point, I was a skeptic.

Since then, I've worked on countless cases involving missing and murdered children and missing people. I've partnered with law enforcement officers around the country and even founded The National Institute for Law and Justice (NILJ) alongside long-time partner, decorated NYPD (Ret) Detective, Mark Pucci. NILJ is a registered 501c3 nonprofit whose mission is to help manage (at no cost) investigative services for crime victims and their families.

Over the years, what's become clear is that I don't operate the way most psychic mediums do. Here's what I mean: I volunteer on cases for NILJ, and I channel messages from children in spirit who then either guide their parents to me or guide me to reach out to their parents or law enforcement. All the work I do as a medium is on a volunteer basis.

For those of you wondering how to vet if a particular psychic medium is the real deal, I have two suggestions: First, pay attention to your own intuition while researching the medium. Does your stomach feel like it's in knots? Do you feel calm when you look at their photo? Pay attention to the physical signs of intuition to determine which psychic counselor is right for you. Secondly, if they talk of curses and ask for unbelievable amounts of money to help rid you of one, run. They may indeed be gifted at mediumship, but they likely aren't very heart-centered. I fully believe mediums should be able to charge for their work; however, there's a difference between taking advantage of someone and operating from a place of truth and love.

As you traverse the world of woo-woo, you might notice that many mediums claim to have been tested by specific agencies. Their accuracy scores are proudly posted on their websites. I do believe that this type of study is helpful, but it also creates a limiting box for those out there like me. My intuition doesn't work within the confines of the test. Because I mostly channel children who've been murdered or died suddenly—and I rely on them to step forward—I doubt I could conjure answers to questions about what I'm seeing on the other side of the door, etc.

This is good news for anyone interested in strengthening their mediumship skills. Knowing that intuition shows up for me in very specific ways that aren't conducive to metaphysical study means that intuition is not one-size-fits-all. We all have our own path, skills, and purpose.

I'm living proof that even scientifically minded skeptics can find their way to and through the light. Now, at the ripe old age of 49, I believe that intuition is a roadmap we can choose to follow or ignore. In my case, I'm beyond grateful that I embraced the unknown—for myself, for the kids, and for generations of skeptics yet to be born. Maybe one day they'll read about a furniture designer/carpenter/CEO turned medium who proved to herself and others that intuitive gifts and paranormal experiences aren't things of make-believe. Turns out, the paranormal is actually, well, normal.

Bio: *Kiersten Parsons Hathcock, author of Little Voices: How Kids in Spirit Helped a Reluctant Medium Escape and Heal from Abuse, is an award-winning self-taught carpenter/furniture designer, and founder of Mod Mom Furniture, a kids' furniture company featured on ABC's Shark Tank. She's also a TEDx speaker and an intuitive medium who works for the National Institute for Law and Justice helping detectives and families uncover the truth in missing persons and homicide cases. In her previous work life, Kiersten was a staff writer for Northern Arizona University and TV marketing executive for A&E TV Network and The History Channel. An Ohio native, she now resides in Phoenix, Arizona with her husband, Scott, daughters, Natalie and Grace, and pup, Scout. You can find her at www.kierstenhathcock.*

Kitty Janusz

Author, Paranormal Investigator, Reiki Master, Psychic Medium

People can't help but initially ask me, "When did you become interested in the paranormal?"

Of course, I smile and tell them, "I grew up in a haunted house." The envy of any aspiring ghost hunter, right?

Spending your childhood in a paranormally active house isn't as cool as you might think. First of all, it doesn't dawn on you right away that the peculiar happenings at home are really that peculiar. The bumps are simply the cat playing with his toys and the footsteps are just my dad walking down the hallway...in his boots...on what sounds like a hardwood floor...even though the house was carpeted...right?

On pretty much a daily basis my brother, sister, and I would see or hear something out of the ordinary. I was probably around six years of age when I first noticed funny things happening in our house. Objects would disappear only to reappear in what I thought were strange places. A heavy glass ashtray that sat on the end table vanished only to mysteriously be found days later perched on the edge of a door frame. Another item was my prized green plastic pirate treasure chest. I stored all my worldly goods inside. I had managed to save up seven whole dollars and I was going to spend every cent at the Rock Shoppe in Knott's Berry Farm. Saturday came and the pirate chest was nowhere to be found. I

KNOW I had set it on the table right before bed. We tore the house apart looking for my seven dollars of Rock Shoppe money. My parents were frustrated as now we were running late. What's this? High atop the refrigerator sat my green plastic pirate chest! Me being all of 6 years old, I couldn't have possibly stashed it way up there and I know my parents didn't because they tore the house up looking for it. How did it get there, and why?

At first, it seemed like small annoying stuff. The occasional object moved. The footsteps we mistook for one of our parents. Nothing too scary.

Until we started to have things happen when we were all in the same room, or worse yet, when we were home alone.

Coming home to find all the water in the house running full blast? Check.

Sitting in a room that had windows on three sides and have all three full-length drapes blow inward at the same time? With the windows closed? Check.

Watching the cat's eyes dilate black as he stares towards the creepy hallway because he hears the same phantom footsteps you hear? Check.

Being just a kid, I came to assume that every house must have some sort of ghost. The ghost must have been someone who lived in the area and was like having a weird uncle hanging around the house. That is until I tried to ask the neighborhood kids about their ghosts. Apparently, they didn't have their own resident spirit. And once they learned there might be some spirits in our home, it not surprisingly, put them on edge. I remember one afternoon some schoolmates and I were hanging out in the living room when poof...there went the drapes blowing a good four feet into the room from all sides of the room. I've never seen those kids run so fast!

I thought over time I was comfortable with some unseen specter abiding in my home. I thought I could handle having what felt like a large man standing right behind me in the creepy hallway. But no, not quite. I bolted down that hallway every time, just to get out of there. Day or night, always right behind me, making the hairs stand up on my neck.

Then one night it happened: As I was getting into bed, I felt a familiar pounce on the bed. I thought it was one of the cats coming to join me. But this pounce suddenly felt different. I continued to feel a weight pressing down on the corner of the bed. I bolted upright and stared as the edge of my bed continued to press downward as if someone was sitting on my bed! Without thinking, I yelled out, "Don't do that!" And just that quickly, I could no longer feel the weight pressing down and the indentation went away.

That was my little epiphany. I communicated with something I couldn't see or hear but it understood me. It didn't mean to frighten me. Spirits can see us and hear us. And now I discovered that the living could communicate with the dead.

The years passed and we came to a sort of understanding. Whatever was in the house no longer invaded our personal space and we tolerated the occasional object missing and hearing the boot steps clomping up and down the hallway.

By the time I was nine, my parents ran a small antique business. Our house became filled with beautiful treasures from the past. I loved simply holding an antique object in my hands and pondering who may have owned it before me. I would admire the craftsmanship and think about how long someone may have saved to purchase such a wondrous thing. Was it a gift for a lover? A beloved child's toy, passed down from generations? I could almost see the stories each antique item held within its fabric. Even all these years later, I still love antiques. My house has many treasures I've acquired over the years. Each has a story to tell.

I also developed a love for historic places. I would walk the halls of old homes and admire the woodwork, craftsmanship, and attention to detail. I toured battleships, museums, and California's early missions. My family would travel on "antiques buying trips" and we'd visit Gettysburg and Mount Vernon and so many historic places along the way. What a childhood. I loved it all. It might seem weird to some to have always had such a love for antiques and old places. But I was somehow always drawn to them. I could feel their energy. I could hear their stories...

We all have our own story on how we began actually investigating the spirits and documenting paranormal activity. As you can see, I kind of grew up with it.

Hanging around old places, you really get a sense of their energy, how a place feels and how a location makes YOU feel. I am creeped out by some places. I am drawn back again and again to others. Most know the RMS *Queen Mary* is my favorite. Locations can feel different from room to room, floor to floor, and day to day. This is one reason why someone can have incredible experiences and gather amazing evidence and the next person hardly believes that location to be haunted at all, they feel nothing and may get no evidence.

When I first started conducting paranormal investigations I just started with the basics. I had a notebook, a flashlight, and a couple digital recorders. Formal investigative teams were something unheard of to me 30-odd years ago so I explored on my own and went on instinct. I was a natural at psychometry; I could hold an object and I'd get visuals of past owners. If the item was very special to them, I might connect with their spirit and have a short conversation. Spirits might tell me who gave them this item or how much they cherished it. I think most of the time if you are drawn to an object, spirits can sense this, and you connect with them through this object. You have a mutual appreciation for its beauty, and it is felt on both sides of the veil.

Talk to museum docents and security guards. They work in historic locations every day. They know the place and they must enjoy being there or they wouldn't stay. These folks have stories to share. I wish I could go into more detail about Stone Tape Theory, Ley lines, geomagnetic anomalies, and the plethora of theories describing WHY locations seem to be haunted but that would take up more space than I am allotted within this book.

This mutual admiration for paranormally active locations is important. In my experience, spirits stay for a reason. Either they, too, love the place and feel they need to protect it and its residents, or they are somehow trapped or bound to the location. This is where a paranormal investigator's work begins. Approach every investigation with empathy, respect, curiosity, and most importantly, personal boundaries.

Like me, I think most paranormal investigators love old places. Many investigators also become empathic to the extent they are cognizant of energy shifts in the environment even before their equipment detects it. Inventors created devices to detect and document, and thereby validate, what the investigator was already experiencing.

It seems every paranormal investigator finds their niche. I know researchers who always seem to capture photographic evidence. Others easily experience physical phenomena. My forte is finding Class A EVPs during many recording sessions. I seem to be able to ask the right questions, I guess. Even with simple digital recorders, I often capture several responses during short burst sessions.

I believe investigating the paranormal is basically energy work. The soul is pure energy, our experiences can imprint energetically into the very matter of a location. If we record evidence of a residual haunting, we are gathering evidence of an imprinted energy that plays over and over again. If we are lucky to capture an experience with an intelligent haunting, we are communicating with the pure energy of spirit.

We get excited when this happens, but we must be cautious. In energy work, there is a light and a dark. Many locations are haunted because of traumatic events. These events and emotions can permeate a location and negatively affect you, the investigator. Souls may feel trapped and reach out for help. And then there are the darker entities. Be that they are elementals or something lower, these can be drawn to the light of our energy, another spirit's energy, and these entities can drain the light from a soul.

There's so much out there that we still don't know. I've seen some crazy stuff over the years. I've had fellow investigators physically attacked. I've witnessed mood swings and had investigators become fearful and nauseous only to be relieved when they leave the location. I saw people's health deteriorating. The layers of pain and trauma at some locations can continue to affect the living.

I wrote my first book on the paranormal, *When the Dead Speak: The Art and Science of Paranormal Communication* because I noticed with ALL the paranormal teams out there, with all the TV shows and gathered evidence, there was a big something that wasn't often addressed. I noticed little attention was being paid to the fact we are dealing with situations that can affect our physical and emotional well-being. It's human nature to get caught up in the moment. We're in a dark and spooky place. Our adrenaline is pumping, and our senses are on high alert. But like layers of an onion, the emotions, the pain, and the trauma of haunted locations can cling to our physical bodies. Over the years, I've witnessed these layers lead to mood changes, depression, and worse. I have seen investigators feeling "drawn" toward dark, negative, "demonic" locations. Their demeanor and personality change. They become withdrawn and moody and aggressive. Many investigators leave the field altogether because of what it has done to their personal lives, and their home lives. In the worst-case scenario, I lost two dear friends whom I will say were negatively affected by years of investigating without any personal energetic boundaries.

Some say it was merely domestic violence. Those who knew them saw the changes. In the end, the layers of negative spaces and provoking dark forces just layered upon them.

They died in a murder-suicide.

I felt it was important to focus on the long-term effects of dealing with such energies. I wanted to find ways to protect myself as well as other investigators by using personal boundaries and how to utilize cleansing techniques to not only cleanse a location but ourselves as well.

One of the best tools I found for energy work was Reiki. Reiki, which loosely translates as universal energy, allows a practitioner to channel the energy around us and help restore balance. You can use it to help a body heal or even send Reiki throughout a room to raise the vibration. What I found Reiki especially useful for during investigations was it taught me how to, I'd say, identify the intention of energy, and with that, the intention of spirit energy. Was this really the spirit of a child, or did my gut tell me something is not right about this spirit? Reiki training amped my gut feeling tenfold.

Along with Reiki, a skeptical yet open mind and just plain respect for those who came before us are the cornerstones for paranormal investigators.

Learn what paranormal equipment detects and HOW it detects anomalies. Visit a location multiple times if possible. Get a feel for a location. Don't think you've failed somehow if you don't capture evidence during every investigation. If evidence is questionable or can be easily recreated, toss it out.

Remember WHY you started investigating haunted places.

Be curious. Have respect. Show compassion. Maintain healthy boundaries.

Bio: *Kitty Janusz's book, When the Dead Speak: The Art and Science of Paranormal Investigation won first place honors in the Los Angeles Festival of Books, the largest book festival in the United States. She has also penned an award-winning book geared towards the YA reader and based on true paranormal events, Secrets Buried in the Lemon Grove. Kitty Janusz is a Reiki Master and works on honing her skills as a psychic medium. She has over 25 years of experience in the paranormal field and has investigated with notable paranormal celebrities such as Jason Hawes, Grant Wilson, Chip Coffey, Mark and Debby Constantino as well as the Ghost Adventures crew. Her television appearances include The Graber Olive House episode of Ghost Adventures and Terror Twins episode of Haunted Hospitals. For more information on Kitty Janusz check out her website at www.kittyjanusz.com and find her books on Amazon.*

Lisa Krick

Paranormal Investigator, Paranormal Tour Guide, Reiki Master, Ghostly-Voices.com

I've been having experiences since I was very young and I've always been fascinated with things that go bump in the night but terrified of them at the same time. I'm never so happy as when I'm scaring the shit out of myself with a horror movie or walking around in a haunted location waiting for something to happen.

I don't consider myself an adrenaline junkie, but really, that's what we are ... tiptoeing through a dark hallway with the moonlight offering slivers of respite from the absolute absence of light in the corners just waiting for something or someone to step out from the shadows and scare the bejesus out of us. However, what separates us from the rest of the crowd is that everyone else would experience this and run screaming from the building. We, as researchers and investigators, run *toward* the sound or image, trying to figure out logically what just happened. We stand our ground and debunk. We experiment to see if we can make it happen again. We talk it through to ensure that what we saw/felt/heard was *really* what we saw/felt/heard. In the moment of heightened awareness, we sometimes try to fit a square peg into a round hole.

I used to be motivated to prove to the world that the paranormal exists. Not so much anymore. I know that it exists. I've had too many experiences not to believe that it exists. But it's not my job to prove to anyone else that it's there. My motivation is to learn from those on the other side. There's always a lesson to be learned from others. My search is from a more personal point of view these days.

I've had several experiences that have fueled my interest. Probably my first experiences fueled me without me even knowing that's what was happening. When I was very young (from about 4-11), my grandparents had a home in which none of the children would sleep in the back bedroom (except my sister, but that's a story for another time). We'd start off back there and then always end up in the big bed in our grandparents' room. I was leery of that room. Didn't even like going to the bathroom because I could feel someone watching me from the shadows in that room. I also hated the basement of that house. I could never even go to the back landing where the stairs to the basement started without being absolutely scared stiff. I never understood that. So, when I was an adult, I asked my "Nanny" (grandma) about that house. I didn't tell her why I was asking but just asked if she knew the history. She told me that all she knew was that there were two sisters who lived in the house right before them. One of them had died in the back bedroom and the other had died in the basement. Shivers. That told me everything I needed to know. I have since talked to my cousins about this house and they've had similar feelings/reactions there as well. Nobody ever tried to hurt me. It could be that the sisters were trying to reach out to me to communicate, but I was too young to understand that. Regardless, I still have nightmares about that house today.

I don't do nearly as much research as I'd like to by digging through courthouse documents and such, but I do find as much out online as I can and then take that information with a grain of salt. I like to find the history of the location (because for the most part, my team and I investigate locations, not people) and how it's changed through the years. How many times has the building changed hands or how many businesses (and what kind) have occupied the location through the years? How far back are the hauntings documented? Is everyone experiencing the same phenomenon? There are so many paths one can take in the actual research portion of the investigation. If I'm investigating a residence or former residence, I also like to visit the cemetery where the folks who lived there in the past are laid to rest and have a chat with them before ever stepping foot in the location. To me, it's respectful to let them know that we'll be in their home. I also ask for their assistance at this time if they'd like to join us. I don't know if this helps, but it certainly doesn't hurt. Once at the location, we conduct the investigation by scientific means ... baseline readings, a walk-through taking photographs and visualizing where everything is located and scouting out where to set equipment for the evening. When I'm with my team, we work methodically with different equipment. When I'm alone (and by alone, I mean working with other teams or new people that I'm not used to investigating with), I tend to go "old school" reverting back to using just an audio recorder, a flashlight, and my own intuition to guide me through the evening.

My team is the American Spectral Society (ASS). We've been around for probably ten years or so. However, I began researching/investigating with a team around 2005. I was a member of the GRS or Ghost Research Society and that's where I learned how to investigate a location scientifically, and methodically. From set up to break down to filing reports afterward, learning about the paranormal isn't just about running amok in a haunted location. There's so much more to it than that. Most people don't know about that...or follow it through. The team I'm with now, ASS (yeah, I know), is an amazing mix of people and we work very well together. I think we get better results because we're so well-attuned to each other. We also have a website called ghostly-voices.com...it's a repository of our best EVP evidence and also our Estes Method sessions, along with a bit of history on the locations we've visited and some team pictures.

Most of the locations I've been to have taught me something. Probably the scariest/most active location consistently for me would be the Monroe House in Hartford City, Indiana. There's an entity there who has tried to actually possess me twice now. Not cool. But that house draws me in. And most times, I'm there with a group who will come to the "safe room" to tell me they're getting my name on the spirit box. The house knows me as well.

The woman I admire in this field above all others is Rosemary Ellen Guiley. She was investigating/researching before it was cool. She was a rock star in this field who knew much about every subject of the paranormal/supernatural and she was happy to teach others. She was my mentor and my friend and I was honored to learn at her knee. Sadly, she passed away in the summer of 2019. Happily, she's still with us. I can't count the times that people have said that they've been in contact with her since she's passed. I am one of those lucky people. Rosemary wrote over 65 books regarding the supernatural and was on countless documentaries, radio, and TV programs talking about her knowledge of the paranormal.

I also work with Troy Taylor's American Hauntings group in which I will lead public investigations in different haunted locations for people who either don't have their own teams or who can't or don't want to rent a venue on their own. Most of these locations I've already vetted and know that they're truly haunted. I don't like taking people to locations that I wouldn't want to go to on my own. These folks are spending their hard-earned money to visit these locations. I want them to at least have a chance to experience something paranormal if they can. It helps if the venue is actually active. I will give my group the history of the location, and the history of the haunting(s), walk them around the location to get them familiar with the layout of the venue, and then let them go to experience it on their own. If they need me, they know where to find me, but I don't like to insert myself unless I'm needed. At some point, people will normally come back to me to let me know that something's going on or that they need for me to help them with something.

I'm becoming pretty proficient with dark mirror scrying and using the Estes Method of communication. People genuinely like to learn those methods and I'm happy to teach them. The main takeaway for my public investigations is that I want my guests to have an enjoyable evening out that hopefully includes something happening to them that they just can't explain away scientifically. Although there are literally scores of right ways to investigate the paranormal, there are, indeed, wrong ways as well. If I can educate along the way, it's a bonus.

While I believe that we're all born with psychic abilities, some are good at it and others, not so much. It's a skill that needs to be developed...like free throws in basketball...the more you practice your skill, the better developed it becomes. I actually discovered my skills pretty recently. Or more accurately, I accepted my skills. I still have doubts sometimes and I've been told that I'm my own worst critic and that I need to believe in myself and what spirit is telling me. But, gosh, it's hard sometimes.

I've never actually done a "sit down and read someone for money thing." But I have (and do) read people on the fly... normally it's someone from the other side who is pestering me with one sentence over and over in my head until I blurt it out to whoever is standing in front of me. Then, my entire body gets chills. That's the spirit's way of telling me what I said was right. It's really weird and probably weirder to put it in writing but that's how it works for me. I'm guessing that every psychic is different. So, I guess I'm a medium and not a psychic. I cannot read the future, but I get information from dead people in the form of pictures in my head or someone speaking to me in my head.

I work with a paranormal team called the American Spectral Society. But my role is not that of a medium. My role is that of an investigator. If something comes through psychically, cool. If not, cool. I'm not the only one on my team who has had their skills developing over the last several years, but I won't name names because she still doubts herself, even though I know she's got skills with the woo-woo.

I have recently become a Reiki Master, which I hope helps bring my paranormal experiences to the next level. Only time will tell.

I'd like to thank Nicole Strickland for inviting me to participate in this amazing project. She and I go back a fair piece (not way back though, because neither one of us is old enough for that!) and has been a constant friend and sounding board throughout my paranormal journey. Much love, Nicole! Here's to many more years of tiptoeing through dark hallways!

Bio: *Lisa was born and raised on the south side of Indianapolis, Indiana. She lived, for a time in a suburb of Chicago, and now resides in a small town in deep southern Georgia, about two hours south of Savannah. Lisa grew up immersed in all the things that go bump in the night, experiencing the hauntings in her grandparents' house. It was there that she would get her first taste of the paranormal, not even knowing that it was out of the norm. She has always had an interest in the subject but has only been formally investigating for around 20 years. She's investigated all over the United States, Ireland, and Scotland. She'll be adding Wales and England to that list in the summer of 2024.*

She is not only a fledgling psychic medium and Reiki Master but also an ordained minister as well. She is a realtor in her day-to-day life. Lisa is also an End-of-Life Doula. She helps families in hospice situations with the transition from life to death and beyond.

Lisa is a member of several paranormal groups around the world. Her team is the American Spectral Society, based out of Chicago, Illinois. She is also a team member of Ghost Searchers Ireland as the United States representative. She's a new member of the Association of Paranormal Study, based in Virginia, as the Georgia representative. Last, but certainly not least, she's a member of American Hauntings, based out of the Illinois/Missouri area, where she leads groups of people into haunted locations to investigate all over the United States. Lisa offers workshops on dark mirror scrying and the Estes Method.

Lisa has investigated hundreds of locations, including private homes, mental asylums, hospitals, poor farms, prisons, graveyards, department stores, libraries, bed and breakfasts, pubs, restaurants, hotels, battlefields, theaters, bowling alleys, etc. Lisa, along with her paranormal partner in crime, Nicole Tito, hosts a website called Ghostly Voices where they showcase their audio evidence. The website can be found at www.ghostly-voices.com.

Heather Leigh Carroll-Landon, PhD

Founder of Exploration Paranormal,
Talk Radio Host, Author

Looking back on my life, I often reflect on what motivated me to start researching the paranormal. I look upon these memories with love and heartache, like many who study the afterlife due to a lost loved one. My grandfather, Archie, was a significant part of my life for as long as I can remember. I spent a lot of time with him, including sitting on the counter at the hardware store he worked at, being pushed around his wheelbarrow in the backyard, and lying on his legs propped up on a stool.

I have very few memories about the day he passed, but I was five years old and did remember playing outside in the snow with him. Whether it is memories of the events or my mind making sense of what occurred that afternoon, I have visions of him going stiff and falling face-first into the snow. My family rushed me away, and the next thing I remember was being told he had died.

After the mourning time had passed, I continued with life as expected, and it was not until I was 17 that all the memories of my grandfather returned. After his death, we moved into a new home with my grandmother, which is why I thought it was weird at the time that I would start having visions of my grandfather more than ten years after his death and in a place he had never been.

His spirit would appear at the foot of my bed, on a chair by my bed, in the bathroom mirror, and walking down the hallway. There was no pattern to seeing his spirit, and I do not recall him ever saying anything. He would silently appear.

This incident sparked my interest in the paranormal. I started checking out as many books as I could on the subject. It was a difficult time to research the field because we had to rely on ghost stories being shared and books. There was no Internet, nor did we have the television shows today to get information. And even with all the resources available today, we are limited in the number of reputable resources available about paranormal research.

After experiencing several years of peace, with no further visits from my grandfather, my family took a trip to Gettysburg in my early 20s. While there, I had several paranormal encounters, including one where I could see a soldier looking out of the window overlooking an outdoor cafe I stopped at for coffee and rest from exploring. Gettysburg would become my favorite place to vacation.

Another experience I had was one of my most memorable paranormal encounters ever. I was exploring Devil's Den and taking lots of photographs (I was a photography major in college). As I turned around one of the more giant boulders in the area, I encountered a man dressed in full Confederate attire. He tipped his hat and walked silently past me. Because there was a reenactment happening that weekend in Gettysburg, I thought it was one of the reenactors and quickly chased him for a photo. However, when I turned back around the boulder, he was gone. He vanished in thin air. I would have seen him walking or running away because, from that area, there was nowhere to go without being seen.

Later I realized this was the soldier pictured in Matthew Brady's famous photo of the confederate sniper at Devil's Den. Then upon further, more recent research, I learned the photo was staged, and his body was moved from the main battlefield into position at his sniper's perch. But that is another story all on its own.

One other experience I had when visiting Gettysburg that year was at Spangler's Spring. While down in the spring, all of my camera equipment malfunctioned. My camera batteries died in the same camera twice and once in my backup camera. Additionally, I could not keep the film (yeah, this experience is that old) from rewinding after taking a single photo. I wasted four rolls of film there. Then, as I was changing the film in the camera, something pulled down and back on my right shoulder. When I looked around, there was not a single living soul within fifty feet of me.

Gettysburg was an exciting vacation, and I always look forward to returning for the history and paranormal encounters.

As I continued to research more into why I was seeing my grandfather and why I had seen the apparition in Gettysburg, I grew closer to becoming the paranormal investigator and researcher I am today. My continued research is why I have dedicated myself to helping those who suffer from paranormal attachments and activity and educating others. So, they are no longer afraid of the spirits who follow them around.

As part of my educating others about the paranormal field, my ultimate goal is for researchers to use a form of the scientific method. I know we cannot 100 percent follow this method, but we can do what we can to create hypotheses, test them through experiments, and document all of our responses. While keeping that goal in mind, I would love to see paranormal science no longer considered pseudoscience with a universal and standardized method to conduct authentic scientific research. However, for that to occur, we must first learn to work together, share ideas, and as a whole, stop being selfish with our research.

To start using a paranormally-adapted scientific method, I have begun implementing many aspects of the process into my paranormal investigating techniques. First, it is imperative to document everything; this includes a written log, audio, photographs, and video. We must also collect scientific data, such as humidity levels, geographic location, moon phase, weather conditions, EMF levels, geothermal data, ley lines, etc. This list is just the beginning of what we need to collect and document our personal experiences.

From there, we must place this information somewhere it can be helpful, such as in a spreadsheet or graph. This information can help us document a specific investigation and compare that data with the data from future and past experiments. Without data, we do not have enough scientific value in our research or the results we achieve.

Do not get me wrong; I love a good (touristy) haunted location like many paranormal researchers do. However, visiting these locations is more for the feeling and the history behind the paranormal activity. Some of my favorite places to explore and learn more about the ghosts who roam these locations include Gettysburg, Savannah, Charleston, Williamsburg, and John's Pass (Madeira Beach, FL). There are so many fantastic stories from these locations, offering a different view of the history and landscape, which genuinely makes them some of the best places for paranormal researchers to put down their tools, turn off their cameras, and forget about trying to communicate with the spirits. Instead, just enjoy each of these towns' beauty and historical value. When you are not trying to get experiences, that is when they will happen.

Though I have been researching the paranormal for more than 30 years, my dream of becoming a published author has finally become a reality. My book *Haunted Southern Nevada Ghost Towns* from History Press was released in the Fall of 2022, along with *Ghosts and Legends of the Vegas Valley* (Spring 2023) and *Haunted Florida Lighthouses* (Fall 2024). I loved the idea of writing these books because I not only shared my personal experiences at several locations throughout Nevada, but I also shared the history behind why many ghost towns are labeled as haunted. My favorite thing about writing these books and my upcoming books is to share these stories and help reduce the fear so many people have when dealing with the paranormal.

Ultimately, the central message of my books is to help preserve the haunted history of historical locations and show others how to investigate these locations properly and safely. Additionally, these books share exciting stories, are easy to read, and help readers connect with me by sharing my own experiences.

Bio: *I am the founder of Exploration Paranormal, a paranormal research team consisting of myself, my husband, and our son in South-Central Florida. We focus more on the scientific aspect of paranormal research, collecting and plotting data while conducting and developing scientific experiments. My team was featured in the documentaries Real Haunts: Ghost Towns and Real Haunts 3 and I made an appearance on Ghost Adventures: Lake of Death.*

I am the host of Exploring the Paranormal, co-host of Passport to the Paranormal, and Ghost Education 101 (on Facebook and YouTube). I have written several books, including Haunted Southern Nevada Ghost Towns, Ghosts and Legends of the Vegas Valley, Haunted Florida Lighthouses, and Haunted Florida Ghost Towns (Spring 2024).

Shannon LeGro

Radio Host, Author, Founder of Beyond The Fray Publishing, Host of Small Town Monsters, On The Trail of UFOs

My inception into the world of the paranormal occurred when I was 12 years old, and I was not at all seeking to have an experience. My father owned a cabin in Duck Creek, Utah. And on this particular day, he had gone down to Cedar City for errands leaving myself, my brother, and my stepbrother to entertain ourselves. This was easy to do as we had access to our favorite toys. Our four-wheelers. With my dad away, I decided to forego my stifling helmet as the day was quite warm and sunny, and dust kicked up as we buzzed around the grid-patterned roads. To this day, there are still plenty of open lots in Duck Creek, Utah...even more so back then.

Eat My Dust was a very popular sticker to put on your quad, but I wasn't in the mood to actually do so. So, I hung back from my brothers as they rode in front of me. At one point I looked to my right into the aspen tree-filled forest...and running parallel to me, about 30 feet in, were four figures. For the most part, very human-shaped, and all around 6 feet tall. However-instantly, I knew something was very wrong. They were completely devoid of light...as if no illumination of any kind could find them, not from the sun through the trees above or any of the ambient light around. They were literally animated cut-outs from the blackest, most completely starless night...implanted into this beautiful sunny day. They were also running alongside me at the same pace as my four-wheeler. Also, the trees that should have been in their way seemed to be non-existent and they were not disturbing any foliage on the ground. The last thing I noticed in these five-second sightings was that their arms and legs were moving exactly as a person's would. This very normal motion stuck out to me right away.

They never looked my way, their "faces" were trained always in front of them. I have to wonder if they did glance over at me, would there have been anything to see that resembled a face anyway? I watched them for at least a count of five, and I then turned my eyes back to my path of travel. I glanced back to where these odd runners would be, only to find them completely gone.

I quickly caught up to my brothers, telling them my desire to return to the cabin. I was done riding for the day. After telling my dad what I saw, he told me it was simply military men executing an exercise. I knew though, these were not people. Not people who were part of our world anyway. Those few seconds obliterated and rearranged what I thought our reality was, and what is lurking just on the other side of what we normally see with our conscience mind. To this day, I can see them in my mind as plainly as I did all those years ago and I wonder, "Why me?" And why did I see them only once?

This sighting turned into an obsession even at that young age. I passed around a sheet of paper to friends and family so they could write down any odd experiences and would shift conversations into Ouija boards and ghosts whenever possible. I was a collector of stories, even back then. I wanted to know I wasn't alone.

Many years later, my multi-topic show *Into the Fray* was born. This afforded me the opportunity to curate stories on an epic scale. From cryptids, and UFOs, to general high strangeness, I cover it all. In regard to my show, I see my role strictly as a curator. It isn't my job to vet the people who come on because in reality, how in the world could I? The only encounters I know for certain happened are my own. It is up to the listener to decide what they believe once the *Electus* outro song begins its first notes.

Though Bigfoot is my favorite subject, some of the most memorable experiences people have shared on *Into the Fray* are those you can't neatly fit into any box. They are creatures or (seemingly) paranormal entities that blow the lid off your "run of the mill" shadow person or Sasquatch encounter. An episode that garnered a lot of attention was "85: An Unfounded Call." It featured an ex-Deputy Sheriff who ventured into an abandoned house after several unidentifiable calls from the location. His first contact inside was with a tall shadow figure in an upstairs bedroom. He blacked out, then regained consciousness while driving. He does not remember leaving the home and quickly pulled over to call his superior after feeling faint and sick. His story quickly gained even more strange momentum when two men showed up the next day demanding his badge and a signature on a release from duty form. His superiors called him after he didn't show, claiming they expected him at work that day. The paper he signed for the two odd gentlemen had vanished, taking proof they'd ever existed with them. Strange physical ailments included ringing in the ears, dizziness, and even hearing loss. Interestingly, the doctors told him there was an unidentifiable blockage in his left ear. To this day, not only does he continue to have health issues, but is unable to get hired back on with any law enforcement agency. There are no definitive answers as to why.

I have been lucky enough to investigate some hotspots when it comes to anomalous happenings. Bigfoot, UFOs, and even hauntings. Not every location produces activity, and this is certainly not surprising. Expecting lightning to strike is the wrong way to go about it. But I have encountered some very interesting things in my travels. What follows is an account of one of my trips to an active Bigfoot location.

In 2014, I headed to Washington State with Wes Germer of *Sasquatch Chronicles* to visit the Brown property. They and others in the area had witnessed Bigfoot on several occasions, with Sara Brown herself seeing one within a frightening distance.

On our first night, we headed to a portion of the property that boasted two abandoned buildings. When it began to rain heavily, we took shelter in the open-sided but well-roofed larger building. Minutes later, we noticed a light coming towards us through the woods on the other side of the ravine. We all wondered who would be walking in cold, rainy weather at this late hour of the night. After watching this light for a few seconds, it took a dive toward the ground. It was as if it noticed us, noticing it. Researcher, Kirk Brandenburg, had a very expensive thermal imager with him and was trying to ascertain what it was. He informed us, it was not a person as no heat signature of any kind came up. We all fled out quickly in an attempt to get closer when three very loud slaps rang out as something hit the metal-sided building that sat next to the one we just sheltered in. We couldn't locate the light, its source, or the culprit of the building slap. Night one was plenty eventful.

The second night after dark we decided to implement a tactic, we'd all heard about: playing baby cries. Sasquatch beings are known to not only respond to these sounds but have also been reported to use them themselves seemingly in an attempt to get people out into the woods to investigate. Yikes.

As darkness came about, we located a bay cry loop and let it rip. It was not being blasted over a loudspeaker, but simply through a cell phone. Keep in mind, we were not deep in the woods in the middle of nowhere, but right in the Brown's backyard. At a certain point, we were all going a bit crazy listening to this baby cry loop...but it paid off. Something began making whooping sounds off to our right. It came in groups of three, and it sounded quite sing-song in nature. In fact, we all agreed it sounded feminine. The whoops continued but did not move location. Eventually, the phone battery died, and the phone shut off, and the moment it did...so did the whoops. Not a sound was heard the rest of the night.

So, what is the takeaway from my years as a researcher and story collector? Well, between traveling to various filming locations for *On the Trail of UFOs*, visiting active Bigfoot areas to research, and collecting encounters from hundreds of people for *Into the Fray*, I can absolutely say I only have more questions than answers. The incredible mystery and depth of it all keeps me going. And, as long as I have people willing to tell me their stories, I'll be here to listen.

Bio: *Shannon has been interested in the paranormal since she was a teen, after her own personal sighting of something truly anomalous. And although it's not what her encounter entailed, one of her passions is the subject of Sasquatch. Her weekly show, Into the Fray, has Shannon speaking to witnesses of cryptids, UFOs, and various aspects of the paranormal. She has co-authored books on both Bigfoot and the paranormal and founded Beyond the Fray Publishing with best-selling author, G. Michael Hopf. You can also see Shannon as the host for the Small Town Monsters production, On the Trail of UFOs: Seasons 1-3 on Amazon Prime.*

Dr. Heather Lynn

Historian, Author, Podcaster, Professor & Academic, Historical Consultant For History Channel's Ancient Aliens

The night sky of the Mojave Desert seemed to lift me right off the rusted hood of my Pontiac Sunbird. "I think we're not gonna crack stuff like UFO abductions and that sort of thing unless we admit the psychedelic evidence. And if we do admit it, suddenly the whole thing begins to look very, very different" Dr. Lynn goes on to say. I sat up to gain my bearings, as my attention ebbed from the dizzying tide of celestial bodies to the voices flowing from the car radio. "What on *earth* is this guy saying?"

Questions about time, space, the origins of consciousness, and alien life swirled in my brain. I suspect anything of sufficient mystery and interest would have captured my attention at that time. I was looking for a distraction. It was after *Midnight in the Desert,* and I was a runaway teenager, seeking answers to life's greatest mysteries by the dashboard light. Being homeless and on the run was isolating with little sources of comfort. The voices of late-night talk radio kept me company on those chilly nights when worry and fear kept me from sleeping.

I used to imagine how amazing it would be to have conversations with interesting, albeit eccentric people, musing on paranormal topics like aliens, ghosts, time travel, or even the nature of reality itself. Little could I have known, that over 20 years later, I'd find myself doing just that. After many strange adventures, good and bad, I found my way back to college and studied archaeology, history, technology, and education science, earning my doctorate. Though I walked a traditional path, I never stopped exploring the boundaries of the status quo.

Over time, I discovered that the academy had some dark secrets, corruption, and political motivations. I found that shadowy organizations, wealthy individuals, and multinational corporations were funding projects at important research institutions and universities around the world. These "hidden hands" tightly held secrets while institutions operating in the public trust were not being transparent about their intentions, donors, or discoveries. While this may not be news to most of you, it was to me at the time.

After leaving school, I took a more serious look at occult history and alternative archaeology. I wanted to know what, if anything, was being kept secret. Popular theories often ranged from the mundane to the fantastic, with claims of giants, extraterrestrials, ancient technology, and so on. I felt humanity had a right to know the truth because by keeping it cloaked in secrecy, all we would gain is increasingly extraordinary speculation, misinformation, and a framework of distrust for society. I eventually started writing on fringe topics considered too threatening to the established historical narrative. For almost a decade, I appeared on many shows, contributed articles to websites and magazines, spoke at events, and published books. I was fortunate to get to know the very authors and researchers I had read when I was younger. I found myself sitting on the other side of that late-night radio microphone, speaking to George Noory on *Coast-to-Coast AM*. I was finally an eccentric guest on late-night radio, having come full circle. Is this what they mean by "synchronicity?"

I have been asked, why I spend my time on the fringe of historical and archaeological research. The answer I always give is a quote from Sir Isaac Newton: "No great discovery was ever made without a bold guess." Newton, often regarded as the father of modern science and one of the founders of the scientific revolution, was also an occultist. Newton wrote at length on subjects like alchemy, astrology, and eschatology over his lifetime. Few people knew about this side of Newton's research until his alchemical papers came up for auction in 1936. The economist John Maynard Keynes bought the papers and later declared:

"Newton was not the first of the age of reason. He was the last of the magicians, the last of the Babylonians and Sumerians, the last great mind that looked out on the visible and intellectual world with the same eyes as those who began to build our intellectual inheritance less than 10,000 years ago."

History and archaeology are vital to the field of paranormal study because they give us frameworks and methodologies for uncovering and understanding our intellectual inheritance as human beings. While they left no written record, there is valuable insight available from an examination of prehistoric cultures. Their artifacts and monuments present mythological truths that are certainly not rational, but neither are they irrational. The language of myth, as seen through the arts, is pre-rational. It is the language of dreams, symbols, and archetypes and exactly how the ancients shared their universal truths and world views with each other, and eventually us. While ancient humans may not have had a highly developed third-tier cosmology, they did have an apparent proto-spirituality, one that viewed paranormal creatures as an important bridge between the spirit world and the natural world. The creatures of the natural world transformed into the gods of the sanctuary. The psychedelic dreams of the shamans and prehistoric magicians would find their way out of the caves and into the spiritual lives of semi-settled Neolithic people.

Historically, the lines between magic and science were often blurred. What may seem like mere superstition on the part of ancient man may, in actuality, be the seeds of a budding mythology and belief system, the kinds we see in ancient civilizations like Sumer. The Sumerians left behind the first written record, making them the civilization at the very beginning of history. History, as Napoléon Bonaparte famously quipped is "a fable agreed upon." Fables have value. We can admit that without agreeing with or endorsing all fringe ideas. There is value in seeing nuance and many potential dimensions of a problem. However, people often cast aside thoughts that deviate from the norm for fear of "rocking the boat." I say, let's discuss these strange ideas, like our ancestors did, sitting around a fire with our eyes fixed on the cosmos. Let the free flow of ideas inspire others to ask new questions about old problems. We need to stop being afraid of rocking boats and being judged by those who are too afraid to navigate the sea of possibility that will raise humanity to its highest potential. From the Mojave Desert to the college lecture hall and beyond, I have unearthed many things, but my journey of discovery is far from over.

Bio: *Dr. Heather Lynn is a historian of the human mind, internationally published author, and host of The Midnight Academy podcast. She is a professor teaching undergraduate courses in humanities, society, and other special topics. Her academic work concentrates on cognitive archaeology, consciousness, artificial intelligence, symbolism, iconography, and the exploration of myth and art through a Jungian conceptual framework. Heather also writes books and articles on fringe topics including hidden history, ancient mysteries, mythology, the occult, and paleocontact theory. She is a regular guest on podcasts and radio programs like Coast-to-Coast AM and has been a historical consultant for television programs, including History Channel's Ancient Aliens. For more information, visit: www.drheatherlynn.com.*

Tonya Madia

Medium, Reiki Master Teacher, Certified Hypnotherapist, Author

From the time I was a child, family, teachers, and friends had told me I had a vivid imagination. Although I felt certain that the disembodied footsteps and voices I was hearing were not just my imagination, over time I began to believe, as I had been told, that my experiences were nothing more than figments of my imagination. As a teenager, I used to play a game with my friends in which I would hold their hands and tell them what they had done that morning—everything from what they had for breakfast, to their thought process when picking out clothes for the day. The information would play out like a color film in my mind's eye and was often accompanied by words, feelings, or just a *knowing*. My friends were always amazed. However, at the time I really didn't consider what I was doing anything more than an amusing parlor trick and I didn't give much thought as to how I was able to access the information.

It wouldn't be for many years, until after my third Reiki attunement in 2009, that I began to once again believe that my experiences were more than my imagination. Spirit people began to show up regularly during sessions. At first, I dismissed them as my imagination. However, as it continued happening, I began to share with my clients the information I received from these visitors. Inevitably, my clients would validate my experiences by saying things like, "You've just described my mother; I was just thinking of her this morning because this is the anniversary of her passing!" or "That sounds like my brother; he looked exactly like what you described!" The more this happened, the more I began to trust in my experiences.

Finally, in 2016, my husband and I had the opportunity to spend two years investigating the paranormally active Webb Memorial Library in North Carolina. It was my experiences during those two years, more than anything else, that allowed me to accept—without a doubt—that I was tuning into frequencies beyond the average three-dimensional experience of our world. On 75 nights, for a total of more than 150 hours, we conducted our investigation, which was open to the public. Among our 525 guest investigators were a dozen or so gifted mediums and many sensitives. The data gathered were so compelling that our longtime mentor, Rosemary Ellen Guiley, asked us to write a book, *Watch Out for the Hallway: Our Two-Year Investigation of the Most Haunted Library in North Carolina*. The book also describes in detail how I came to trust that the spirit people I was encountering were not my imagination.

As a medium, I have often had people tell me they are nervous when they first meet me because they are afraid I will have access to their private thoughts or feelings or be able to "pick up things" around them. I remember one man in particular, with whom we were having dinner before a presentation, who looked at me across the table and said, "I know you're reading my mind. All the mediums do." I always assure these individuals (especially our dinner host) that I never read anyone without their permission, and to do so is an invasion of privacy that I equate to rummaging through someone's personal effects. This usually puts people at ease. I also meet the occasional cynic who insists that all mediums are frauds—including me. No amount of validated information will ever be enough for such individuals, so I simply choose not to engage with them. It is, however, unfortunate that their cynicism (which is different from skepticism—the healthy, questioning approach to the paranormal) may be fueled by unscrupulous individuals who are not authentic mediums.

Because mediumship works differently for everyone, there isn't one specific thing one can look for in terms of authenticity; however, one of the most important things one can do is trust their instincts. If you feel comfortable and at ease with the medium, that is a good sign. When I do a reading for a client, I like to start off by asking them to tell me as little as possible; the less I know about the person I'm reading for, the better. I also use this approach when assisting people experiencing hauntings in their homes and businesses. Notice how sure the medium is about the information being offered. When I offer a description of the spirit person with whom I'm connecting, clients often want to try to make the person "fit" who it is that they want to hear from. When I stick to my guns, in terms of whom I'm seeing and the information I'm receiving, my clients often eventually realize who was coming through and are pleasantly surprised. An inauthentic medium might be more inclined to simply change the description to fit the client's expectations. Be on the lookout for this type of approach, as well as lots of questions or leading statements. An unfortunate trick used by unscrupulous "mediums" is to try to hook you into frequent repeat readings. I prefer to teach my clients how to connect with their loved ones on their own, so eventually, they don't need the services of a medium.

I consider the opportunity to do a reading for someone a great honor. I approach it with reverence and respect. Before I do a reading, I meditate for thirty minutes and set the intention that whatever is most valuable for the person I'm reading for is who or what will come through. As I sit with my client, I take a few moments to tune into their energy field in the same way I connect with my Reiki clients. I find this particularly helpful, especially since, again, my first communication from spirit people as an adult came through during Reiki sessions. I relay the information as it is told, or shown to me, without trying to add my own interpretations. The information is, after all, for my client and not for me.

I have never really been a fan of the term "psychic" because I believe it implies that there are special abilities that some possess and others do not. We all have the natural ability to tune into the spirit realm, and I always take the opportunity to let my clients know that they can communicate with their deceased loved ones whenever they like. My first book, *Living the Intuitive Life*, is a guide to learning to tap into these natural abilities to enhance your life. I take time daily to meditate and connect with my loved ones on the other side to ask them for guidance and messages. I also keep a dream journal as well as a journal of animal totems, messages, and synchronicities. For fellow paranormal investigators, my best advice is that your body is your best piece of equipment. During an investigation, trust what you're sensing, feeling, seeing, and experiencing; it is valuable information.

My husband Joey and I work as a team. We are fortunate to be in contact with a wide array of other paranormal investigators with whom we often consult regarding data collected during an investigation. This has proven extremely helpful when deciphering information, such as photo anomalies, EVPs, and incidents of high strangeness. I firmly believe that having multiple insights, experiences, and opinions is invaluable to gaining perspective, and formulating a potential narrative as to the nature of the phenomena we are investigating. This is especially true because Joey and I do not investigate sites simply to collect anomalous data. We are committed to mediating between the living and the dead and helping them coexist, if at all possible, in peaceful, productive ways. This is the focus of our second book together, *Roommates from Beyond: How to Live in a Haunted Home*, which includes the world's first Paranormal Bill of Rights.

In addition to drawing on the education and experience of other investigators, I think it is important to incorporate a diverse toolbox when doing paranormal research. Joey and I have found it extremely helpful to read books on, and have a basic understanding of, fields such as metaphysics, consciousness studies, and quantum physics, as each of these can offer insights and possibilities into the nature of phenomena such as hauntings, sightings, and instances of high strangeness.

As a lifelong experiencer and paranormal investigator, I have noticed that there seems to be an increase in the number of people experiencing unexplained phenomena, such as hauntings and visitations, as well as instances of missing time and time slips. Although there is no way to know for certain what is causing the uptick in these experiences, I have identified several factors that I believe are playing a role. The first is the popularity of paranormal television shows and podcasts. The wide availability of information on the subject has made discussing these topics less taboo, and I believe that the increase in reporting, to some extent, is simply because more people are comfortable sharing their experiences.

Additionally, I often wonder whether experiments attempting to open portals into parallel universes, such as those performed at Oak Ridge National Laboratory in Tennessee, and with CERN's Large Hadron Collider (the largest and most powerful particle accelerator in the world), might be playing a role in the thinning of the veil. It is hard to dismiss the increase in incidents of high strangeness experienced by myself and many close to me shortly after CERN first fired up the LHC in 2008. The sheer amount of electromagnetic energy added to the atmosphere because of routers, modems, cell phones, and the like is almost certainly contributing as well.

Finally, I believe that many people have become interested in topics such as meditation, yoga, remote viewing, and mediumship over the past several decades, and, as a result, have succeeded in increasing their own natural intuitive abilities. Because of this, an increasing portion of the population is now able to tune into frequencies that previously may have gone un-noticed. I do believe these abilities were once readily available to us all, particularly when human beings lived more closely in harmony with nature. Regaining these abilities is an important step in evolving into a more compassionate species. Hopefully, it will lead us to become a civilization that lives in harmony with the natural world, rather than one that seeks to dominate it.

Bio: *Tonya Madia is a medium, Reiki Master Teacher, certified hypnotherapist (with specialties in past life regression and soul contact), author, and life-long experiencer who believes in the importance of cultivating and trusting your intuition. She has seen firsthand how practices such as yoga, meditation, and Reiki lead to a deeper awareness and understanding of the natural intuitive abilities we all possess, and she now teaches others how to develop these life-enhancing skills. She is the author of* Living the Intuitive Life: Cultivating Extraordinary Awareness, *and co-author of* Watch Out for the Hallway: Our Two-Year Investigation of the Most Haunted Library in North Carolina, *and* Roommates from

Beyond: How to Live in a Haunted Home. Tonya and her husband Joey have been invited to talk about their books and paranormal research methods on more than 60 podcasts and radio shows, including Coast to Coast AM, and have spoken at numerous conferences, festivals, and events. Tonya co-hosted more than 100 episodes of the weekly livestream Into the Outer Realms.

T.J. MacGregor
Author and Podcaster

Border. Outlier. Fringe.

When I was a kid, I realized I lived on the fringe. There was a huge tree in our backyard in Maracaibo, Venezuela, where we lived, and I used to climb up into the higher branches to talk to a greater power. I had no name for this power.

I often stood at my bedroom window, searching the night sky for UFOs. Cemeteries fascinated me. I figured that spirits and ghosts hung out there and if I walked through the place, I might glimpse a ghost or talk to one. I loved hearing about anything paranormal. Coincidences intrigued me. My favorite TV shows, which we watched in Spanish, were *Twilight Zone* and *One Step Beyond.*

While peering out a dormitory window one night when I was 16 and in boarding school, I finally saw a UFO. But not until I was 18 did I find any explanation for coincidence. A friend gave me the Richard Wilhelm edition of the *I Ching,* to which Carl Jung wrote the forward. In it, he introduced his concept of synchronicity and how it works in the *I Ching* – and in other divination systems.

He defined it as the coming together of inner and outer events in a way that can't be explained by cause and effect and is meaningful to the observer - i.e., you, the person who experienced it. In other words, a meaningful coincidence. I later read Jung's autobiography, *Memories, Dreams, and Reflections*, learned to use the *I Ching*, studied tarot and astrology, and eventually wrote books about those topics.

As a 25-year-old social worker in Indian River County, Florida, I planned a trip to Europe with a colleague, Chris. It would last six weeks. We listed the countries we wanted to see, whether to travel by train or plane and the cost of it all. I had two absolutely *must-see* spots - Carl Jung's castle on Lake Zurich in Bollingen, Switzerland, and Arles, France, where van Gogh had spent a couple of years in a nuthouse and created some of his most memorable work.

I understood the Jung part of the plan. I wanted to see the place Jung had built on the shores of Lake Zurich after his wife had died. He lived there alone, without electricity or modern conveniences and it was where spooky synchronistic stuff happened to him.

The day Chris and I were finally in the Geneva, Switzerland train station, ready to head to Bollingen, we got lost. We missed our train and caught a later train. This missed connection proved to be significant.

Chris and I walked through Bollingen, which back then was fairly small, from what I remember. At some point, I asked a man on the street where Carl Jung's castle was located. He nodded enthusiastically, pointed up the street, and gave us directions.

When we arrived at Jung's place, we walked around to the back to take a look at the lake. But a man was in the yard, tossing a ball to a dog. I walked up to the fence and asked him if this was where Jung had lived. He said it was and introduced himself as Jung's grandson.

I was blown away.

He resembled photos of a younger Jung. He said he was visiting his parents, who lived in the castle, and the place now had electricity. I explained my fascination with Jung and synchronicity and told him I'd specifically come to Bollingen to see the castle. I also remember saying that if we hadn't missed our train in Geneva, he might not have been in the backyard.

He smiled. "Synchronicity."

So, for 20 or 30 minutes, we stood there talking about UFOs, spirits, the paranormal, divination systems, Jung and synchronicity. I hate to admit that I no longer remember the particulars of his stories. But I remember how they made me feel like it was all a manifestation of a dream I didn't know I had.

Then Chris and his dog got impatient. He recommended a place for lunch, I thanked him for his time, and on our way we went.

Synchronicity has been woven into the fabric of my life ever since. It's how I met my husband, Rob, who figures into our daughter's birth, to the jobs I worked, to finding an agent, selling my first novel to Ballantine Books, and the many sales afterward. Synchronicity has always been present.

By the time Rob and I wrote our first synchronicity book - *The 7 Secrets of Synchronicity* - we'd spent a decade writing 13 books a year for Sydney Omar's series of annual astrology books for NAL. We had written – jointly or alone – books on the tarot, meditation, yoga, magic, and dreams. I'd written eight of my own astrology books. We both had written dozens of novels and mine were usually paranormal – and still are. We'd both won the Edgar Allan Poe Award from the Mystery Writers of America. But *7 Secrets* was the first book we wrote that explored the phenomenon of synchronicity in depth.

I was steeped in the idea that synchronicity hints at a deeper order that physicist David Bohm called the implicate or enfolded order, a kind of primal soup that births everything in the universe. He referred to our external reality as the explicate order. I suddenly understood that synchronicity flourishes at the border between the implicate and the explicate, the inner and the outer.

I've found that the phenomenon runs through everything - daily life, pivotal points like birth, marriage, divorce, death, significant moves, creativity, illness, UFO encounters and abductions, spirit contact, and travel. It occurs in global mass events like 9-11, the pandemic, crashes of commercial airlines, the sinking of ships, the invasion of sovereign countries, and disappearances of people. These days, if it's news all over social media and TV, it's likely that synchronicity is embedded somewhere in the events.

In novels, non-fiction books, works of art, in photography, synchronicity often manifests itself as precognition. It can act as a warning or a confirmation, is sometimes a trickster, but always when it happens, you feel like you have been touched by magic.

The beauty of synchronicity is that it's an equal-opportunity phenomenon. It happens regardless of ethnicity, religion, beliefs, gender, age, culture, or anything else. It's a vital part of the collective consciousness, perhaps even an archetype.

A book falls at your feet - and that somehow hurls open a door to a lifelong friendship between you and the author. You hear a certain song on the radio that addresses a concern you have, you get lost in a city, you miss a train or a flight, and experience synchronicity because of it. You write a novel and parts of it actually happen. The night you hear of a friend's death, there's a loud explosion in your house that doesn't have a physical cause. On a flight, you experience a cluster of certain numbers that reflect the reality that the vacation is actually an escape from a situation.

In the years since I first realized I was an outlier, a woman on the fringe, synchronicity has been my ally, navigator, messenger, trickster, and friend. I've found books on what it is and is not and its supposed source. Some people attribute it to God, some provide scientific theories, and some dismiss it as "just a coincidence." But in the end, synchronicity is our most personal invitation to dive into who we are. Because it exists along the border between David Bohm's implicate and explicate order, it's our internal selves made manifest.

Oh. The Arles/van Gogh part of the trip? That's another part of synchronicity - when a passion you have seems to confirm a related past life. But that's a whole other story!

Bio: *Trish MacGregor – as T.J. MacGregor, Alison Drake, and several other names - is the author of 43 paranormal suspense novels and several dozen nonfiction books on synchronicity, astrology, tarot, and dreams. Her most recent novel, White Crows, was published by Crossroad Press in May 2022. She won the Edgar Allan Poe Award in 2003 for her novel, Out of Sight. For a decade, she co-authored the Sydney Omar series of astrology books for New American Library, which featured daily predictions for the 12 signs. She also has written 8 astrology books on creativity, soul mates, transits and other facets of astrology. Her most recent non-fiction book, co-authored with her husband, Rob MacGregor, is The Shift: Report from the Mystical Underground published by Crossroad Press. She and Rob* *host a weekly podcast, The Mystical Underground, which features authors, artists, researchers, astrologers, and experts in the paranormal field.*

http://themysticalunderground.com/

https://soundcloud.com/themysticalunderground

email: trishjmacgregor@gmail.com

Instagram:trishandrobmacgregor

Facebook: https://www.facebook.com/trish.macgregor.7?fref=ts

KAREN MCAFEE

PSYCHIC, MEDIUM, CHANNELER

If anyone had told me that I was going become a psychic medium one day, I would most likely have returned their gaze with that of a deer in the headlights on a dark winter night. Because I was raised in a very conservative Catholic home, reincarnation was unheard of and the only afterlife there was only included Heaven or Hell (and Purgatory for some).

But, while en route to my mother's hospital room on a late-night Delta flight in January of 2001, I must have drifted off for a moment or two, because in my mind's eye, I saw my mother in a pale blue nightgown walking across what seemed to be a theater stage. Smokey pale clouds billowed around her and the words, "Now I can rest" popped into my head. I felt something touch my forehead, much like when she kissed us goodnight as children. Then, an incredible sense of peace washed over me, and I woke up and I was shocked to see that 20 minutes had passed. When I arrived at the hospital, I told my sister what had happened on the plane, and she said that she remembered looking at my father's watch as my mother took her last breath at around 11:10 p.m. – the same time I told her she came to me on the plane.

Soon after her passing, I started noticing things that could only be taken as signs from her. Some signs were subtle but finding a 1968 red

Camaro convertible just like she drove was a huge wake-up call and she totally caught my attention. So, I started asking her for specific signs, and even to this day, when I ask her for a sand dollar at the beach, she always delivers. I must have 50 of them by now.

In 2005, my father decided that he had done enough dialysis and asked my sister, a nurse, what would happen if he stopped going. In the gentlest way possible, she told him that his kidneys would begin to shut down, and that he would eventually fall asleep and not wake up. So, he decided that he would stop dialysis, and on July 4, 2005, he joined his beloved wife in the spirit world. I was not able to be with my mother when she left, but I was beside my father this night, holding his hand, and I will never forget the look of awe on his face as he left—it was if he was a child gazing upon the face of God (or even better, seeing the love of his life again).

A year later, my sister, Kathie, left this world for the next after a courageous five-year battle with cancer. She lived in Texas at the time, and I know in my heart she waited for me to arrive before leaving us. She will always hold a special place in my heart because she stood up for me and encouraged me and always had the best words of wisdom I needed to hear whenever times were hard. Even now, when I struggle, she whispers to me and gives me strength.

The Paranormal Years

A couple of years later, my husband decided to join a paranormal investigation group, and my life changed dramatically. My husband and I would watch the shows like *Ghost Hunters* and *Ghost Adventures* on television, and while he was intrigued, I wasn't buying it.

I remember the very first time I went out with his group on a historic tour of a nearby town. I spent most of my time peering into storefronts and challenging the ghosts to show themselves, which of course they didn't. But when we arrived at the historic jail, someone noticed that the door was open, and a few people went inside. As I approached the door, though, *something* stopped me from going into the jail, as if an invisible hand was holding me back. I was trying to see inside of the jail when all of a sudden it seemed like a gust of wind came *out* of the jail and went straight into my chest. I began to feel somehow different—I looked all around me and didn't recognize where I was, and I noticed that my stomach began to hurt...as if I had been stabbed. My eyes began to water like they did when I saw my mother on the airplane. The medium came out of the jail, took one look at me, and quickly asked me if I believed in God. I said I did, so he got some Holy Water out of his backpack and started saying the prayer of St. Michael and sprinkling me with it. I exhaled a minute later, my shoulders dropped, and I seemed to return to normal. I was exhausted. And, let me just say that I didn't leave that man's side for the rest of the tour, which apparently was now heading over to the old cemetery, and since I was too afraid to stay in my car alone, I reluctantly agreed to go along.

A few weeks later, I went on my first real investigation, and the same thing happened there, too. While the TriField meters were whining, chills were climbing up my spine –not once, but twice—and then on the third time, the energy I was feeling came around my side, through my navel chakra, and went straight to my throat and tried to speak. She could not make my vocal cords work, though, but the tears were there just like the other times, and so the tears became a physical symbol of a spirit person joining me physically.

The weirdest thing about both of these first encounters was that I wasn't scared. But I was curious. I spent more than a decade trying to learn how all of this supernatural stuff worked. If I couldn't explain how it happened for me in the physical, then I couldn't accept it until I figured it out. For example, why could some people smell a particular smell, like coffee, or hear their name called out, while others did not while on an investigation? How could two different people see the same ghost at the same time and perfectly describe what they saw in unison? What was a "ghost" anyway and what was it made from that made only certain people able to recognize it? Who were my guides and how do I meet them? Why was this happening to me?

Ah, yes. Because Mom woke me up in 2001—and Mom wouldn't lie to me, right? Right. So, I spent many years re-examining and rebuilding my spiritual foundation so that I could include all of the new things I was learning about energy, the blending of consciousness, and my new role as someone who could seemingly step between the two worlds.

About three years after my father passed, I saw him in one of my meditations, wearing his favorite Houndstooth jacket and sitting at a table at the top of some stairs, sipping tea and reading the newspaper. There was no interaction between us at that time, but a medium I had met told me that I needed to be patient because my father was working on things "behind the scenes" for me. She described him as holding a bow and arrow, poised to shoot. The next time I saw him during a meditation, he was standing at the beginning of a boardwalk that led into a jungle, seemingly waiting for me to catch up.

I soon learned that my time as a paranormal investigator was over, and a different set of spiritual lessons were about to begin. It was also around this time that I discovered that my hands would move on their own during meditation or when I was in an altered state of awareness. I used to think that they moved to release excess energy, but I learned years later that I wasn't quite right about that.

My father became my primary spiritual guide around this time. He led me to people who taught me what I needed to understand in order to move forward on this metaphysical journey, the most influential of whom was a man from Brazil who taught me about the indigenous ways and culture (the Red Road) of North American Indians. I learned about the different healing properties of the sweat lodge ceremony, drumming circles, sacred herbs, and the special relationship that the Indigenous have as stewards of our planet. By this time, all of my guides were indigenous, and I felt like I had come home in so many ways, so I will always be grateful for my time with him and the lessons he taught me. I can't help but wonder if this was why the medium saw my father holding a bow and arrow (and I saw him on the first step of the board-walk leading into a jungle).

When I was involved in the paranormal world and so many different things were happening to me spontaneously, I spent a lot of time trying to figure out if I was a trance medium, a physical medium, a channeler, etc., because I didn't seem to fit into any one particular category. So, I decided to take my first psychic development class, and while doing my first practice readings at home, I discovered that I would take on the mannerisms, accents, or other physical attributes of some of the spirit people who came through. The first time my teacher saw me do this in class, well, let's just say he was surprised and leave it at that.

I spent the next several years taking monthly classes and learning about all of the different modalities of energy, energy healing, divination with wands and pendulums, learning to do psychometry (how to read the energy of places and things) and reading auras...I could go on and on. But when I found out that a class in Shamanism was being offered at a local metaphysical store, I signed up for it immediately. It was in this class that I learned the reason why my hands moved seemingly on their own in the past.

Because I have spent the better part of my life outside, I especially feel connected to the Earth and its energy. I have always said that being outside is like my church, and walking a beach anywhere is my medicine. When I weed, for example, the answers to questions I have been seeking often come to me. When I weed, I watch the bugs, birds and animals interact with their environment, and they teach me the connectedness we all have with Earth, air, and water. When we keep our hands busy, we allow our consciousness to travel and to shed the human constraints that keep us disconnected to our environment. It's one of the reasons we can travel anywhere in our dreams and receive those especially vivid dreams from those in the spirit world.

A shamanic journey is when a person listens to a drumbeat, which then alters the normal brainwaves and allows a person to go to a different state of consciousness. While in this altered state, the person can either visit the Upper World (Spirit) or the Lower World (Animal Guides, etc.) to receive information, gain spiritual knowledge, or conduct healing for others. We live in the Middle World, between the Upper and the Lower. I remember being told once that my father was working on making a bridge for me so that I would have "one foot in the real world and one foot in the spirit world."

It was easy for me to get into this altered state of consciousness and journey for another person. Sometimes the person was looking for a specific answer to a question—whether it was if they were going to move, find a new job, or just what was coming up for them in the future. Journeying for me was always in pictures of recognizable places or things that meant something to the other person. Sometimes, however, I would feel my hands moving, and because I had surrendered to this peculiarity many years before, I stopped questioning why they did. One day, one of the mentors came over to me and asked me if I was aware that my hands moved while I journeyed. I said I was aware, but I didn't know what they were doing or why. He told me that I was doing Reiki. I said I didn't know how to do Reiki, and he assured me that I was as he did Reiki himself. I thought that was pretty cool, but it sent me back to trying to describe who I am or why I do what I do.

And then I decided it really didn't matter how I label myself.

All I need to do is get into that altered state of being, which allows another to see with my eyes, hear with my ears, or speak with my vocal cords – or in the case of a healer like when I journey, use my hands to direct the healing energy. I am always present and aware of what I am doing, and in control of the energy exchange. I work for the healing of others and trust my guides to help me affect that change. But let me be clear: it doesn't always happen the same way for everyone. As they say in this field, "You don't always get what you want, but you almost always get what you need."

I'm just a conduit.

The most important thing I have learned is that healing can take place between our two worlds, for both the person sitting across from me as well as for the person next to me in the spirit world.

It really is all about the love.

Bio: *Karen McAfee is a psychic, medium, and channeler for the recently departed, healers, and teachers who want to communicate with those here in the physical world. She also enjoys hiking and making her own walking sticks, photography, and gardening. She and her husband and son live in Atlanta, GA. If you would like a reading with her, message her on Facebook at Psychic Medium Karen McAfee.*

Jackie Meador

Paranormal Researcher, Host, Writer & Producer of Paranormal Journeys

What motivated you to research the paranormal?

Well, in the beginning, I never actually thought of it as research, to be honest. You know, being young, dumb, and wanting to hunt ghosts but having no idea what you're doing but going ahead anyway. But once you get started, it's like taking the next logical step in the research investigation process. I wanted to know more...to see if there was a connection between the paranormal activity and the site's history. Sometimes there is and it can make your investigation more meaningful and relevant.

Case in point: An alleged haunted house in California sits on an acre of rural land. Residents experience the usual phantom footsteps, doors opening/closing, lights flickering, heavy breathing, etc. So, you go in, investigate, and get some unusual photos with anomalies that can't be explained, and your recorder captures low voices and whispers speaking Spanish. All of that is interesting but doesn't answer the question of "why" and that you need to do your research on the property. Come to find out, the house was once a bunkhouse for migrant workers on a large ranch. And since no actual communication or interaction with the spirits occurred, the conclusion was a residual haunting, which we know will eventually fade away. Then again, sometimes there is no connection whatsoever and gee, aren't those fun? Not.

Did you have an experience(s) that fueled your interest?

Absolutely not! I'm one of those rare few, who will actually admit to never having had a paranormal experience prior to starting this journey. Did you know that someone once told me that because I never had a paranormal experience and I wasn't psychic, I could never be an investigator? Stupid and short-sighted, right? Never saw her again and I bet she's not in any book. HA! So, what did fuel my interest?

It was *The Canterville Ghost* (Paramount, 1944) one Saturday morning. The burning question of a then 10-year-old that put me on this path was, "Why didn't the ghost just go to Heaven?" From there I watched and read everything that had a ghost in it or anything with a supernatural flair. From there I expanded my interest to horror, cryptids, UFOs, and anything Sci-Fi where there was an unknown element and a mystery to solve. Hey, I'm a Virgo, what can I say?

What is your role as a paranormal researcher?

There are two answers that define my role as a paranormal researcher: To explore the unknown to find the answers to whether ghosts exist, and why. It's not just ghost hunting, it's the answers I want. My role is to exhaust every possible probability through research, experimentation, and investigation work, then what's left, is the possibility.

My other role is to teach what I know, and what I've experienced and pass that on to others asking the same questions. One thing I tell my students is to read and not just about ghosts and hauntings. There are so many layers to investigating an alleged haunting, you will need to know the basics in astronomy, physics, geography, anthropology, sociology, geology, and writing or at least know how to Google those subjects. All of these will come into play at one time or another; not all at once of course, but I can't tell you how many times I needed to know about geology, physics, sociology, etc. It's great to see a classroom full of bright, shiny faces with the same passion that I have and willing to step out of their comfort zone and be open to possibilities. My job here is done.

What types of methodologies do you utilize and why?

It's not enough anymore to just go and investigate alleged haunted sites, not if you want to be taken seriously. Sure, there are those, who opt for the thrills and chills and nothing else and that is ok because it can help in the overall scheme of things. But if you want to help, actually help people understand what is going on around them, you have to have a plan or method of investigating. I am a Virgo and such an organizer that I learned from the beginning I needed a method not just for me but for my team and our client, so they know what to expect. Knowing the basics of paranormal investigating can help in forming your methodology and how you want to proceed. I love the scientific method but really, it can't be 100% because so much of what we look for is unknown. Owning that up front, I start with the questions, what comes first, second, and so on? What is the goal? What equipment will you need? How does it help the client? I start with client interviews including signing waivers and release of liability forms. Then comes the research of the site's history. On the night of the investigation, I make sure there is a controlled environment, concentrate on the hot spots where most of the activity has occurred, set up the equipment, and take base readings for temperature and electromagnetic field fluctuations. After that comes analyzing the data and I use certain criteria to determine if a place is haunted or just experiencing unexplained/paranormal activity. My team looks at the following indicators to help us acquire a better idea of what's occurring:
1. Photographic evidence
2. Electronic Voice Phenomena (EVP)
3. Electromagnetic field disruptions
4. Temperature fluctuations
5. Odors
6. Physical movement of inanimate objects
7. Physical contact

After the investigation comes the written report that will be given to the client. Based on the seven indicators, listed above, I proceed as follows:

1-3 indicators – inconclusive

4-5 indicators – paranormal activity

6-7 indicators – haunted status

What would you like to see changed or improved in the field of supernatural research?

Hmmm, that's a good question. I mean, I've been at this for almost 25 years. I've seen groups come and go, watched celebrity ghost hunters appear on TV shows then fade away, listened to investigators lecture(s), then not be heard from again, etc. I've concluded it's all a big popularity contest and all the drama that comes with being part of a clique. Very few have made the transition from a ghost hunter to a veteran research investigator. And I have to give them credit for staying in this field for the long haul. It's not easy and demands continual adjustments, changes, honing your skills, and refining your expertise.

Ah, but I digress...what would I like to see changed or improved? There is so much knowledge out there from all levels of investigators and unfortunately, a "mine, mine, mine" attitude is prevalent. But I would love to see more sharing of data, information, and perhaps a central database, like a supernatural library, where investigators can upload data that researchers can tap into for research. Just Googling a question, can be frustrating with a lot of false/incorrect information and so many articles, it takes an eternity to read them all. Case in point: I researched a site that was heavy in mineral and ore deposits, such as sulfur and heavy metals, nickel, vanadium, lead, chromium, mercury, and also arsenic, selenium, and other toxic elements that cause halluci-nations. That was when I found there was an abandoned military ammunition site on top of a mountain above the site. This was an issue that needed to be diagnosed by their medical doctors. But to make my point, I could've uploaded that info into the library database for others to use given the same set of circumstances and a possible link between hallucinations and paranormal activity.

How do you go about investigating the paranormal?

The most important and first priority is the client. Getting to know our clients, the environment, the paranormal events, and the witnesses. This is where you start. Then it's the research of the site, whether it's a house, land, or a person/object. Next is the investigation, if warranted. And I say that because not all interviews lead to an actual investigation. A good research investigator will know the difference between a possible haunting/spirit activity and a one-time consultation. Next, decide what equipment to use and that will depend on the type of activity being reported. And by the way, know your equipment, study the specs, and know how it works and why. I try to keep to a scientific approach to each investigation, such as a controlled environment, marking all exits, debunking incidents if possible, identifying extraneous sounds, like dogs barking, traffic, water pipes, and taking notes, etc. I keep all notes, photos, EVP recordings, and research in a folder, as a way to document findings along with the finished report. There have been a couple of times I've had to refer to a past investigation because something similar is happening in a current one.

Below is my procedure for a paranormal investigation:

1. Initial contact with the client
    a. Screen potential client(s).
    b. Have client(s) complete the client questionnaire.
    c. Set the daytime preliminary interview, if local.
    2. Preliminary investigation
    a. Conduct the interview with residents/witnesses.
    b. Identify the hot spots.
    c. Capture site photos and diagrams.
    d. Get the required consent/permission forms signed.
    e. Set the second investigation date.
    3. Site research
    4. Investigation
    a. Confirm the second date and time three days prior.
    b. Arrive at the site.
    c. Prepare and set up the equipment.

5. Post investigation

a. Analyze the data from video and audio tapes.

b. Team members have 30 days from the investigation date to hand in their report.

6. Prepare the report

a. Correlate validated activity regarding pictures, EVP, and other evidence from team members.

b. Write about the history and conclusions.

c. Make recommendations for the client(s).

7. Report to client

a. Turn in the final written report to the client(s) within 60 days of the investigation.

Top cases? Favorite locations?

Oh my, there have been so many. You can investigate many sites over a period of a year and get, maybe a half dozen pieces of validated evidence that makes you proud to be a paranormal research investigator. But in between? There are long periods of waiting and watching in the dark, taking photos, collecting recordings, and then long hours of analyzing the data. However, some are more memorable, maybe not for the amount of evidence captured but rather those that made an impact on the client and me.

Regarding a house in Sanger, CA: A co-worker asked if I would take a look at a photo, she took at her grandmother's birthday party. She sent me the photo and I took a good hard look and thought, "Now that's funny, I've never seen that before." What I was seeing or better yet, what I was feeling was a rocking spirit orb. Ok, now I know orbs are controversial, but I believe some are spirit orbs, especially if they meet certain criteria and you have corroborating evidence to back them up.

So, I met with my co-worker and knowing how silly it sounded, explained to her what I was seeing. She started crying and I thought, "OMG, what the heck did I do?" She then explained that her grandfather had passed before the photo was taken but he had a very special habit: he would rock back and forth, like bowing 3 or 4 times when entering a room and those actually were her happy tears. This is one of those memorable times you feel all warm and gooey inside doing what you love and knowing you've made a difference. There are other cases that make my top ten hit parade that are just as memorable, but the authors of this book would roll their eyes because I would be way over my word count limit. In any case, I do want to talk about one of my favorite locations, The Sierra Sky Ranch. It is my home away from home. I have been investigating this place since 2005. I take my paranormal studies students there for their overnight field trip, I get the best night's sleep and it is a verified haunted site. I've organized and hosted four paranormal seminars, filmed an episode of *Paranormal Journeys* there, and well, I just don't get tired of this place. I might add, the owners and managers are very supportive and open to our investigations.

The Sierra Sky Ranch, Oakhurst, CA

There is never a dull moment at the ranch, something happening all the time both inside and outside. With seven spirits to contend with, it can be quite the night. We have the nurse who loves to come into rooms, stand by the bedside with a tray of meds; the old cowboy, who loves to play pranks; the two children, who like to run up and down the hallways late at night; the chef in the kitchen along with the pantry chef, both of whom hate each other and fight constantly and finally the young man in the downstairs suite, who gazes out the window, afraid to move on. They all co-exist, have the run of the place and most of them are aware of each other, which makes for an interesting investigation. There are so many validated photos that it blows my mind and the electronic voice recordings (EVPs) are off the chart, and awesome with many Class A and B varieties. So much evidence, I can safely say with a certain degree of certainty, this place is haunted.

Talk about the research team you're on.

As of this writing, the CCPI organization is on active status but because of the pandemic, is in a holding pattern. From 2005 through 2019, my awesome team conducted over 300 investigations of homes and businesses, etc. Most of my team members have gone on to other interests during this time and I have moved on to new adventures. For the last nine years, I've been producing and co-hosting a local TV show, *Paranormal Journeys,* including haunted locations. We have a lot of fun talking about weird and strange stuff on the show and highlighting those who travel the same journey as I do. CCPI will always be here, and I am currently investigating locations with friends and continue doing what I love, which is paranormal research investigation work. But I fear times have changed, as they always do...for the better? We shall see.

Who do you admire in the field and why?

In 1999, I was fortunate to have veteran investigator Gloria Young of Ghost Trackers, as a mentor. For the next three years, we traveled everywhere. She taught me the basics of researching and got me started on this path until I was ready to hang my own CCPI shingle, long before it was popular. Sadly, she has passed away.

One other who has the most influential impact on me is Dale Kaczmarek, of the Ghost Research Society. His investigation work and analysis of evidence are so instrumental in the way I conduct my work now. Many of his methods I've adopted and I respect his integrity, credibility, and professionalism.

Bio: *Jackie Meador is the founder and chief investigator for Central California Paranormal Investigations or CCPI. She has been researching*

ghosts and hauntings for over 24 years. She has been published in trade magazines, newspapers, and books, and appeared in numerous newscasts, radio programs, TV specials, and A&E's Psychic Kids series.

Besides research and investigation work, she has taught Paranormal Studies 101 and 102 for nine years. She also organized a program for gifted children titled, "The Light Explorers," planned fundraisers for historical sites, and was involved in other special events throughout the community. She continues to organize seminars and workshops.

She was the producer behind the popular series of special documentaries called, Hauntings in Central California, which aired on MyTV 53 | KMSG TV from 2009 – 2012. The series earned a Gold Award at the 2009 International AVA Awards. She also writes and produces the TV talk show Paranormal Journeys on Fresno's Community Access TV station CMAC. She and her co-host interview other paranormal researchers about ghosts, Sasquatch, UFOs, metaphysical mysteries, cryptids, etc.

Nicknamed "The Paranormal Hub," Jackie continues to lead CCPI as the foremost authority in paranormal research and investigation throughout Central California.

Her favorite cartoon is Casper, the Friendly Ghost.

Ashley Moreno

Founder of Haunted Travels
Paranormal, Podcaster, UINI Research
Team Investigator

Since a young age, the paranormal has been an interest and a large part of my life. One thing people do not know about me, especially in this field, is that when I was 7 years old, I lost someone incredibly important in my life. I watched her endure a long and painful 13-month battle with stage 4 stomach cancer, which unfortunately claimed her life at an early age. Being so young, I had to learn, cope, and adapt to the "new world" around me. With her death came questions, such as uncertainty, anger, and fear of what was next. Days after her death, I had my first experience: it was late at night, and my father was asleep on the couch, where he had spent most nights since her death. I walked down the hall, turned the corner into the living room and that is where I saw her! My mother, watched over my father as he slept; her appearance and demeanor were as if nothing had happened. She looked me dead in the eyes (no pun intended) and began to speak. In a soft, soothing voice she began to tell me everything would be ok, not to worry and she would see me again; she promised!

I could not believe my eyes as she looked incredible, youthful, and no longer sick. It all happened so quickly and within minutes, she was gone. It was at this exact moment that it began - my "obsession" with the other side - the unknown, the paranormal. I needed answers, I needed justification, I needed her! Her death left me empty in so many ways, voids that can't be filled, a sadness that can't be forgotten. The paranormal has not only given me hope but the justification that there is so much more out there. It has provided relief and serenity in the thought of loss and death.

It was not until later in life that I finally had the opportunity to truly explore my interests and abilities. Joining a paranormal investigation team and heading to several infamous haunted locations throughout the East Coast seeking evidence and answers awakened a part of me that I had buried a long time ago, a part of me that many saw as crazy, weird, or overly spiritual. To date, I have founded two paranormal investigations teams and am currently working on building the brand of Haunted Travels Paranormal. I also created a true crime / paranormal podcast called *Realm of Darkness* on WLTK-db and am also an investigator with The Uini Research Team. Haunted Travels Paranormal is a different type of team as we do not go looking for scare factors, or typical Hollywood effects. We focus on the location, a few individuals who may still "reside" at the location and we strive to bring their story to light, no matter what that means! We continue to focus on the history of a location and the town in which it sits. Many haunted locations tend to have ties to the town and/or city and these untold stories and truths are what we hope to share through paranormal research.

With that being said, we as investigators, work hard to bring truth and honesty to the field. Unfortunately, there are numerous media outlets that show or give the wrong impression of the paranormal world and we want to show the public it is not something to be feared but something we can learn from. The paranormal has been an incredible healing journey for most investigators, leading to heightened abilities, stronger beliefs, and open spirituality. It allows your mind to find comfort in those we have lost, knowing they are still out there, and it wasn't lights out, you're done kind of scenario. The Uini Research Team is scientific based. Focusing on the use of experiments, data, and continuous information logs not only to deliver hard evidence but proof and justification that there are trends within the paranormal.

Showing the environment, time of day, weather, etc., can all influence paranormal spikes.

The Hinsdale house in New York is not only one of my favorite locations but also a location unlike any other: it reads you, studies you, and shows you exactly what you need at that moment. Hinsdale is where I experienced a lot at first, including disembodied voices, a partial possession (or so we thought), objects moving, shadows, EVPS that made our blood run cold, and sights/visions that left some in tears. Hinsdale was a location I swore to never return. However, the history, the authenticity and the activity are incredible and to this day it continues to draw me in. In fact, I have returned five times and counting.

Through my journey in the paranormal field, I have seen the work of many incredible, talented, and extremely intelligent people. Many who I have had the pleasure to meet and work with. Throughout my years, it has been hard to pick one person or one team that I would say I admire because each team and each person I have met brought something new to the table. I have learned different methods of investigating, communicating, ways to open not only spiritually but mentally, ways of protection and ways to ground myself. Each person I have worked with has truly given me a piece that has allowed me to better myself, my investigating and further my knowledge and for that I am forever grateful.

Bio: *Ashley Moreno is the Founder of Haunted Travels Paranormal, co-founder of Beyond the Dimensions, a PARAFlixx exclusive, and host/writer of Realm of Darkness Podcast on WLTK-db Talk Radio. Ashley has investigated some of the world's most infamous locations, not only as a paranormal series cast member and investigator but has also taken part in events. She brings the public together and teaches the proper and safe ways to investigate while shedding light on the true side of the paranormal. She is currently working alongside the UINI research team as an investigator, editor, cinematographer, and narrator. The filming for Season 2 of Beyond the Dimensions, Resurrection will begin in late September 2023 and can be found on PARAFlixx. You can also find Ashley in a brand-new female investigator series, The P.I.T., an Angry Trolls Production that will begin filming in late 2023 and will be available across many streaming platforms. You can find her on Facebook, Instagram / TikTok at Ashley.Moreno4*

LINDA MYERS

SHAMANISM TEACHER, PSYCHIC & TAROT
READINGS, REIKI MASTER, PARANORMAL
INVESTIGATOR

What motivated you to research the paranormal?

I have always felt that there was something just outside my reach that could possibly explain things that I had seen and felt at an early age. It seems to me looking back, that I was always looking around the corner for something, not knowing what but feeling there was something if I could just catch it. I would spend hours as a young adult questioning and wondering the why of things that happened.

Did you have a personal experience?

At age 19, I had what I believe was a visit/message from the other side from my brother Les, who had passed away. I was visiting friends during a very intense thunder and lightning storm. I went to bed, and I had a dream about my brother. He was in a cave-like room with handmade furniture, he was facing me, and he had a bow and arrow in his hand. He looked at me and spoke saying he could shoot the arrow into my heart and it would stop but I would not die.

I believe the message was for me to understand that our bodies die however we do not. He also visited one more time. I was lying down resting between two jobs; I felt a push on my back and said, "Stop Les." Then I remembered he was gone. I went outside to go to work and found that someone had punctured my tires and I believe I was warned to wake up. I would have to say that the above occurrences led me to become more deeply involved. I have had several other instances, two of which involved full-bodied apparitions. I was in my new home and was lying in bed thinking about the house. I looked to the corner of the room and saw a man and a woman dressed in old farm clothing. As the woman smiled and walked toward me, I had to admit to being spooked and hid my head under the covers. When I looked again, they were gone. The next incident was in Sedona, Arizona. I was hiking with friends to a large medicine wheel and was wondering how much further we had to go. I then noticed a native woman walking towards me, so I stopped and asked her how far to the wheel. She smiled and said, "Not far." I walked a few steps further and turned to tell my friends what she had said, and she wasn't there. I could see the whole trail; she had just disappeared. I have on a couple of occasions seen the shadows of spirits during our investigations.

My current role as a researcher.

I am the co-team lead of Olympic Peninsula Paranormal Society. I help with setting up investigations and have been doing some of the training of new people on the team. I also lead and participate in the inspections.

Methodologies used:

I use my natural abilities as a psychic intuitive. I also have several pieces of technical equipment that I use. I have researched extensively which pieces that I have found to be accurate. I do however depend on my natural abilities most of the time and use the tech often for confirmation. Some of the technical pieces are a recorder, EMF detector, SLS camera, pendulum, dowsing rods, and IR (infrared) camera. Also, if I know a specific thing about a location, I will use a pendulum and dowsing rods to locate potential hot spots. I use my senses to first investigate a location as I have found my first impressions are important. I utilize my recorder to record my first impressions, which provides me a record.

As far as changes, I would like to see in paranormal research, I would like to see more investigators/teams use standardized training when introducing new people to the field. At Port Gamble Paranormal Conference this year, I taught a class called, "How to Conduct a Paranormal Investigation" from start to finish. Feedback on this class was that people wished they had this kind of training prior to doing any investigations.

I first do any necessary research for location background and team safety. I will try to do a daylight visit so I can look for things that may interfere with team safety. I will then set up my team by experience based on the level of difficulty at the location. I will brief the team on what I have found, and we discuss team equipment, setup, and safety.

Top cases include:

Conducting investigations at the Walker Ames located in Port Gamble, Washington

Participating in locating missing persons with a team

Investigating the Pioneer Saloon in Goodsprings, Nevada and St. Ignatius Hospital in Colfax, Washington

Current research team:

My current team is Olympic Peninsula Paranormal Society. This team was formed 15 years ago. I joined the group three years ago. It is comprised of 12 members varying in age and experience. We are currently resuming home investigations after two years of COVID-19. We are a local team that assists in the Port Gamble Paranormal Conference conducting the investigations that are done at The Walker Ames House. We also assist at the Port Townsend Paranormal Festival conducting investigations at local haunted locations. We have been busy recently doing home investigations for people who are having things happen in their homes. We provide them with options to assist in either removal or how to peacefully coexist.

I admire the following paranormal investigators:

Loyd Auerbach: I respect his approach and teaching methods.

Catherine Crowe 1780-1872: author of *The Night Side of Nature*

Amy Bruni: She doesn't do drama and tries to find the cause.

Nicole Strickland: I respect her no-nonsense approach to the paranormal and her willingness to approach the paranormal without judgment.

Todd Bates: He brings tons of value and teachings via his radio station.

Michael La Chiana: paranormal researcher and documentary producer.

Pete Orbea: He brings the paranormal to the Pacific Northwest via his podcast and asks the hard questions.

Bio: *Linda Myers has been interested in the paranormal since the age of 19 when she experienced several unusual events after the death of her brother during the daytime and while dreaming. She is currently a member of the Olympic Peninsula Paranormal Society and a past member of Conscious Paranormal Research and Investigation and Desert Paranormal. Linda has been active in several paranormal conferences and has taught classes on paranormal boot camp, dowsing, and pendulums. She has been tested by the Edgar Cayce Foundation and found to be intuitive.*

Linda has also been involved in both the study and teaching of

Shamanism. She does psychic and tarot readings and is also a Reiki Master. She is currently involved in investigations and after mostly intu-itive work, is exploring some of the new devices available for paranormal research. She has a commitment to exploring the afterlife after her own experiences.

June Antionette Nixon

Vice President/Client Coordinator – AGHOST, Paranormal Researcher

What motivated you to research the paranormal?

I've always been fascinated by the paranormal but was not one of these kids that had any ghostly experiences. I've just been drawn to it. It might have been because my mom's dad died when I was 5 years old and I had to stay in the room with his body until the coroner came to pick him up, or that I saw my dog killed when I was 6 years old. I got a little obsessed with what happened to them. I also got a little obsessed with anything scary at that age (started off with *Scooby Doo*) then graduated to old Hammer Horror movies. After my divorce, I was watching a ghost hunting show and thought, hey I would love to do that. I started taking classes and then found my first group, King County Paranormal Investigators.

Did you have any experiences that fueled your interest?

Like I had said before, nothing when I was really young, but as I got older had some strange things happen with a Ouija board at slumber parties or during *Light as a Feather Stiff as a Board* that actually worked. When I was in college, I went over to a friend's house and the planchette flew out of her hands (or she might have thrown it, just not sure to this day) but at the same time, all the lights went out. I was terrified but it even fueled my interest more. My first big experience that sealed the deal, so to speak, was at the Walker Ames House in Port Gamble, WA. I was on the 2nd floor when I saw a shadow standing in the little hallway. The sun was still shining, and as I walked toward it, it came toward me and disappeared. I tried everything to debunk it but to no avail. I had to accept it was a shadow that was not connected to any living person. It fueled my desire even more.

What is your role as a paranormal researcher?

I'm the Vice President and Client Coordinator of the Advanced Ghost Hunters of Seattle Tacoma (AGHOST). I talk to a lot of people, find out what is going on, and see if we can help them. Eight out of ten times, people really don't want an investigation, they just want to talk to someone who won't judge them. I am a very good listener and can be very compassionate.

This is the third team I have been on and the last one I will ever be on. It was founded by Ross Allison in 2000 making it one of the oldest continuously running paranormal research teams in the Pacific Northwest. We have an amazing drama-free team who are all professional and caring people. I'm very fortunate to be a part of such an incredible group and feel like they are my family. We really look out for each other. Our website is AGHOST.org.

What types of methodologies do you utilize and why?

I do not have any "psychic" abilities but I do have a good feel for people. I think I have a good sense of BS and when someone is telling the truth. I do use a lot of equipment in investigating and I think the best evidence consists of EVPs and not from a Ghost Box or Ovilus. Although I have had some interesting experiences, and do not discount the Ghost Box completely, I believe these are too suggestive and you can pull out anything you want from it. I call it the "Instant Ghost." I feel if your investigation is getting a little boring, you can pull out this device and usually, you will get something. Using white noise would be more effective and impressive, in my book. I've heard whole sentences come out at times from just that.

What would you like to see changed or improved in the field of supernatural research?

Well, I would love to see some of these television shows cancelled. They are definitely for entertainment purposes only. I wish there was a way for all paranormal researchers to be on the same page and have the same values and check system. But there are too many egos and too many paranormal celebrity wannabes. I would like to see true paranormal scientific methods. Ross Allison's documentary *ParaSense* really delves into this.

How do you go about investigating the paranormal?

When I go into a business or home, I go in with a lot of respect and humbleness. I tell them why we are there; I promise them that we are not there to get rid of the energies (I don't believe anyone can get rid of spirits if they do not want to go) or harm them. We usually go room to room asking if there is a message we can get to someone, or if they want us to do anything for them. We try to find out their name and talk to them compassionately. We never provoke.

One of my favorite locations is The Walker Ames House in Port Gamble, WA. We have had so many different experiences in that house. It makes it one of my favorite places to investigate. The USS *Turner Joy* in Bremerton, WA is another favorite. It's a retired Naval battleship and we've had so many amazing experiences on its decks. People can book a tour or overnight on the ship by contacting SpookedinSeattle.com It is incredible. Roslyn Castle in Scotland was incredible. We stayed there for four days and got to investigate the four tiers underneath the castle. Sicignano degli Alburni in Italy is a castle ruin not too far from Naples. It is an incredible place and bed and breakfast that we stayed at not too far away. There are so many other places that would take too long to name.

Who do you admire in the field and why?

I admire our roots in the paranormal such as Eleanor Sidgwick (one of the first women scientific pioneers in ghost hunting in the late 1800s), Harry Price, Hans Holzer, Dr. Barry Taft, Loyd Auerbach, etc. They opened the doors for paranormal research and over the years made it more acceptable in mainstream culture (the show *Ghost Hunters* did too in the beginning seasons). I do acknowledge Ed and Lorraine Warren also, but I am going to say something controversial here: I am not a fan of them, everything to them is a demon and I believe they fabricated a lot of stories just for media attention. I know so many people admire them but the more research I have seen on them, it makes me angry and irritated that they have gotten so much notoriety and people don't even know anything about them.

Bio: *June Antoinette Nixon is the Vice President and Client Coordinator for the Advanced Ghost Hunters of Seattle Tacoma (AGHOST), the Northwest's oldest operating paranormal team established in 2000. The group has over 20 years of being involved in the paranormal community.*

June has also lectured on paranormal topics for various conferences, public libraries, and other social events. These include women in the ghost hunting field to haunted travels around the world. She has also assisted in public ghost hunts and educational venues for Seattle's leading tour company, Spooked in Seattle. Her passion for the paranormal and the things that go bump in the night have taken her on travels all around the world with renowned ghost hunter Ross Allison, including paranormal investigations of some of the most haunted castles, cemeteries, and houses throughout Europe. It seems that she just can't get enough of the culture, history, and spookiness that keeps drawing her in.

Rev. Lezli A. Polm, DD

Psychic/Sensitive, Teacher, Lecturer and Workshop Facilitator, Author

When I was a little girl, I often heard the adults in my life, both family and friends use one word to describe me: "Precocious." That was the word they all chose. I didn't know what it meant, but it didn't feel like a compliment. I know they were confounded by my behavior. I had visions, memories from a past life, saw apparitions, had conversations with people no one else could see.

I often felt dismissed when I tried to explain it to others. Everyone from family to teachers chalked up my strangeness to an overactive imagination. When I was just three years old, I encountered my first full-body apparition; in layman's terms, a ghost. I was not alone when this specter appeared. I was with my best friend Joyce. She saw this ghost as well. It was a woman that suddenly appeared while we were playing with dolls. I felt her before I saw her. Just before her arrival, my vision became blurry, then I heard my friend let out a gasp. I turned to look at her. She was staring toward the door, which was across the room from where we sat on the floor. In the doorway stood a woman wearing a long black skirt and a long-sleeved white blouse, her dark hair was pulled up into a bun. She didn't move and just stood there staring at us.

At first, we were scared, shocked and didn't know what to do. But she didn't seem menacing at all. She gave off a nurturing vibe that had a calming effect. We saw her on several other occasions and although she gave us the impression that she wouldn't hurt us, we were both afraid to be alone with her. We thought for some reason that she might take us away with her. One day Joyce's mother couldn't find her, and I was convinced that the lady had taken her. Luckily, I didn't voice this opinion since I'm sure no one would have believed me. A short time later, Joyce's mom found her in the broom closet downstairs playing her own little game of "hide and seek."

When puberty hit, I had crazy poltergeist activity follow me around. Items flew off of walls, things fell off of tables and other surfaces when I walked into the room. Not all the time, not even every day, but often enough to be noticeable. This was weird enough that one of my friends would no longer enter my bedroom when they came over. My room was the focus of the majority of the activity. One day I came home from school to an empty house, which was normal for me. I was a latch-key kid. My mom worked and I carried a house key. That day was like any other until my mother got home and went into the bathroom to take a bath. I had been in there after school but hadn't paid any attention to the bathtub. The shower curtain was drawn closed, and everything seemed fine. When my mom went in to take a bath, she pulled back the curtain and screamed. I ran in to see what was going on. The entire wall behind the tub was covered in a very strange script. It wasn't English and we couldn't decipher it. Accompanying the writing were drawings of face-like structures with eyes, but they didn't look like anything human or animal that I've ever seen.

My parents demanded an explanation, and of course I didn't have one. At that time, I had a few books that I had checked out of the library and a few that I owned about ghosts and the unexplained. I decided to do some research. Earlier that year, I received a Ouija board as a gift. My friends and I had been goofing around with it. Everything I read led me to wonder if we had accidentally summoned something with that Ouija board. We stopped playing around with it for a long time.

As a teen, my paranormal experiences slowed down considerably. This was a big relief for me because I really wanted to fit in. During this time, I hardly noticed my psychic ability. I was much too busy with school, extracurricular endeavors and of course having fun. That's not to say that I didn't have an occasional odd experience. I bought a magazine once that had an article about ESP or extrasensory perception. Along with the article were pages that you could cut out to make a set of cards with which you could test your ESP.

That sounded like fun, so I cut them out and proceeded to follow the directions. Basically, it was a matching game. One was supposed to guess which cards were the same without looking. I ran through the exercise doing fairly well at guessing the matches. It was an entertaining little game, yet it wasn't really a very good test of my ESP because the test would vary each time I took it. I got frustrated and put it away in my dresser drawer. I never saw it again. When I went back to that drawer to show it to a friend who wanted to take the test, it wasn't there. We looked everywhere and it never was found. I had no siblings, and my parents swore they hadn't touched them. Weird.

As I moved into adulthood, the activity picked back up but was less unpredictable and made more sense to me. I knew to trust my intuition. That was until I was married. I then found myself in a very religious family. Like many young brides, I really wanted to please my new mother-in-law. At her behest, I became more involved with the church. I had to back away from anything that might be considered a part of the occult. I spent a decade basically denying my own identity. Eventually I left the church and went through a period of isolation from my husband's family. I was ostracized and demonized until it became inconvenient for them to do so. After several months, they began to soften, and I was able to forgive. Since then, both of his parents have passed, and the family is much more open minded.

Since that time, I have found my spiritual community and have the support that I did not have at earlier times in my life. Together we have witnessed some pretty interesting occurrences. For instance, we were once called to help an elderly neighbor who needed us to pick up her weekly box of food from the food bank. Three of our group members volunteered. When we pulled up in front of her single-wide mobile home, I saw her shuffling out to the mailbox. I waved and finished parking the car. No one was paying much attention to what was going on outside of the car as we were gathering our things and her food box.

When we exited the car, she was nowhere to be seen. I figured she had gone back inside and proceeded to the door. I knocked, rang the buzzer, and waited. She never came to the door. One of us tried the knob, but the door was locked. We didn't want to leave the box outside, so we left, hoping that she would call us back. After a day passed, one of our members tried calling her. There was no answer and no voice mail or message machine. A few days later one of us saw her obituary in the newspaper. She had died two days before we made the delivery. I must have witnessed a little ghostly visit to check the mail.

A recent encounter happened when we were on vacation. My husband and I were visiting our oldest daughter and her family. We were staying in our granddaughter's bedroom. After a fun day of doing touristy things, we went to bed. In the middle of the night, I was awakened by something. I don't know if it was a sound, a feeling, or something else. When I first opened my eyes, I was facing my husband's back and he was fast asleep. Beyond him was a large window facing the street. The curtains were blowing gently and the blinds behind them were vibrating, creating a little fluttering noise. I knew that this was caused by the standing fan oscillating in the corner of the room. I was not alarmed at all.

Since I was awake, I thought that I might as well get up and use the bathroom, and maybe get a drink of water. I turned over and froze. Next to the bed, standing in front of the bedside table was a figure. It was solid black, not very tall, maybe five feet. The figure was thin, with long arms. Longer than normal for your average human. The head was long and narrow, the face without features except for two glowing white eyes that were staring down at me. The entity was slightly bent over as if it were inspecting me carefully. It had an air of concern, even tilting its head in a way that reminded me of my pup when she is confused.

I immediately recognized the being as a "shadow person." I have read and heard of people seeing these creatures, but having never seen one myself, I was skeptical. I lay there frozen for a few seconds or maybe a few minutes; time is relative when you are in the middle of something inexplicable. As my paralysis began to abate, I was able to close my eyes and slowly turn over. I hoped that if I turned my back on the figure, it might go away. I waited. After I got the courage, I turned back toward the shadow. It was gone. Now, I had full view of the door, which had been closed when we went to bed. It now stood open about six inches.

I have to say that this visitation left me a bit rattled. I don't have many answers for the things that I have seen and experienced, but I am always learning that the more I know, the more I don't know. At present, I continue to nurture my intuition. I have occasional visitations and get messages often through various methods of divination such as tarot cards. I also found others interested in investigating paranormal activity and together we formed an investigative team called SOS Paranormal.

We have done several investigations, some in which we picked up some really good EVPs. A few years ago, at the behest of my family, I wrote a memoir about my experiences and adventures in the realm of the paranormal and metaphysical. You can read more about my personal journey in *Thin Is The Veil: A Haunting Memoir.*

I believe that we have so much more to discover about this world, this reality, this dimension. Sharing our stories can help further our knowledge and understanding as well as support and encourage our fellow psychics, mediums and seekers of all mysteries.

Bio: *Lezli A. Polm is a life-long psychic/sensitive, teacher, lecturer, and workshop facilitator. Her professional background began with a*

career in nursing and holistic healing. Later she obtained a Doctor of Divinity from National Interfaith Seminary and became an Ordained Interfaith Minister.

She owns a business with her husband and has authored non-fiction as well as fiction and children's books. She resides in Arizona with her husband and very spoiled pets.

DeEtte Ranae

Psychic Medium, Medical Intuitive, International Teacher, Radio Host

When did you discover that you have psychic abilities?

When I look over my life, I would have to say I always had abilities. As a child, I always knew there was something in the room with me. I didn't see it or hear it, but knew it was there. I would keep the covers tight up against my neck and when I would be scared if I had to go to the bathroom, I remember counting to ten throwing the covers back, and running as fast as I could to the bathroom just to slam the door behind me. And then when I had to come back it was even more scary as I would fly in my bed and grab those covers, fling with my head and shiver myself to sleep.

Throughout the years, I always seemed to know things prior to the question being asked or before anybody ever told me anything. I was considered and known as the know-it-all not only in my family but also within my school. It wasn't until I got into my college years that the instructor finally told me to put my hand down. As I grew into adulthood, I would say things happening throughout the day prior to that part of the day occurring. It brought on a curiosity of things regarding divination. But it wasn't until I got into my 30s when I went to go see another psychic and he told me that I was better than he was. After that, I actually started to study and look into what those abilities were.

On a mediumship scale of it though it's a totally different story. When I was nine years old my grandmother was in the hospital and back in those days unless you were 13 you weren't allowed to go upstairs. So, I didn't know what the hospital looked like. In a dream, she had come to me one night and walked me through the hospital. I was having a conversation with me now to say I wasn't really listening to her at that point. I was just really looking at all the things that were in the hospital. When we got to the last room, she opened up the door and had me look inside. There was an older woman lying in a bed with tubes and wires connected to her. She asked me who the woman was, and I told her, "That's you, grandma." Then she asked me who I am. I stood there and looked at her and I was confused, and I told her just that. And that's when she told me the difference between the body and a soul. That's when she told me that her body was no longer working and that her soul was going to heaven. She then proceeded to tell me to not be afraid. I woke up that morning and told my mom that my grandma died. And she told me that she had not or else she would've received the call. Surely there after, my mom got the call that grandma had died.

Sometime after that experience, I started having dreams of people passing away. It took me years to realize that it was just the beginning. It wasn't until I got into my 40s that I took my first class and was blown away by what I was able to hear and see. Within a few years, I have done thousands of readings and talked to thousands of souls.

How can you tell when a psychic medium is authentic?

To tell if someone is being authentic is to watch them and their energy. When a person is positioning their body to push their energy toward the client, they are going in psychically. Some people who claim to be mediums will do this and not actually connect to a loved one. They are receiving all the information from the client's aura. So, watching body position is one thing. Another is to watch if they are leading the client. A good car salesman can appear to be psychic just by watching bodily cues and responding to them. Also, with a medium, it should touch on an emotional cord. And at the end of the day, neither of these should ever tell a person what to do. It is up to the client to make those decisions.

I never approach someone to do a reading. If someone wants a reading, they will come to me. If the question is more of how I do a reading, I explain to the client how I read. Even if someone has had many readings, they may never have had one with me. I want them to be comfortable knowing what to expect before we start.

How do you incorporate psychic mediumship?

In a reading, I ask what the client is looking for – about their life, deceased loved ones or health. If they are unsure, I simply ask if they would like to go wherever the spirit leads. I do not mix them though. Meaning I do psychic, then mediumship, then medical intuitive. Not necessarily in that order. I live a spirit-filled life. I truly believe that things happen for a reason and that I can always ask my guides for assistance or guidance.

Do you work with a paranormal team?

I have worked with a few teams as the guest medium, including The Shadow Hunters out of Illinois and The Ghost Finders. Recently, I was accepted into the Warrens Legacy Foundation to work cases internationally by connecting to the client, location, and to remote view. A continuation of Lorraine's passion, I assist with helping mentor some of the others within their psychic support group.

Some people believe that incorporating metaphysical studies in paranormal research is important. Do you agree and why so?

I do agree. I strongly feel they should work together. However, at the same time work separately. What I mean by that, is a medium needs to walk into the situation blind. Not knowing anything about what has happened or information about the location. That way they keep themselves out of what they get. Then report to the team regarding the information he or she receives. At that time, the medium should join the team. The results the team receives can collaborate on what the medium received, and they can further work together. It helps to get the full story and not just pieces of it.

Do you think there's a cosmic shift going on that's causing an influx of paranormal activity?

Honestly, not within the stars. I do feel the shift is a willingness and increased curiosity of what else there is. People are open to the idea of what more there is. With the shift within people, I do believe they are noticing more. Things we used to ignore or brush off as the wind are now being questioned. People are opening up to their own abilities, which they were once told were in their minds, and that has increased the desire to know more. When they know they can communicate, they want to do it more. Don't we all want to know if there is more after this mortal body has finished its time on earth or that grandma is okay? We want to know if what we want to believe in is true.

What are some ways to incorporate metaphysics in a paranormal case study?

As I wrote earlier, it's beneficial to have a medium go into an investigation prior to the team to just receive what she does without the interference of possible knowledge of the location. I feel this can truly help to understand the information the investigators will receive. When they come together, you find the medium is able to help fill in the holes. It truly helps to give a much fuller picture of what is going on. It also helps if the medium is able to connect with the spirits that are there and help them find peace if that is something they seek.

What is your podcast/radio show about?

My show is a paranormal show in the broader sense of it. It isn't the bump in the night show. It is called *Schooled Thru Spirit.* I bring in guests to talk about their journey, why they got into the paranormal, and how their journey has progressed.

What motivates you to have a radio show/podcast about the paranormal?

I found so many had questions about what I do and how I do it. When really, they wanted to know if they were normal, because they have many similar things happening with them. The show is helping people to know that they are not alone and that there are resources available to help them understand themselves more.

Why is radio/podcasting a good medium to educate about paranormal phenomena?

The show is very broad in the guests that I have come on. It truly is anything paranormal and is educational and full of stories. So, my listeners keep an interest and keep coming back. I also find they will share it with others they know if that person has a commonality with that particular guest.

What is the main message(s) you want to convey?

The message here is that we are all normal and it is not in our head or imagination. As people, we are waking up and understanding the old thought patterns of "shh" and "ignore it" are over. That imaginary friend may be one of your guides. The random things you hear in your mind are your loved ones. Your interests in different things may be from a past life and the comfort in knowing that you will not be persecuted for being who you are.

Bio: *Sharing messages from spirit, DeEtte Ranae is an acclaimed psychic medium, medical intuitive, and teacher who serves international clientele as she travels throughout the world, including the United States, Mexico, and Scotland. She has continued her studies and in 2018 was certified through Lisa William's school as a Master Teacher for Psychic and Medi-*

umship Development. Earning her certifications has allowed her to both ensure quality within her readings as well as allow her to educate others and hold them to the same high standard of Lisa's expectations through her teaching of students in mediumship development.

DeEtte is the host of Schooled Through Spirit and Unfiltered, two weekly radio shows on WLTK-db.

You can check out her appearances on The Ghost Finders (episodes 1, 2, 3, and 4 of season 11) and in the Light in the Darkness documentary, where she discussed how she used spirituality to heal from PTSD. You can learn more or contact DeEtte at www.DeEtteRanae.com or on Facebook at www.facebook.com/DeEtteRanae

Andi Roe

Paranormal Researcher & Investigator

My name is Andi, and I have been a paranormal investigator for ten years now, and part of a wonderful team based in Wichita, KS called Road Trip Paranormal. We have an amazing team that investigates all over the United States. I have had paranormal experiences from a young age, and never fully understood it, until I got older. What I have experienced has left me knowing that there is more to the paranormal, ghosts/spirits, etc. It left me with many questions and being intrigued, excited, and maybe a little nervous.

I have learned since being around Road Trip Paranormal in my early days of investigating, to rely on my senses. Your senses are called into action when investigating- your eyes, ears, sense of smell, touch, temperature changes, etc. For example, the eyes are used often in the dark to look for shadows or anything out of the ordinary. The sense of smell is used no matter what location we are in and most of us notice some places have a scent and some do not. As an investigator, I use my sense of smell as it helps to know when there could suddenly be a scent. I've had cases when I sensed nothing, then all of a sudden, got a perfume aroma out of nowhere or smelled cigars or cigarettes.

I was around eight or nine when I first remembered seeing and hearing things. After my grandfather's sudden passing, his death was the first I personally had experienced. I had not really understood death until that point in life. Although now that both of my grandpas have passed on, I know they are around, and they do give me signs. I know, now, what I was experiencing at home back then were both of my grandpas. I have gained a lot of knowledge being around amazing investigators and learning from them. We honor every individual's approach and what we each and collectively bring to the table.

One of my favorite stories comes from my parent's home that I grew up in, located in Derby, Kansas. We had moved into the house when I was seven or maybe eight in the late 80s and had moved to Derby from Wichita. I have had many experiences at our new home, and never fully understood what was happening until I was older. I thought maybe I was crazy and just seeing and hearing things, but boy, was I wrong!

It all started with seeing a full-body black shadow. It was not a very tall shadow, but as a child, it made me nervous because it was taller than me, but not by much. The shadow was around 5'6 to 5'7; I could make out the head, shoulders, arms, legs, and feet. I could not really make out features such as the eyes, nose, or mouth. Our home was a quad-level house, and from the living room, you could look into the kitchen and the staircase going upstairs. There was a loft upstairs overlooking the living room. I often saw the shadow on the stairs, the upstairs hallway loft, and downstairs in the family room. When I was younger, it scared me a little, but I never had a bad or heavy feeling as it was more of a feeling of being protected. As the years passed, I would see it off and on.

Fast forward to the early 2000s, when I was home alone one afternoon. My parents were both at work, and my brother was out on his own. I was working the second shift at that time and had some time before I had to go to work. I had gone outside into the walkout basement off of the downstairs family room. I opened the sliding door and stepped into the family room. I paused as I saw the shadow walking down the stairs. It got to the bottom, stopped, and stood there for about 40 seconds. I was in shock as that was the longest time, I had ever seen it. It then turned and walked down the hallway.

I said out loud, "Dad, Mom, who is here?" Thinking I was losing my mind and one of my parents had come home suddenly for some reason, I then walked down the hall and searched the bathroom and downstairs bedroom and could not find anyone. I searched the whole house and garage and no one had come home. It was just me and the shadow. I felt that whatever it was, was simply letting me know it was around. As the years passed, and I would be back home visiting, I would often hear the shadow spirit talk to me from time to time.

Our team works with an amazing psychic, Lena, with Peaceful Whispers, LLC. Lena is a psychic medium who offers intuitive tarot card readings with the assistance of her spirit guide and has over 20 years of experience. I have had many readings with Lena, and she has been amazing! There are things that she has seen and said in my readings, those that she could never have known about me or my family. During one of my readings with Lena in 2020, she said, "There is a man in your house." I knew immediately that she was referring to the shadow I had seen at home over the years, and was shocked and thankful to have the assurance of what I had seen most of my life. I must have had a shocked look on my face because she said, "You have seen him."

Lena told me that it was a man who was either tied to the property or the home. He was a very nice man and he watched out for us. She relayed that he felt he could show himself to me, and that he does often talk to me. I do not know his name, but we have had some conversations since then. I know he is still around, and I have thanked him for looking out for my family and for being nice to us. I have let him know that he is welcome. I am looking forward to hearing from him, hopefully getting his name, and finding out any information about his life.

I feel that all spirts are people, obviously no longer living. But every one of them has a name, has a story, and has a part in history. I believe they, or at least some of them, want to share their story in some way. I, for one, am going to try my best to find out who this man is. Is he tied to my dad's house or property? We have been given a chance to speak to the past through our investigations. It gives us a chance to learn, to grow, and to help those who have departed this earthly life.

Bio: *Andi is a lifelong Kansas resident and works by day as a billing specialist for a company that serves people with disabilities. She loves her job and being able to help the people she serves live a better life, help them build life skills, provide job opportunities, and take them out into the community for various activities. She spends a lot of time with family and loves bonfires, music, and fishing. She loves to travel and Hawaii is one of her favorite places. She loves meeting new people and experiencing different cultures.*

She has been a professional paranormal investigator for ten years and is a member of a paranormal team called Road Trip Paranormal based in Wichita, Kansas. The group collectively has investigated many places around the United States. Helping clients, they do private in-home and public investigations and love what they do. Part of being an investigator includes studying history because each place the team goes to has a historical tale as well as the people and spirits they encounter. I never thought that being an investigator could be as rewarding as it is. It is an honor to be a part of such an amazing team, where each teammate brings something different to the table.

Atheria (Carrie Jane Ryan)

Trance Medium, ET Contactee

I was born Carrie Jane Ryan in Rochester, NY in 1996 but became Atheria in 1999. Well, I was given the name Atheria by an unseen voice in 1998 but fought it (I'm stubborn) for many months. Atheria felt way too exotic for me, but when my unseen friends wanted me to do something, they got aggressive. I had heard this loud voice above me say, "You are not really Carrie Ryan, you are Atheria" during meditation one afternoon. When I responded with a shocked, "What?!" the voice repeated it. Then I said, "Spell it." It spelled A-T-H-E-R-I-A. In March 1999 during the span of one week, everywhere I went strangers and neighbors walked up to me and said, "You know, I changed my name, and it was the best thing I ever did." It kept happening! When I finally gave up and accepted the name, my life opened up that day. Opportunities arose immediately. Interestingly, a very good psychic medium in 1994 said to me the first minute he met me, "You need to change your name. It's so wrong for you, it's literally causing you harm." I disregarded Rodolfo Silva's words and forgot about them until 1998's loud voice.

My normal life had gotten weird in 1996 due to some healing sessions with very gifted Dr. Eric Pearl in West Hollywood, CA. Up to that point, I'd never considered myself psychic, but as a kid, I was very interested in all things paranormal. We neighborhood kids would hold séances in my house's basement. I loved the TV show, *In Search Of*. I would listen to late-night radio shows about ghosts and such. I do recall having some dreams come true, and one night my eyes jolted open when I felt my face belovingly held by two hands. I saw the upper part of a dark-haired lady float through my bedroom and through the wall or door. Occasionally, I'd have someone pop into my head I'd not talked to in years and my phone would ring with them calling to catch up. But I basically considered myself to be a normal person. I had gone to see Eric for healing after a bad neck injury in 1995 that triggered a constant horrible headache. How I was sent to him is a whole story in and of itself. He worked on me three days in a row and amazing things happened while I was on his table. I felt hands touching me that were not his. I felt my soul twirling around inside my physical body. I had visions of eyes flying at my face. I felt the wind blowing across me. During the first session, I felt myself lift out of my body into the light as I started uncontrollably giggling from pure, unadulterated bliss. It was incredible!

After the third healing session, not only did a lump I had in my breast shrink dramatically, but I got a period 28 days later for the first time in years. (I had hormone issues.) I was amazed at the magical things that happened during the sessions, but thought I was still the same Carrie Ryan. Wrong. During the night, that third time, I had a major out-of-body experience. My soul slammed so hard back into my physical body that it threw me half off the bed and onto the floor. It freaked me out! As I laid back on the bed, I was like, "What was that about?" I also felt like I was being watched. I could strongly feel that my room was full of spirits. I pulled my covers over my head and somehow fell back to sleep. But, starting the next morning, I suddenly started hearing clairaudient voices, started having clairvoyant visions, and just knew things I couldn't explain how I knew...but I knew information that should have been impossible.

Besides being given the name Atheria in 1998, I had my first remembered alien abduction while living in the Hollywood Hills. I realize now that I probably have been taken by ETs my whole life, but this was clear and dramatic. Another abduction happened about 1-2 weeks later by a not-friendly group of ETs. The first group treated me very much as an equal as they took me to a laboratory underneath downtown Los Angeles to show me hybrid baby experiments they were doing. 1998 was also the year Taos, NM showed up for me, calling me to it. I didn't know it was a town in New Mexico until a friend told me. I visited for the first time in August 1998 and had more life-altering events happen. That's definitely a story in itself.

In 2000, I went to someone to be hypnotized and regressed to see if I could better clear out the ongoing head pain problem (for some reason, that didn't respond to the healing sessions) by digging through past lives. I have been killed by my neck in numerous lives, including being hung on July 19, 1692, during the Salem Witch Trials.

Everything was going normally for this novice hypnotherapist until BAM! I was suddenly pushed outside and to the right of my body. Voices that were not mine, spoke through me and I could not control, interrupt, or stop them. They talked about, "Your true work will be important in 12 years" and how I used to live on Lemuria. In 2000, I had never heard of the Mayan Calendar or Mu. I had to look this stuff up later. That was my introduction to doing verbal channeling. I found a meeting where these students of the fabulous channel, Shawn Randall, were going to demonstrate what they could do regarding trance mediumship/channeling and went to it out of curiosity. Unexpectedly while sitting in the audience, I went into full trance and kind of took over the event.

When I came out of it, the other students said, "You need to take Shawn's class! You have a gift!" I did end up taking classes with Shawn and she really helped me learn how to handle the strong energies that came through. All these years later, I still struggle with some of them but also don't practice as much as I should. I'm an unruly psychic at times.

I used to do some readings for people but stopped as it became very stressful for me. I really want to do a good job if I'm doing a reading and would put too much pressure on myself so that it wasn't fun for me. That being said, spirit does want me to stop being a wuss and do what I was sent here to do. Now, I do have a blog I enjoy writing and a YouTube channel where I post some channeling sessions, but I have a demanding day job with a long commute and it's hard to find the time and energy to do spiritual work. I actually like giving what I call "drive-by" messages to people when I'm out and about...just quick spirit messages.

I need to be more careful about that. It's not always welcome and I should ask permission first. Also, to walk around too open, energetically, isn't great for me. I used to be called a "walking antenna" by my British medium teachers years ago and they didn't approve. It can be very draining and sometimes dangerous. I accidentally brought home a spirit attachment one day that I'd gotten from spending an evening at a coworker's house where she was not mentally well and had been playing with Lenormand cards, which triggered an entity to take her over.

I didn't realize the being came home with me and I started getting these odd obsessive thoughts about Denver and Boulder that I'd never had before...but the coworker was very connected to Boulder. It took an Apache medicine man to notice that something was attached to me. He did a thorough cleansing of my Albuquerque house and me and this entity got yanked out of my solar plexus chakra, flew across the room, and out the wall. He calmly looked at me and said, "Yeah, I thought so." The next morning, all of the obsessive thoughts I'd had for weeks disappeared. Doing protection when you are a psychic medium is very important. Actually, everyone should do energetic protection every morning before they go out and about. When I lived in Los Angeles, I would feel so bombarded with millions of people's energy that it was very draining and not good for me.

When you are a psychic medium and channeler, I don't think being male or female makes much of a difference in terms of how many in society view you. A lot of people think I'm nuts. Some didn't believe in what I do at first, but then witnessed some cool things, and became less skeptical converts. Some love what I do. I will say it's a bit isolating having this gift because I'm just not like most other people and quickly lose interest in average life things. I have zero interest in sports, for a simple example. I don't relate to a large percentage of people. I'd much rather hike in the woods than go to restaurants or movies. I prefer animals over people and am also a vegan. I actually think my veganism and love of animals come from my life in Lemuria.

I feel a tremendous amount of pressure to make a big difference in the world, and as a kid would stress myself out worrying that I was running out of time and needed to hurry. Now, at 57, I've not done much and I am kind of rotting. I'm feeling a bit lost and don't have as much oomph to get up off my butt and do something or do anything. I feel some guilt about not doing something to help the world, but also don't know exactly what I'm supposed to be doing. I really wish my spirit guides would give me specifics, but that's not totally their job.

I am feisty and can't put up with total skeptics who refuse to have an open mind about all things paranormal. When other psychics, mediums, ET contactees, etc., are mocked or attacked, I get very angry. I need to work on not caring and letting things go, but it's hard. Sometimes I wish I was average, but other times, I've experienced such glorious spiritual events that I'm grateful to be who I am with what I have. In 1996, I went from living in black and white to living in color. I don't want to give that up.

Bio: *Atheria is a psychic medium and trance channel currently living in Santa Fe, NM. She grew up in Rochester, NY, and lived in Los Angeles, CA for many years, with shorter stints in Lake Oswego, OR, West Linn, OR, Westminster, CO, Albuquerque, NM, and Pojoaque, NM. Her special place is powerful Taos, NM and she also resonates strongly with New Orleans, LA, and Savannah, GA. She suspects a very good past life she had in the 1800s took place in Savannah. Atheria is still a SAG-*

AFTRA member from her Hollywood days and is a long-term vegan animal lover with a special affinity with cats and horses. She embraces the term "crazy cat lady" and wears it as a badge of honor. She adores tiny houses and is into minimalism...living with no furniture other than a mattress topper on the floor, a $10 folding chair, and an $11 folding TV dinner table for a few years not long ago. Her soul is that of a nomad and if she could talk the cats into riding in her backpack, would travel around the world to places like Tibet, Nepal, Peru, Japan, Ireland, India, etc. New Mexico has called her three times now, and it annoys her to no end that she's been brought to a state with long, freezing cold winters. Couldn't she have found jobs in tropical/warm Costa Rica? But, alas, the Land of Enchantment wants her here at this time in her soul's journey. Oh, it should be mentioned that Atheria is a double Libra. Don't ask her to make decisions (sun and rising) with a Capricorn moon. Without the grounding of Capricorn, she'd be up in the ethers all of the time! Her blog is www.bridge4spirit.wordpress.com and she can be emailed at 20october@ gmail.com

Jyl Straub

Co-Founder of White Light Paranormal Insight, Haunted Walking Tour Director & Host

I believe once you are bitten by that paranormal bug, you are bitten for life. I also have seen that there are more women in the field than men and it always makes me question these ghost shows even more as they bring in these big-chested men who scream at their own shadows. I've seen amazing and intelligent women in this field who I respect immensely. They are my true heroes.

I have had an interest in the supernatural since I was a child living above my grandparents' funeral home. Death for me was just a normal part of life. As a toddler, I had an invisible friend who I affectionately called "Dorny." She shared space in the funeral home and I remember one incident of baby powder getting spilled all over the bathroom and the heater getting turned up on several occasions. I would conveniently blame her when things of that nature happened. I would tell my parents that "Dorny did it!" Looking back, I often wonder if "Dorny" was a visiting spirit, an earthbound spirit or a possible spirit guide. I guess that I will never know for sure.

Sometimes children are more open to paranormal experiences because they have a much greater sense of awareness. I do recall having lucid dreams and was known to sleepwalk while living there. My mom even found me on top of the pool table one morning and there was no explanation of how I got up there. While I don't live at the funeral home anymore, I am sometimes called to style hair for those who have passed on. Whenever I tell people this, they usually say, "Well, at least they don't complain." In my experience, at least a couple have! I was just about finished with one lady when I heard her clairaudiently say, "Too poofy." Another one said, "Too much hair spray." As a hairstylist of 36 years, I am extremely meticulous and really care about making my clients happy whether they are living or have passed on. I can usually feel them watching me while I try to make them look their best for their open casket showing. Another time, I believe that I picked up on one of the spirits empathically. While I held her hand to paint her nails, it was as if there was an energetic cord between us. The woman was young and had committed suicide, leaving a baby and husband behind. I believe that I had picked up on all of her sadness, excruciating pain, and mental anguish that she must have felt inside. It stuck with me, merging with my energy field. After I left, I sobbed uncontrollably for a couple of hours. I am not a crier by nature, and it took me a while to shake it. In all of the years, this was the only funeral home job that really got to me.

Bigfoot, UFOs, ghosts...you name it, I saved my allowance to purchase these types of reading materials at the elementary school book fair. Since a child, I have always had a passion for anything otherworldly. When on a family weekend getaway around the age of ten, I opened a bathroom cabinet and saw a little black dog pushing an empty food bowl with its nose. When I opened the door again, it had vanished, leaving me to believe that I had just encountered a ghost dog.

As a teen, I would practice psychic-type games with my cousin. I remember picking up a copy of *The Enquirer* at the grocery store while on a beach trip to Lincoln City. It had an article about psychic Uri Geller who was popular at the time. We would practice trying to bend spoons with our minds as instructed in the magazine. We would spend hours playing with homemade Zener cards, which are used to conduct experiments for extrasensory perception. In addition, we would write words and numbers down and try to send psychic messages to each other. We actually got quite a few right!

Shortly after graduating high school, I purchased the *You Are Psychic* book by Pete Sanders Jr. This was one of my favorite books.

Never in my wildest dreams did I expect him to say "yes" to being in the documentary, *All Around Us* decades later. The documentary features my fiancé Seth Michael and shows a glimpse into what life is like being a natural-born psychic medium. Many of our colleagues from the Pacific Northwest paranormal community are in the film as well. One thing that we had in common was that before Seth and I met each other in person, we discovered that we both owned a copy of this book. We both really respect Pete. He is an MIT-trained scientist with a proven program for expanding psychic abilities. If it weren't for ghosts, we would have never met so many incredible colleagues who have become lifelong close friends.

I have had many metaphysical experiences in my lifetime ranging from psychic to paranormal, and even experienced an overwhelming awareness of the presence of my guardian angel when I was going through an extremely difficult time in my life. One day, out of the blue, a psychic who went by the name "Amethyst" walked into my salon to get a haircut. She told me that she was guided there for some reason. I did her hair that day and had a strong intuition to set up a reading with her. During my reading with the psychic at her house, I felt a huge warm loving glow behind me and I started crying uncontrollably. Again, I am not normally a crier and tend to bottle up my feelings. The psychic said that the angel's name was Rachel; she was golden yellow, and she wanted me to let my pain out rather than hold it inside. All of this was proof of the celestial being that I had felt around me for quite some time. At that point, I knew I wasn't in this alone and that I was going to be ok.

In 2010, I met my soulmate Seth Michael and I wholeheartedly believe that we met through divine intervention. I have always been a sensitive empath and after meeting him, I began to understand myself on a much deeper level. I was also having negative paranormal activity in my home after my daughter's guy friends found and messed with an old Ouija board that I had purchased as a teen at the local toy store. The board had been put away and I told my girls prior not to mess with it. Although it is a tool used in the paranormal field, I do believe that it can open a door or gateway to the spirit world and caution should be used.

The activity in our home was intense and affected my daughters so much that they had to move to my parent's house. Seth and I would often hear marbles being thrown at the wall, dropping, and rolling across the floor. Much to our surprise, we could never find any marbles. One day, there was a triangle formation of marbles on the floor. We believe that there was a negative entity in the closet of the upstairs bedroom that seemed to be a portal. It gave Seth intelligent answers to questions. The entity communicated a legit Portland, Oregon phone number that we called, and the person said that they had just recently moved into a new house. To this day, we still do not know what that phone number was about, and it will be one of those things that remains a mystery.

It took a while to energetically clear the house that I lived in, but it sparked a passion and motivated us to start our own paranormal investigation team so that we could help others who were having unexplained occurrences. Co-founded by Seth Michael and me and established in 2011, that is how White Light Paranormal Insight was born. You could say that we turned a negative situation into a positive one. I feel that it is really important to be of service to others and help people whenever possible. "Guiding spirits and empowering people" is our team motto and we have two sides to our team, the investigative side and the spiritual resolve side. I do a little bit of everything on our team including client interviews and relations, investigating, medium assistance, taking notes and photos, historical research, evidence review, etc., mostly on the resolve side. I work closely with Seth and the other mediums on our team.

We take a respectful and compassionate approach with each situation and strive to resolve any spiritual issues for those that have passed on whenever possible. For equipment, we use a digital voice recorder, which we often catch EVPs on. We keep it pretty simple, mostly concentrating on communicating with the spirit or spirits using our natural psychic abilities. Our investigative side uses many types of paranormal equipment and tries to identify the source of the activity. Everyone deserves a safe place to call home and not be bothered by things that they can't see.

I feel that if there could be any improvement in the paranormal field, I wish that more mediums would help families going through a hard time. So many television shows concentrate on fear and documenting that a location is scary and haunted. In the end, sometimes those families are told that their house is indeed haunted and there is a lack of help for them in my humble opinion.

We have been doing paranormal research for over a decade. We took a fantastic workshop at our local historical museum with lots of tips on researching locations. About five years ago, we started a "Ghosts and Spirits Haunted Walking Tour" in downtown Camas, WA. Our team has investigated some of the locations featured on the tour such as the hotel, antique store, and a chiropractic office. We research the history of the buildings, collect paranormal experiences of staff and clients, and also have our team mediums write down any psychic impressions that they get. This makes up all of the elements of our tour along with a couple of stops for spooky snacks and a spirit drink at the end. We donate any profits to our downtown association.

Our lead investigator on WLPI, Kristen, leads a monthly haunted basement tour at Kenton Station in Portland, OR. It is a fascinating tour with plenty of history on the building and lots of paranormal experiences and stories collected by our team and tour guests. I don't really have a favorite location to investigate because I love to keep exploring new and different places. But since we help with the tours and have been there well over a hundred times, Kenton Station is definitely at the top. Each experience is different, and we have captured some really great Class A EVPs and some incredible photos. None of it is proof of the paranormal, but we have had some really interesting things happen in that dirt-floor basement known for the speakeasy and where underground boxing used to take place. There will always be skeptics and it is not our job to make someone a believer. Maybe they are more closed off to the paranormal or maybe they just haven't had their own personal experience.

We have investigated lots of interesting places with our team and also on our own. Homes, businesses, hotels, bars, a prior mortuary, a church, antique stores, and even a gas station/food mart just to name a few. My favorite case started out with a family having paranormal activity and ended up being tied to the spirit of a missing person. We strongly believe that he (the spirit) wants our help and we have spent hours upon hours, even years, trying to solve the mysterious disappearance. With a lot of the cases that our team takes on, the clients end up becoming like family. We try to keep in touch with many of them and check in to see how they are doing.

I am very blessed to be able to follow my paranormal passion and create a life with lots of adventures. I feel so grateful for Seth, our teammates and all of our extended para-family.

As far as projects, we are working on our October tours and collecting more stories and I hope to write a book someday. We were recently on the cover of *Beyond the Gravestones* paranormal magazine and it includes an interview with Seth Michael (Issue 9), which is available on Amazon. The *All Around Us* documentary, directed by Tristan David Luciotti, includes interviews with Seth, me, teammates, other psychic mediums, and clients and is out on DVD and available to stream. You can purchase your copy at www.allaroundusfilm.com.

Bio: *Jyl Straub is based in the Pacific Northwest and lived above her family's funeral home in Camas, WA as a child. She co-founded the paranormal team White Light Paranormal Insight in 2011 with her fiancé Seth Michael. Client relations, interviews, medium/resolve assistance, research, and investigating are just some of the jobs that she's contributed to on the team. The group also runs the Kenton Station haunted basement tour in Portland, Oregon. "Guiding spirits and empowering people" is White Light Paranormal Insight's motto.*

Naturally intuitive and empathic, Jyl has assisted and helped organize many gallery and group readings for Seth Michael. She was a part of The Vision Collective, the All Around Us documentary, and has been involved with the Oregon Ghost Conference since it first started. Jyl researched, wrote, sponsored, and directed the Ghosts and Spirits Downtown Camas Haunted Walking Tour, which was a dream come true. Validating other people's experiences and attempting to resolve them is a passion along with working at her hair salon, The Wild Hair, which is coincidentally on the same street as the funeral home.

Sophia Temperilli

Paranormal Investigator, Host Of Live Paranormal's The Ghost Host Since The Age of 12

My name is Sophia Temperilli. I'm a 24-year-old radio host, known as *The Ghost Host* on LiveParanormal.com/GhostHunting.com; I started on-air at the age of twelve. I have always had a passion for the unknown and the paranormal field ever since I could remember, beginning mainly with, watching *Scooby Doo* and anything and everything related to Halloween. With all of these early interests, a true passion for the field began when my parents attended a dinner ghost tour aboard the *Queen Mary* when I was eight years old for their ten-year wedding anniversary in April of 2007. Before my parents left for the tour, I became jealous of what they might experience without me. The day after my parents' anniversary, they let me know how great the ghost tour was aboard the ship.

When I was finally able to attend Peter James' hosted tour, and after investigating the infamous haunted areas of the *Queen Mary* for myself, I quickly realized how drawn I was to the paranormal field. The next day, my father wrote Peter to thank him for including me on his tour, and that is when he asked my dad to co-author his book. Unfortunately, Peter James passed away before his book was finished, yet due to the popularity of the long-awaited release of his work, our family was included in many events and overnight investigations, starting in 2009.

However, after being in the field for about a year at that point, I began to notice strange instances that were happening in our family home. Essentially, during this period, the paranormal became permanently cemented into my life, shaping who I would become moving forward.

My family home I lived in until 11 years of age, was once where my grandfather passed away in the late 90s; however, he was not the ghost who would become my tormentor. My dad was adopted in the early '70s, yet his adoptive father developed paranoid schizophrenia by the late 1970s, which sadly, forced my grandmother to remove my dad from the home as a child. My grandfather was placed under county guardianship within the home. When he passed away in 1996, my parents spent a year preparing the house, married in 1997, and had me in 1999. Though, the prior information being a quick summary of the history of the home, the details are important to explain the paranormal activity experienced by many (mainly females) in the residence.

Over the eleven years on my LiveParanormal.com / GhostHunting.com show, I am often joined by seasoned paranormal investigators who detail similar personal encounters with home haunting activity, and I am able to share my experiences with them on-air. One story I rarely share, involves the accounts of my parents and grandmother together when each watched me as a toddler frequently go into our old dark laundry room. I was told I would stand with my back against the door staring into the distance frozen, unable to move until my mom would physically touch my hand to get me to move. To this day, I have no memory of this ever happening.

Fast forwarding to when I was around 4 years old, my dad wanted to surprise me with an autographed photo of actress Drew Barrymore since I absolutely loved the *Charlie's Angels* movie. My favorite character was Barrymore playing "Dylan." However, when the personalized image was received and mounted on a wall near my old sliding closet, the head-shot picture scared me. I made my parents take the image down immediately; due to the fact, I had the feeling of being watched by Drew's photo. When further detailing personal experiences on-air, my father often talks about a New Year's Eve encounter he and my mother had in the former kitchen, and a small piece of metal was thrown from the sink window sill at my mom's back six feet away; then, the part continued to slide across the floor. My parents further tried to reenact the moment, and my dad tossed the same piece of metal on the part of my mom's back, but each time they tried, the part would not go as far across the floor.

Starting at age nine, I began to feel as if I was being watched when I entered my parents' bedroom. The eerie sensation felt as if eyes covered every square inch of the walls, ceiling, and everything in between. The intense feeling progressed over a few months, until one day, I was suddenly taken aback when I saw a man in my mom's vanity closet in a white t-shirt and blue jeans. At that moment, I knew he wasn't a living person, but rather a ghost, and from that point forward, I knew our house was haunted. Following the discovery, and after telling my parents, my mom didn't know what to think; though, she never told me I was wrong. My dad, on the other hand, didn't believe me, and felt all of the experiences at that time were just my imagination.

As time went on, so did the intensity and frequency of the activity; and, it quickly became apparent to everyone living in, or visiting our home. My female cousin from Chicago came out to stay on a trip and was talking to my mom in my parents' room when both heard three knocks on the closet door. Obviously, that should not be happening, so my mom called for my dad to bring in a digital recorder to see if they could capture an EVP. After starting a recording session, they gathered a Class A voice of a man upon playback, which verified everything I had been telling my parents. From there forward, the activity quickly escalated. My cousin on the same trip, saw a man in a white t-shirt and blue jeans standing over both her and me in my room one night, and my mom began feeling daily buzzing sensations when walking through rooms where the ghost was standing.

Numerous other personal experiences were shared by many during that time, and the activity continued to target females rather than males; though, one instance in particular, involved a psychic family friend within the paranormal field. While visiting from out of town, intuitive Rod Shelton wanted to see what he could gather in our home, and he included some of his Southern California friends to conduct a livestreamed investigation. On the evening everyone arrived, I attempted to share a secret with my mother that I had not let anyone know at that point in time.

I started to tell my mother about what I experienced two days prior. For context, when I was younger, I would sleep on a couch bed mainly because I thought it was fun; yet one day, my mom decided it was time to change the sheets and clean up the couch. So, I spent that night in my actual loft bed. The evening was the first realization that the ghost would look around my room for me, but never actually found me in my loft bed. Finally, I felt safe knowing he couldn't find me high above. One night, however, I was going to bed as normal, feeling the only amount of solace I could in my loft bed when suddenly I felt his presence. The ghost had climbed my loft bed ladder and was watching me sleep! I'm not sure how I fell asleep that night, knowing my last shred of comfort had been taken away.

I'm unsure why I kept the details from my mom leading up to Rod's investigation. Though the prior scary event was my secret, I still didn't get to express everything to my mother so easily that night. With everyone in our home busy with the livestream investigation, I went to reveal it to my mom, and she said, "Not right now, we have company over." So, I pulled a family friend over who had known me my entire life at that point and had personal experiences in the home, herself to detail to Rod and explained my secret to her. When our friend heard my entire secret about the loft bed ladder experience, she immediately pulled my mother over to tell her everything I said. Now, my mom, our family friend, and I were the only ones who knew my secret, until...

Rod started his investigation of our home, and at the moment we reached my room, one of his psychic friends looked inside and said, "There's a man on that loft bed ladder!" Due to the fear, my parents felt for how close the man had gotten to me, that was to be the last night I slept in my room and ultimately, they had me sleep on a couch in their room until we moved out. So, over the course of Rod's investigation with the crew, equipment anomalies sent some members fleeing out of our home, other personal experiences and evidential captures transpired, and we still discuss the events with Rod during times on my show. Even though any personal encounters ceased when I left the house, I still have

PTSD-type trauma from everything I went through while being stalked by the ghost.

After moving from the Long Beach home, my father was asked by the founder of LiveParanormal.com to start a broadcast, which he declined several times over a few years. When situated in a new residence, and 12 years old at the time, I asked my dad to see if Rob Szarek (LiveParanormal.com site founder), would let me start a show instead and fortunately, Rob loved the idea. I initially started *The Ghost Host* show on LiveParanormal.com to see if I could find other kids with experiences like mine, who also grew up in haunted houses; yet surprisingly, I was unable to find any. Instead, I started booking renowned figures within the paranormal field. Author Alexandra Holzer was my first live guest in June of 2011 and the show took off with guests from there.

Today, I have one of the highest-rated programs on Live Paranormal, and the second longest-running broadcast on the network. Over the past eleven years, I have interviewed thousands of individuals and teams, including the cast of *Kindred Spirits, Destination Fear, Ghost Hunters, The Ghost Brothers,* and many more. The *Ghost Host* show has allowed me to have many great experiences, including conducting live red-carpet interviews, becoming a columnist for *Haunted Path* magazine, being featured as presenter/overnight investigator at national events, being a moderator for *Ghostbusters* Fan-Fest at Sony Studios, being featured on Los Angeles' area newscasts/newspaper articles, a guest paranormal investigator on the *Ghost Adventures Queen Mary* episode, and now with this book, a contributing author.

Bio: *Sophia Temperilli is currently a 24-year-old paranormal investigator and radio host. She started investigating the unknown at the age of eight. After attending a ghost tour aboard the infamously haunted RMS Queen Mary, Sophia quickly fell in love with the paranormal field. Along with her interests in all things supernatural, she additionally lived in an actively haunted house; where within, personal experiences changed her life forever. At 12 years of age, Sophia started her own podcast, The Ghost Host on www.LiveParanormal/GhostHunting.com in 2011; where currently, she continues to interview renowned figures within the field. With over half of her life in the world of the paranormal, Sophia cannot imagine her passion for the unknown ever going away.*

The Ghost Host Sophia Temperilli on LiveParanormal.com/Facebook fan page

YouTube: The Ghost Host Sophia Temperilli
Twitter: @GhostHostShow/@SophiaTemperili
Instagram: @SophiaTemperilli
LiveParanormal.com/GhostHunting.com

Nicole Tito

Paranormal Investigator, Creator of www.Ghostly-Voices.com, Author

Growing up on the Southside of Chicago, there are numerous local ghostly tales from Resurrection Mary to Bachelor's Grove. From an early age, I enjoyed listening to these spooky tales and visiting the locations (my family is buried in the same cemetery as Resurrection Mary). I don't have a first experience in paranormal that stands out to me. It was more of a collective calling from myself and those around me that pulled me into this field. I genuinely wanted to make sure that the evidence I captured couldn't be easily explained by normal phenomena.

I don't label myself as an expert since there are so many ways to investigate locations, but I navigate towards audio work including conducting EVP sessions and recently doing research with the Estes Method both in-person and remotely.

While it is great to have a personal experience at a location, it is better to capture that with some sort of proof to demonstrate what happened later. I don't suggest that investigators go out and get all the equipment as it can be expensive and too complicated. Sometimes, having less tools during an investigation is better. I usually take an audio recorder, a full spectrum or infrared camera, and a temperature and/or EMF device to try and obtain evidence. I found myself too into all my equipment that I felt like I was missing something or not feeling the location. I don't claim to be a psychic or sensitive, but after investigating so many locations, you start to develop a feeling about the paranormal. You can feel the energy or lack of it in a location. You know when things are going to happen. You know when the air is charged. I believe that everyone has some sort of heightened environmental feelings depending on the situation that they are in, and these skills can be improved with time.

While I understand that the paranormal field is far away from being truly scientific as paranormal events cannot be tested and replicated easily in a controlled setting, I do believe that researchers should try to create some sort of process in how they review their work and what they consider paranormal. I am a skeptic regarding most orb pictures that are labeled as paranormal. In my experience, I have found most orb pictures to be dust, insects, pollen, water particles, or reflections off a surface. Before something is labeled as paranormal, one should stop to think about the situation and the environment when that picture was taken. If it cannot be explained, I recommend sharing the picture among friends, both paranormal and non-paranormal, to get a second opinion. They may uncover something that you didn't realize that can explain the situation. This is one of the main reasons why during my EVP sessions or if someone is filming a location, I will announce myself if I enter the room with the camera, especially if I am off screen so that we don't accidentally label my noises as paranormal upon review. With EVP sessions, I tag sounds as they occur in real time so again, I don't accidentally label it as paranormal. You would be surprised at how much an empty stomach sounds like an angry demon emerging from the deepest level of hell. We need to question our evidence and if we cannot explain it then share it with the community, too.

As previously mentioned, I find myself drawn to collecting audio evidence. Depending on the location, I do have different ways of investigating the situation. If it is a local case within a home or location that might not be well known, I let the person who set up the investigation take charge of the case. I recommend that they limit the amount of information told to the team until we get to do a walk-through of the location and discuss any findings that might have been uncovered. I don't like it when too many people are already biased or have a preconceived notion about a site. I think that diminishes the investigation abilities of those present and can do a disservice to the individual who owns the property. In these cases, I like to have the team walk around and record any weird or odd areas. I also like the team to take any baseline pictures or temperatures. This is also a great time to investigate any natural or human-made sources of paranormal activity. We once investigated a home that was right under a power line and certain parts of the residence had such high EMF levels that members of our team were quickly affected after being in the place for a brief period.

High EMF levels can cause a variety of physical symptoms including headaches, irritability, inability to sleep, and even hallucinations. Another time a fish tank and an alarm clock within a person's home caused high EMF fields. These devices can be unplugged and therefore resolve the situation. After the initial walk-through of the location is completed by all team members, we quickly come together as a team and discuss our experiences. Then, the individual who knows the background will update the team. Based on the findings and the background story, that is when we start to set up any equipment quickly and efficiently to begin our investigation. I do say quickly because a lot of my best evidence happened in the first few minutes of an investigation.

I do think it is imperative to be sensitive to the owner depending on his or her fear level. I also never recommend taunting spirits in any situation. First, you truly never know what you are messing with. Second, if you were getting yelled at by someone, would you really want to talk to them? I believe that most ghosts are like humans. They are mostly good and some may have negative qualities, but they don't mean harm. They may be stuck, not want to move onto the next realm, confused about the situation, or a bit upset about what has happened, so they refuse to leave. However, there is the chance that you are messing with something that is not human whether it is unknown or something evil. Again, that is why I don't suggest putting out that negative energy nor ever allowing that spirit to use your own personal energy to manifest. That opens your body for something to latch on, follow you, and suck your energy.

I don't suggest doing a full psychological profile on the owner of the location but be aware of his or her emotions and how he or she acts. Also, note any discrepancies of things that don't add up. There is always the possibility that they are lying. But, as I said, be sensitive to the situation whether the location is active or not. You might love to live in a haunted house if you are reading this book, but many people live in fear for themselves and their children. If you believe that you can help someone safely, do so. If someone wants their home saged or cleansed and you know how to do it properly, then do it. You might be the only person that can help that individual. Make a commitment to come back and help them or get an expert to come and help this person if the situation doesn't get better or gets worse. There is no excuse nowadays to not be able to find someone in this field that can help you. If you are unable, contact me, and I will help you.

I do think most TV shows dramatize bad occurrences during various paranormal investigations and label everything as evil and demonic. However, if you do uncover a situation like this, get help. I have a strong religious background as a Roman Catholic. There are true members of the Catholic Church that can help you. Seek out that help as they are trained in these situations. You are more than likely not, and neither am I.

When investigating more known locations, I already know that I am biased and might want to investigate a certain area based on the stories I know. Therefore, I usually set up my equipment in a location that I believe will be a hotspot especially if I have limited time or know that I might never come back. Utilize your time wisely. Some locations don't allow for long investigations so make sure you don't spend two hours on a tour and only have two hours to investigate. Confirm with the location before you go what time you can come on the grounds, what time you can enter the building, and what time the investigation really goes to. If you can enter the grounds before the project, take your pictures then. Plan with your team on what you are going to do with that investigation.

My favorite paranormal locations have been Waverly Hills, Mansfield, and Lincoln Theater in Decatur, Illinois. Waverly Hills and Mansfield are well-known locations that many investigators strive to visit once. I had multiple paranormal experiences at both locations and captured evidence. At Waverly Hills, I have seen the shadow figures dart in and out of the doorways and come down the hallway at you. I have sat alone in the morgue as fellow investigators wheeled someone on a gurney towards the death tunnel.

At Mansfield, I have captured audio evidence both in real-time and during EVP sessions. I have heard footsteps walk above me on the prison tiers. I have seen shadows. I have felt things. I have been scared. However, I do want to stress that you can go to the most haunted location in the world and not have an experience. It happens and there is nothing that you can do. It doesn't mean that a location is not haunted. There will not always be activity. A few years ago, I went to Mansfield for the fifth time with my husband, our ghost-hunting friend, and his wife. I was excited because none of them had ever been to Mansfield. We went on a public investigation, but it wasn't too crowded, and nothing happened to any of us that night. No pun intended, but it was dead. I didn't capture any audio evidence. Everyone was disappointed. However, I told my husband, our friend, and his wife to give it another chance in the future.

It could have been the energy that night. I do believe that certain people turn off or expel a certain type of energy that may shut down a location. Some people work well together, and I do believe those individuals tend to find each other and make good teams. I work with my paranormal partner in crime, Lisa Krick. We met on our first ghost team and clicked instantly. We have good energy together and get great evidence. I am part of the American Spectral Society and run a website that houses the paranormal evidence captured from various investigations across the country called ghostly-voices.com. Our team is open to anyone who is interested and consists of members from across the country with all interests in the paranormal.

I have and will always admire Rosemary Ellen Guiley. Unfortunately, she passed away several years ago, which is such a hit to the paranormal community. Her books contain such valuable information, and you can tell the amount of time and research she put into authoring them. They provide various information for those old and new in the field. She was such a kind and knowledgeable person, and I was honored to know her and investigate locations with her. She taught me a lot of techniques and how to protect myself. I know she has reached out from beyond the grave and I believe she will continue to do what she can from the other side to help guide and further advance this field as much as she can. We miss and love you, Rosemary!

Bio: *Nicole Tito is a paranormal investigator and creator of the www.Ghostly-Voices.com website. She holds a DPT from Northwestern University and an MBA from Missouri State University. Nicole has been investigating the paranormal for over 20 years and grew up on the South-side of Chicago surrounded by many infamous ghost tales. She loves collecting audio evidence and just sitting in a haunted location feeling its energy. She now resides in the Chicago suburbs with her husband and two children.*

Josie Varga

Author, Blogger, Motivational Speaker, Paranormal Researcher

In life, there is no greater teacher than personal experience. Our experiences and the very memories we keep from them are what shape our lives. Perhaps, nowhere is this more apparent than the field of paranormal investigation.

My catalyst and life-defining moment came in August 2003 when my husband's former boss and friend, who died in the September 11th attacks, came to me in a vivid dream. In it, I saw and felt myself walking down this long hallway. Finally, I walked into a room at the end and saw desks and windows everywhere. Suddenly, I saw Rich—a man I had never met in person before, yet I knew it was unquestionably him.

He looked at me saying, "Josie, thank you for mentioning me in your book." I had talked about Rich in the epilogue of my book, *Footprints in the Sand: A Disabled Woman's Inspiring Journey to Happiness*. For reasons I cannot explain, my response to him was, "Rich, you have to prove to me that this is really you." All communication was telepathic as he walked over to a desk and picked up a cell phone. It was a flip-style phone, which was very popular at that time. On the phone was a picture of him with his wife and son. Showing me the picture, he said, "Boston is okay." I had no idea what this meant but I intuitively understood that this was a message he wanted me to give to his wife.

The next thing I remember is going through what looked like a window and ending up on a street. Rich appeared to be saying, "Now go ahead. Give her the message." He made a motion with his arms as though he was pushing me forward and the next thing I knew I was sitting up in my bed panting and out of breath. I literally felt like something just hit me in my chest. I was shaken up and didn't know what to make of what had just transpired. Jumping out of bed, I quickly checked on my two toddler-aged daughters and then rushed to dial my husband who was already at work.

He reacted as though I had lost my senses. "You want me to call Rich's wife who is grieving the passing of her husband and tell her, 'Boston is okay?' I'm not doing that!" I guess my persistence eventually won him over. By the end of our conversation, I had convinced him to forward an email written by me to Rich's sister-in-law whom my husband knew from working in investment banking.

After John forwarded my email, he was full of regret feeling like she was going to think he was crazy. On the other hand, I had no regrets whatsoever. I knew what I had experienced was real. I was also confident that I did what I was meant to do. Two weeks later, my family and I were on vacation at the Jersey shore when an email came through on my husband's phone. Rich's sister in-law wondered how I could have known about Boston. As it turned out, Rich's wife had a brother in Boston and was considering moving there. His wife felt guilty as she pondered her decision having just recently purchased her current home with her late husband.

As my husband read the email out loud to me that day, I was shocked out of my senses. I had never met Rich or anyone else in his family and certainly did not know that he had a brother in-law living in Boston. In the ensuing weeks, I began investigating the afterlife. My intent at the time was not to write a book but rather to know that I was not alone. As I delved deeper and deeper, I was pleasantly surprised to find so many other accounts so similar yet so different than my own. This led me to write, *Visits from Heaven,* and from there I went on to write other books focusing on different metaphysical topics like near-death experiences and deathbed phenomena.

One day while I was in New York City doing a radio interview, I met a young psychic medium who told me that someone was there for me. When I turned around looking for this mysterious someone, I was told, "No, in spirit." When he described what the person looked like, I realized that it was Rich. That night Rich told me through the psychic medium that my latest book, *Visits to Heaven,* was not going to be released on schedule. In fact, I was told it was coming out two months later. I was also informed that I was led to do what I do. The show's producer then called me into the studio, and I didn't get to finish my conversation with this young medium. But two weeks later, I found out my book was being released in February, not December—two months later just as I was told that night.

More importantly, though, being told that I was led to do what I do served as a validation. I have no doubt that I am fulfilling my life's purpose and I feel privileged to be able to share my message that life truly never ends and love never dies. Death is by no means an end but merely a transition from one form to another. Consider what happens to a glass of water that sits for a long period of time. The water will eventually evaporate changing back to its gaseous form. This is analogous to what happens at death when we transition from the physical to the spiritual.

Some scientists will argue that so-called evidence of the afterlife is anecdotal and therefore both incomplete and unreliable. Anecdotal evidence is a claim based on a personal experience or observation. The scientific method, of course, gives more credence to research data than these personal experiences. Some refuse to look past a materialistic mindset enough to even consider studying parapsychology. This is unfortunate since as Albert Einstein once noted knowledge can only come from experience.

Some say only gullible masses desperate to hear from their deceased loved ones believe in an afterlife. However, this couldn't be further from the truth. As I mentioned earlier, I had never even met Rich and his connection with me was completely spontaneous. Over the years, I have studied the spiritual experiences of thousands across the globe. While knowledge comes from studying these experiences, questioning the results, and collecting data, wisdom is gained through what we learn and how we use the information gained.

I feel very blessed to be part of the parapsychology field. While I've found that more and more people are willing to share their experiences, further work needs to be done. I would love to see more science-backed research. For example, some doctors argue that near-death experiences are simply due to hypoxia in the brain. However, how does that explain seeing deceased loved ones and receiving validated information that was previously unknown?

In studying deathbed visions, it did not surprise me to find how common and widespread these experiences are. It did sadden me, however, to note how often these experiences go unreported due to fear of being ridiculed. Parapsychology should be taught in medical and nursing schools so that both doctors and nurses are more aware of such phenomena and can encourage patients to share their experiences.

Further research also needs to be conducted on both consciousness and the nature of reality. Our reality is based on our perception. Perhaps this is one of the attributes, which connects us in the paranormal field for we have a willingness to both study and see the unseen. And, as I've said many times, it is in studying the spiritual that we will come to better understand the physical.

Looking back, I know I would not be in this field had it not been for my experience with Rich—what I term a visit from heaven. I'm blessed to know so many incredible women in the field of paranormal investigation. Some, like the late Rosemary Ellen Guiley, helped me to understand the importance of this work. Rosemary, who passed in July 2019, was known for her leading role in metaphysical research. She published more than 65 books and was a frequent guest on many radio and television programs. I was blessed, however, to know the wonderful woman off camera and she was truly one of the most caring people I've ever met. Her immense knowledge was surpassed perhaps only by the kindness and love she so willingly gave to others.

Earlier I explained how my experience served as a life-changing catalyst for me. My many years of research may have solidified my belief in an afterlife, but it has also shown me time and time again that life is not what it appears to be. As Fredrich Nietzsche, a well-known German philosopher, once noted, "There are no facts, only interpretations."

Once we understand that life continues, what does that say about the nature of reality? Who are we really? What we perceive as reality is not reality at all but merely how we make sense of our existence. Put another way, there is no such thing as nothingness. Even nothing implies something. Empty space is made up of energy and particles that connect everything and everyone. And at the base of everything that exists is spirit, which always was and always will be.

We are spiritual beings having a human experience. Spirit is primary and the physical is secondary. I am fortunate in that my life experiences have been my greatest teacher. There are many components, which bond those of us in the paranormal community. For one, we are not afraid to ask tough questions and search for answers to the seemingly unknown.

The word "paranormal" literally means beyond normal and implies something that is outside of scientific understanding or explanation. But who's to say what is normal and not normal? Perhaps one day, we will find that the answers were in front of us the entire time. We will come to understand that the paranormal is in fact normal.

Bio: *A celebrated author, blogger, and motivational speaker, Josie Varga has been researching the paranormal for over 20 years. Her books help people worldwide understand why death is only a transition from one form to the next. She also has a popular group on Facebook based on her book, Visits from Heaven, for people to share their spiritual experiences*

and know that they are not alone. Passionate about her life's work, she is committed to changing lives—one story at a time. For more information, please visit her website at www.josievarga.com.

Rev. Donna Voll

Spirit Artist Proves Human Consciousness Survives Permanent Death

True Spirit Art

True Spirit Art occurs when divine unseen forces—or spirit—draw the images of those passed over to prove their continued existence along with evidential messages. The recognizable spirit faces drawn on paper, often matching old photos, are undeniable visual evidence that they are still alive in another unseen place. Visual evidence provided to paranormal research.

The true spirit artist does not draw what is being shown clairvoyantly within his or her mind. The medium drawing is being used by Holy Spirit to demonstrate this form of communication by the unseen artist. This true gift of spirit art is very rare, as it is spirit drawing, not the physical person drawing.

True Spirit Art is not a talent that can be taught by a physical teacher. A true spirit artist is chosen to serve and trained as a vessel for Holy Spirit to help others. I cannot teach others to become a true spirit artist. I may only share my own spiritual journey, which led me to experiencing spirit art phenomena.

My story begins from my earliest memories. A childhood of being aware, seeing, sensing, hearing, and witnessing things others did not. As a small child, this brought no comfort, only concern and nightly fears. My bedroom became a clairvoyant menagerie of multiple experiences. I came into this world clairvoyantly sensitive and, I believe, protected by a mother who taught me to dispel lower negative energy with prayer, replacing my thoughts and attention to higher vibrations of God, prayer, and energy shifts. These are keys I continue to use in my work and life. Nightly, I would call her; nightly, we would pray to dispel the overload of energy, entities, and thought forms invading my room.

Limited offerings of Lutheranism could not help me understand my experiences. At 12 years old, I tried to find my own answers and information to guide me. The search led me to the local library where I found the only paranormal books available at that time written by Hans Holzer. I learned that other people did see an unseen world! The books did not teach how to develop but did offer the knowledge that research existed.

I lived in a paranormal mine field. Across the street was a VA psychiatric ward, a Nike Site with underground missiles, a neighbor man who began the local UFO group, and only few miles away from NASA research labs. In fact, many of my neighbors worked at NASA, too. Our area was a hotbed of UFO sightings. All these odd vibrations, astral and mental, swirled around me. My clairvoyant development continued with more messages, seeing entities, and seeing clairvoyant visions and events before they happened.

One profound vision came as I saw a tornado approach the stadium where I was seated, two hours before it happened! I was overwhelmed with fright. The day was sunny and everyone was having fun, only I was witnessing this scene in my mind. Then suddenly that vision became my horrific reality, with people struggling, running in fear around me. A Fourth of July celebration that went terribly wrong and a night Ohioans still recall.

I experienced an astral man try to attack me in my dreams. Then the same astral scenario began during my waking life. Years later, I discovered that many girls in our little neighborhood had the exact same experience with this entity, as well as discovering none of them wanted to go into their basements either.

As someone open to the paranormal, my neighborhood both activated and created my personal curriculum for spiritual development lessons to come. I married and moved; the area changed but my clairvoyant gifts continued. At 30 years old, and mother of three young children, I needed a better understanding of the unseen world around me. I learned the value of sitting quietly in intentional prayer and came to understand this intuitive part of me was a spiritual gift and not a curse. Meditation raised my own spiritual frequency connection to God, which became my spiritual protection from overwhelming unwanted spirit advances.

I began a journal of what I was seeing, hearing, and witnessing while connecting to my higher self. In addition, I learned to be still and let my own spirit write through me. Advanced insights flowed and more vivid spiritual teachings emerged. At the end of journaling one day, I was led to draw a face. This face was detailed, revealed specific characteristics, and much better than anything I could have attempted drawing my own.

Every meditation included more faces. I understood them to be coming from spirit because I was unable to produce them on my own. I prayed that if these were not of a high spiritual frequency from God then they should stop. Instead, the faces continued and developed more detail. Along with the faces, a written message was added.

I kept these hidden for months until one day after one face was drawn with a detailed message, I was prompted to give it to a woman I knew. As she received the picture, she cried. She recognized the face as her friend who passed over in a violent way. Here is her testimony:

One of the first pictures you ever did was for me. You were not aware that the person who came through was a dear beloved friend who died some ten years earlier. He was a very troubled soul who suffered much emotional and physical trauma. His beautiful eyes were shining like they had when we were young. Charlotte Horvath.

This spirit portrait along with the evidential message brought healing and comfort to her, proving he was alive, healing, and learning. This was a remarkable visual proof of the human consciousness continuing after a physical death. This was paranormal evidence. I began to understand my spiritual gift and the call for service of a true spirit artist.

It was the first step of my 36-year journey of embracing spirit art and exploring a new life.

I began working with the public by having a simple signature on paper. I would pray, meditate, and draw portraits with handwritten letters based on the signature alone. Never having met the people assured me that my own thoughts could not interfere. These finished spirit art portraits would be dropped off at a store or mailed to fulfill the request. This was long before the Internet. Judy Wischmeier had the spirit face of her Uncle Glen presented along with an evidential message only he would know.

Here is her account:

Donna was developing her gift of mediumship (spirit communication) when she proved spirit communication was real to me. Through her mediumship and art, she received a message for my aunt and myself. The message was from my Uncle Glen. Uncle Glen had passed at least 5 years before I had met Donna. Donna had received a picture of a balding man wearing a string tie. She also kept hearing the word 'hots' from him several times. When Donna gave me this message, I knew it was from my Uncle Glen from her description of him. He was balding and wore a bolo string tie most of the time. Donna hearing 'hots' would not have known my uncle's last name was Hotz. Her drawing was of my uncle when he was younger.

The part of the message that was for my aunt was a special word I was to tell her. It didn't make sense to me but I did pass it on. My aunt did not respond at first when I told her the word. I then showed her the drawing Donna had done.

My aunt broke into tears and asked who drew the picture of Glen. I explained to her and then she told me about the special word. The word was how my aunt and uncle said 'I love you' when out in public. My aunt said they never told anyone, not even my cousins. It was just their special word.

As my spirit development continued, the portraits developed as well. Charcoal and pencil drawings gave way to charcoal and pastel. Multiple faces surrounded the main face. These extra faces also were important to the person receiving the portrait. In addition, symbols, words, and scenes were being added on the portraits. The portraits revealed evidence of life after death and shared the messages that had been revealed. They were confirmed with eyewitness testimonies and many people sent old photos as evidence.

Spirit art brought generations together in one visual way, providing proof that the spirit people knew each other on the other side even if they had not met in their physical life. Spirit grandparents talked about meeting their grandchildren prior to their birth, even those spirit children not able to be born from abortion or miscarriage.

I set up consultations to allow spirit to draw and give verbal messages at the same time. The angel came unexpectedly as I worked in a small shop. He was in the physical form as he moved around objects on the counter. I felt an overload of energy and I could barely contain my composure. I knew if I watched he would be transformed to a different being. He asked me simply, who drew the spirit art?

I answered simply, "God does through me."

He asked if I ever drew beings that were never human.

I said "no" firmly, knowing many in my area that told of alien abduction experiences. I did not want to connect with that energy. Remember I grew up near NASA.

Then he said, "Angels are not of this world, and if you hold that belief you could not draw my brothers and sisters." He added, "Angels are sent by God to enlighten and work with humanity and its true souls."

He turned and left! I was compelled to run after him but he literally disappeared.

After meditation I recognized I had put up a barrier out of fear. Instead, I could be specific in prayer how I worked and with whom I worked with spiritually, by determining the vibration with spiritual discernment.

After this angelic visit, the spirit art expanded with full-color pastel chalk and the addition of angelic influences. Spirit faces were drawn around the main portrait of an angel. We then referred to these as Angelic Spirit portraits. My spiritual work needed to expand to ministerial work. The logical place to begin was Spiritualism, where someone with spiritual gifts could be taken seriously and become a spiritual minister. I studied spiritual bodies, spiritual planes, natural law and ministerial ethics. I learned to discern true spirit from fraud. I was ordained. This provided me with opportunities to demonstrate the gift of true spirit art within large groups at church.

But how does a true spirit artist work in a large group of people? Never having seen spirit art demonstrated was a blessing as I allowed the Holy Spirit to direct me to achieve its goals.

This is how it happened: I went to the church 15 minutes prior to service and sat in the front near the altar. I brought my pastel chalk and blank clean pad of paper and I sat in meditation and prayer. As people entered the church to sit down, I was directed by spirit to notice someone. I made a note at the corner of that piece of paper that this was to go out to that person. Quickly, almost miraculously, a full colored portrait was drawn using my hand, but not by me. I set that finished art down and then continued to do another portrait rapidly. Spirit produced 14 full-color pastel art spirit portraits in detail while the service was happening in less than one hour. Near the end was my turn to get up, direct the portrait and messages to the person that was indicated on the art. The messages were accurate and evidential and the recipients recognized the spirit faces on their portraits. It was a remarkable demonstration of how fast spirit could work through me. For me, it is always as if my hands just fly and the energy is hard to contain.

Many ministers and congregations have witnessed these true spirit art portraits. Many people have also reported that additional faces appeared on their portraits after other family members transitioned. Why not? Holy Spirit is the artist drawing and can continue to update the art if so desired.

I would travel to demonstrate spirit art. One portrait was drawn during a church service in St. Louis, MO. The recipient of the portrait copied it along with her father's photograph to show spirit evidence. We noticed even the angle of the pillow behind his head in the photograph was captured by spirit in the portrait. Sometimes the faces look like a mirror image.

True Spirit Art moves beyond any language barrier. As I traveled internationally in Montréal, Québec, Canada, I served many churches during Italian and French services. An interpreter translated my spirit messages and sermons; however, the true drawings spoke for themselves, as people could visually see those, they loved drawn on a portrait. In addition, they developed faces drawn of those still physically alive who are important to the one receiving the portrait and faces drawn of future people who came into the life of the person who received the them.

Spirit drawings reveal those who are important surrounding a soul's past, present, and future. This proves not only that the spirit world is alive and human consciousness continues after death, but that the true spirit is not bound by our sense of time. The portraits show the importance of these souls interconnected with us in many dimensions and planes; that we are part of a greater divine plan.

Spirit art gives evidence to support the multi-universe theory as well. In paranormal terms, it answers why we can have multiple encounters of various timelines in one place. We can be standing in the same place vibrating at different frequencies and interconnect. I still connect with people internationally by phone. The finished artwork is insured and shipped. This method helps me serve people in different time zones and different locations in one day. I do not know all people with whom I have worked, their private concerns or dreams. True Spirit Art does not require me to know. My job is simple. Like my paper, my mind is a clean blank space ready to serve. I never say I will draw your deceased relative or friend, only that I may pray and let God decide how these portraits shall be created.

How many spiritual portraits have been drawn over 36 years of service? If we try to calculate them all, the number would be up into the thousands. They are located all over the world. True Spirit Art is a unique phenomenon proven beyond statistical chance. A true artist of this type is rare in this world and brings valuable and unique visual evidence to be considered in life-after-death paranormal research. I have written eyewitness testimonials from people all over the world who received and confirmed recognizable spirit art faces.

As a groundbreaking woman in paranormal studies, I have proved life after death with actual visual proof. Never has this type of art, which provides photographic evidence, been considered in research into the paranormal. Paranormal events can now be explained when we factor in natural law of vibration, attraction, frequency and cause and effect. Spiritual knowledge must be involved in scientific research to truly understand the living human consciousness here and after physical death.

As a young woman working in the paranormal, I had to develop spiritual gifts on my own. This led me to see how spiritual gifts are tools to access and understand the supernatural or unseen. Being a strong woman was a benefit. As a pioneering woman, I had to stand up against negative slurs and labels of being crazy, satanic, and evil. I was dismissed as being too sensitive. When I think of all those thousands of souls who have benefitted from my many years of art, the insults and judgments directed at me were worth it for the spiritual healing that was offered.

I will continue as a visionary woman in the paranormal by offering spiritual gifts as viable tools for paranormal work. Right now, we often see spiritual versus science in paranormal study. I am determined to bring these two sides together to develop a deeper understanding of paranormal phenomena. We will uncover more information when we use all the tools available to discern what is happening to a family, a home, or an unseen event that seems unrelenting. Imagine spiritual tools offering insight to paranormal sound recordings, visual sightings and phenomena! Without spiritual understanding, and natural law, paranormal studies based on science tools alone can exacerbate already dangerous phenomena. We live in a world of multi-dimensional beings, some positive and others evil. I do extensive work in spiritual warfare and discernment. Integrating spiritual warfare into paranormal work is imperative for the best outcomes.

My next level of groundbreaking paranormal work has just begun!

Bio: *Rev. Donna Voll has been serving God for 36 years, helping thousands of people with her ministry, spiritual counseling, and her unique angelic spirit portraits. These portraits reveal the angels that work with you and include faces of family, friends, and guides who are spiritually influ-*

ential to you. Very often, many of these faces are recognizable as loved ones who have passed over. Rev. Voll's remarkable spiritual gift serves as proof that there is a spiritual life after death and that we are not alone.

Rev. Voll travels internationally sharing her gifts through radio and television interviews, teaching workshops and seminars, serving churches, and private phone consultations. She teaches about spiritual development and gives an extensive angelic seminar on dreams, symbols, and spiritual warfare. Rev. Voll was the host and producer of Spirit Connections, creating over nine years of radio programming, both on network radio and the Internet.

Spirit Connections offered spiritual topics for discussion to advance spiritual interest with researchers and teachers. Archives are still available for free listening, as she is committed to help others who are seeking God, spiritual truth and answers. She is comfortable and capable to speak publicly to large groups, panels, radio or visual media, podcasts, or tele-vised events, and has been a guest on many radio programs. More information, testimonials and portraits with photographic proof, please visit: www.angelstoguideyou.com.

Alexandrea Weis

International Bestselling Author, Screenwriter, Advanced Practice Registered Nurse

Ask any nurse, and they will tell you about that one patient who, right before passing, carried on a conversation with a dead relative, reached out, and seemed so at peace. This is a deathbed vision or DBV. They can occur immediately prior to death or sometimes weeks ahead of time. Nurses are the ones who most often witness them since so many patients die in hospitals, nursing homes, or hospices. For many of us, deathbed visions are a crucial indicator your patient is getting ready to depart.

Many in the medical community would love to chalk up these instances to the last gasps of a dying brain. Still, many of the deathbed visions I have witnessed were with lucid patients who knew they were dying and were aware that the relative in the room with them had already passed on. It is troubling as a health care provider to see such an event, but it is also comforting.

Anecdotes of deathbed visions have appeared in literature and biographies throughout the ages, but it wasn't until the 20th century that the subject received scientific study. Dr. Karlis Osis of the American Society for Psychical Research conducted the most extensive studies. Osis interviewed over one thousand doctors, nurses, and health care providers to the dying. He believed they had the most objective approach to describing this phenomenon.

The spirit encountered is usually someone to whom the dying was closest. The most common sightings are family members who the patient reports have already passed on. Mothers are the most common, followed by grandparents and aunts or uncles. But sometimes young children will see someone hanging around who they have never met before, such as grandparents or, in some instances, great-grandparents. These are the most intriguing events for many health care providers since these children describe the visitor at their bedside, often shocking parents and relatives with their accuracy. One child I tended gave a thorough description of an older woman who smelled of vanilla. The young girl's mother broke down, claiming her grandmother often smelled of vanilla.

The second most frequently appearing figures are angels, religious icons, and even mythical figures. There are many times I've heard patients speak of Jesus coming to get them. The one that stuck with me the most was when I tended a dying child. She expressed surprise that the angel at her bedside had no wings and asked me why that was. This one instance convinced me that deathbed visions are not hallucinations. A child would have described an angel with wings as depicted in art and literature. This child insisted her angel didn't have any and that her angel told her she didn't need wings in her world.

One of my patients was in her last hours and claimed that a dear friend had come to visit. The family reported the friend was still alive and well, casting doubt on the patient's mental status. It wasn't until after the man died that I discovered the friend he'd seen at his bedside had been killed hours before his passing in a car accident.

A few patients don't see people in their visions but beloved pets. A man with not much time left found great comfort in seeing his favorite childhood dog sitting on his bed. He'd even stroke it, moving his hand back and forth, and spoke of the adventures he'd shared with the beloved Labrador.

For some, there are only auditory experiences. Patients often speak of hearing the most beautiful music coming into their room. Or they describe a comforting humming, like the sound of a mother rocking a child to sleep. With a few, there were stories of bright lights, colorful displays of rainbows, and one woman talked about the thunderstorm that played out on her hospital room ceiling, complete with a lightning show and beautiful silky gray clouds.

There are also non-verbal cues that the patient is having a deathbed vision. Some will stare into a corner or laugh out loud without a prompt. You may see them move their eyes about a room as if following something or someone we can't see. They may speak or mouth words, reach out with open arms, or smile, seemingly at peace. It gives you profound reassurance as a health care provider to know they are comfortable in the end.

Many of the experiences I have witnessed had a calming effect on me. Usually, the end of life in a hospital is a chaotic affair where code carts are pulled into rooms, and everyone is fighting to save the patient's life. But when patients in hospice or labeled do not resuscitate, speak about others in the room who have moved on before them, it brings peace to you.

Over the years, I have seen the dying express great happiness. No patient I encountered ever showed signs of distress at seeing loved ones in their room. The dying also seemed quite willing to go with these apparitions. Their mood lifted, and their faces changed after having a deathbed vision. The darkness lifted from their features if they were depressed or consumed by pain. The people having these experiences are not hallucinating or in an altered state of consciousness. Many are aware of their surroundings. Whether or not they believed in where they were going, my patients' reactions remained the same.

Every dying patient I tended changed my preconceived notions of death. When you witness such events, your fear of what may come recedes. You believe there is more after we die because you have seen it in the tranquil smiles of those you have stood by as they take their last breath.

Deathbed visions are unique to every dying patient and can't be explained away by science. If you have been around the dying, you understand that there is more than a physical explanation for these experiences. They are profound and life-altering for the living. For the dying, they are a comforting transition filled with understanding and peace. If all the visions I have had the privilege to behold have taught me one thing, it is that death is never the end. It's a new beginning that begins in love.

Bio: *Alexandrea Weis, RN-CS, PhD, is a multi-award-winning, international bestselling author, screenwriter, and advanced practice registered nurse who was born and raised in the French Quarter of New Orleans. Having grown up in the motion picture industry as the daughter of a director, she learned to tell stories from a different perspective. A member of the Horror Writers Association and International Thriller Writers Association, Weis is also a permitted wildlife rehabber with the Louisiana Wildlife and Fisheries.*

CHAPTER 4

IN REMEMBRANCE

WOMEN PARANORMAL PIONEERS

Linda Godfrey
March 20, 1951 - November 27, 2022

In November of 2022, the world lost a remarkable author, investigator, and artist named Linda Godfrey at the age of 71 who made her mark researching and writing about strange creatures, phenomena, and people. If you met her in the supermarket, you might never imagine such a pretty and sweet woman harbored a longtime passion for the strange and creepy world of cryptozoology, legend and lore. Godfrey was an accomplished author of over 20 books and a frequent guest on radio, television shows and in the press discussing cases of high strangeness that included the legendary "Beast of Bray Road."

She began writing about the beast in 1991 for the Walworth, Wisconsin's county weekly newspaper with her first piece published in December of that year. Soon, the tales of the beast, a wolfish-looking creature that was said to run on two legs, steal chickens, eat roadkill, and scare many a local in the Bray Road area, spread and more reports flooded in, making her the go-to expert on the cryptid. Some were calling the beast a "dogman" and Linda was on the case, delving into the mysterious sightings near the town of Elkhorn and beyond. She eventually dubbed the creature the "Bray Road Beast" and the name stuck.

Godfrey, who had moved to Delavan in 1978 and lived in the Walworth County area until 2016, was soon being interviewed extensively by television crews eager to know about recent sightings and she was even paid by the National Enquirer, along with staff photographer Terry Mayer, to stake out the Bray Road area for any sightings of the beast.

In a story for the 2019 Chicago Tribune, Linda spoke about the beast. "One day I was talking to a local animal control officer and said, 'You hear about this thing people are seeing on Bray Road?' And he pulls a manilla folder out of his desk. It's labeled 'werewolf.' I was a novice reporter then but even I knew if a county official is keeping a folder on possible werewolves, you probably have a story."

This story set the stage for an illustrious and productive career for Godfrey, who became an investigative researcher specializing in cryptozoology, yet she also wrote true crime books and novels. She soon became a world-renowned cryptozoologist, a woman in a man's world, and those who knew her remarked on her generosity, sweet nature, and humor even as she dug into some pretty scary lore and legend. Her research included the mysterious Thunderbird sightings and Wisconsin legend and lore, which she documented in the book *Weird Wisconsin,* and folklore in general. She was also an artist.

Godfrey began speaking all over the country at events and became a popular guest on radio and national television shows, and her work on the Bray Road Beast has become a popular documentary on Amazon Prime, also inspiring many movie scripts. She can be seen discussing her work and in action in the field shows such as *Small Town Monsters,* which did a film titled *The Bray Road Beast, The Unexplained, Inside Edition, Dead Files, Monsters and Mysteries,* and was a regular on many radio shows such as *Coast to Coast AM* and the *Jenny McCarthy Show.*

She died peacefully and leaves behind her husband, two sons, many grandchildren and siblings, and a massive body of work for which she herself has become a legend, including books like *American Monsters* and *I know What I Saw: Modern-Day Encounters with Monsters of New Urban Legend and Ancient Lore.* Those who knew her personally described her as a sweet, generous, fun person with a passion for her work who willingly offered her knowledge, experience and expertise. For a woman in the world of high strangeness and cryptozoology, long known more as the domain of male researchers, she broke new ground and will be a hero to many women following in her footsteps.

Her many blog posts are available for viewing at www.lindagod frey.com.

Rosemary Ellen Guiley
July 8, 1950-July 18, 2019

Rosemary Ellen Guiley was one of the foremost researchers in the fields of the supernatural, metaphysics, and unexplained phenomena. She worked full-time in the paranormal field since 1983. In August of 2015, Guiley became the proud recipient of a Lifetime Achievement Award from Michigan's Upper Peninsula Paranormal Research Society for her leading research into various facets of paranormal study. She served as owner and president of Visionary Living, Inc., a publishing house and media productions corporation, which includes Visionary Living Publishing and its imprints.

In addition to her role as executive editor of *FATE Magazine*, she served on the Paranormal Romance Guild board as well as those of numerous organizations connected to consciousness studies and alien contact. Guiley was on the board of directors for the National Museum of Mysteries and Research and the Foundation for Research into Extraterrestrial Encounters. She was a founding member of the Afterlife Research and Education Institute and taught at the International Insti-tute for Integral Human Sciences in Montreal as a visiting faculty member.

Rosemary was a certified hypnotist with the International Hypnosis Federation, having specialized in bioenergy and Johrei energy healing. Her talents also included tarot reading, dreamwork, intuitive and psychic development, and past-life recollection sessions. As such, she was a Dream Oracle advisor for the DreamSocial.co website.

As a best-selling author of more than 65 books on numerous topics, including nine single-volume encyclopedias and reference works, her knowledge also extended to hauntings, psychic aptitudes, spiritual protection, afterlife studies, spirit communication, cryptozoology, ufology, and exploration into various dimensions. Rosemary's written material has been translated into 17 languages.

Guiley was featured in a myriad of media outlets, including numerous appearances in television, film documentaries, radio, and print. She was interviewed for programs on many networks, including A&E, Animal Planet, Destination America, Discovery, History, SyFy, and Travel Channel. Rosemary was a recurring guest on *Scott Colborn's Exploring Unexplained Phenomena* and *Richard Syrett's The Conspiracy Show*. You may have heard Rosemary in one of her many frequent interviews on George Noory's *Coast to Coast AM*. Along with Noory, she co-authored *Talking to the Dead*, a book that discusses emerging technology utilized for communicating with spirits and other entities. As a spearheading leader in the field of supernatural study, she was an invaluable speaker at conferences and higher education institutions.

As a fellow member of the Ghost Research Society, Nicole Strickland was extremely fortunate to work with Rosemary on investigations of iconic sites, such as Waverly Hills Sanatorium, Lincoln Theater, and the RMS *Queen Mary*. They were both speakers at Troy Taylor's 2011 West Coast Haunted America Conference in San Diego, California. It was an event-packed few days as Rosemary, Lisa Krick, Nicole Tito, and Nicole Strickland also drove up to Long Beach to spend a couple of nights aboard the legendary *Queen Mary*.

Rosemary was also graciously interviewed for a number of Marie D. Jones's books. Her legacy lives on and she remains one of the standout scholars in the field of supernatural study.

Anne Strieber
August 25, 1946 – August 11, 2015

Anne was a school teacher who became a writer, known for her thrillers *An Invisible Woman* (2004) and *Little Town Lies* (2005). It was her marriage to famous UFO contactee Whitley Strieber that helped solidify her own role in the world of ufology, and paranormal radio as the co-host of *Dreamland Radio* and as the managing editor of her husband's website, www.unknowncountry.com, which she also founded. She lectured widely at Mutual UFO Network (MUFON) and other UFO events and appeared on other radio shows such as *Coast to Coast AM* discussing UFOs, abductions and contactees, and Whitley's extensive experiences, and she was even portrayed by actress Lindsay Crouse in the film adaptation of her husband's famous 1987 non-fiction book *Communion,* starring Christopher Walken.

She edited all of Whitley's books before they were published, and she wrote the non-fiction book, *The Communion Letters*, a compendium of letters from witnesses of UFO close encounters Anne read and cataloged in reference to the book and she was the first person to realize that the appearance of what she termed "the visitors" was associated with simultaneous ghostly apparitions, which served as the foundation for the approach that was the basis of Whitley's work and their understanding of close encounter experiences. She also documented her long and courageous struggle with cancer in *Miraculous Journey*. Anne will always be remembered for her extensive knowledge, her inquisitive nature, her kindness, and her generosity of spirit.

Lorraine Warren
January 31, 1927 – April 18, 2019

In the paranormal investigation world, there are few people who haven't heard the name Lorraine Warren. Lorraine was a popular figure in the paranormal world for decades before reality television brought the paranormal world to the attention of a wider audience. The cases the Warrens investigated became the ground floor for dozens of books, movies, and documentary programs. The Warrens also wrote numerous books about their cases.

Although she was part of a team with her husband Ed Warren, she was on equal footing with him in the way she connected with others in the paranormal field. In particular, her talent lay in her abilities as a medium.

Lorraine and Ed founded the New England Society for Psychic Research in 1952. Over the years they investigated cases that grew into nationwide interest and eventually popularized in films and documentaries. Although they investigated cases not related to a claim of demonic activity, many if not all of their well-known cases highlighted their belief that demons are real and caused the hauntings. In particular, they believed those without a religious background were more likely to suffer possession.

In 1968, the Warrens investigated a claim made by two roommates that a Raggedy Ann doll had tormented them. The Warren's took the doll, which was supposedly haunted by the spirit of a young girl named Annabelle Higgins and put it on display at their museum, which housed a considerable number of other haunted objects. The tale behind this doll inspired an entire universe of movies including the *Conjuring Universe* collection of films. In 1971, the Warrens visited a Harrisville, Rhode Island home owned by the Perron family. The entire family had endured many years of paranormal activity. This famous haunting also inspired the *Conjuring Universe* of films.

Probably the most famous investigation Lorraine participated in was the haunting of a home in Amityville, New York. By the time Lorraine and Ed became involved, the house was already well known for a murder case where Ronald DeFeo, Jr. had murdered his family in 1974. The publicity around the haunting resulted in not only numerous fiction and non-fiction books but several motion pictures. Controversy over the validity of the haunting itself is ongoing to this day.

In 1977, the Warrens participated in investigating claims made by a family in Enfield, England that their girls were experiencing poltergeist activity. This case has inspired non-fiction works and fictional works and generated considerable controversy.

Less well-known was the case of Arne Johnson, who was accused of murdering his landlord in 1981. Prior to the murder, the Warrens were called in to deal with an alleged demonic possession of another family member. The situation inspired the movie *The Conjuring: The Devil Made Me Do It* (2021).

From 1974 until 1989, the Smurl family of Pennsylvania claimed they endured a haunting with sizable amounts of activity. At one point, the Warrens became involved. A book, *The Haunted*, and a film of the same name were eventually made about the Smurl's experiences.

In 1986, the Warrens investigated the Snedeker house, a former funeral home. This case engendered not only a movie but several books and mentions in non-fiction paranormal series productions.

Despite the controversy that surrounded Lorraine, she is known by many family members and fellow investigators to have been a warm and helpful individual. She stands out today as one of the most famous female paranormal investigators of all time.

The Future for Women on the Fringe

There will come a day when a person's gender, race, color, or creed won't bear any weight on his or her ability to research and investigate the world of the unknown, but until then, women will continue to break new ground, make new noise, and boldly go where others have not gone before them without thought to their gender. They will use their innate gifts, talents, and skills and their ability to cooperate, collaborate, and corroborate with others to push the edges of the paranormal envelop. Some will become famous or household names, others will become known to their particular fans or audiences, and many will toil in the trenches out of the spotlight of the camera, doing the work they have such great passion for. All are necessary to move the study of the unknown forward. All have something special to bring to the table.

They do what they do because it is who they are. It is their passion, their calling, and a part of how they view themselves and their place in the world. From the little girl who believed in aliens to the teenager who saw a ghost at a friend's house to the woman who discovered she could "see" into the future or across vast distances, the women on the fringe are diverse and unique in so many ways, yet share the common goal of trying to answer questions we have all asked:

Is there anything beyond what we see, hear, smell, feel, and touch?

What happens after we die?

Are we alone in the universe?

Are we capable of transcending space and time?

What is consciousness?

In asking these questions and pursuing the answers, even if those answers elude them in their own lifetimes, women, like their male counterparts, help to map out the unseen realms of reality and find the links, patterns, and signposts of those realities. They are the outliers, the adventurers, the explorers, the speculators, and the Imagineers. They are the children who knew there was more to the story than what met the eye, and decided to find out as much as they could about the vibrant unseen world that they were immersed in and surrounded by. They are the hearts that refused to be told that reality was only what our five senses told us and intuitively understood that the realms we could not see were as vast and rich as those we could – maybe even more so.

As we celebrate and honor the women in this book, we know that there are so many more that have gone nameless or not been mentioned here simply because we didn't have the room, and we celebrate them, too. There are enough out there to fill hundreds of books such as this, and each one has brought something incredible to the table of paranormal research. Whether books, television shows, radio shows and podcasts, working with the government, speaking to the public, field investigations, educational seminars and tours, or a host of other contributions, we thank them for their boldness, their courage, their curiosity, and their passion and we hope they know how appreciated they are for shattering the glass ceiling and forging new paths that the next generation of women, and men, can follow.

We salute them all and we cannot wait to see where their research, investigations, and pursuits lead them, and us, in the years to come.

Let's hear it for the ladies.

Bibliography

Abbott, Karen. "The Fox Sisters and the Rap on Spiritualism," Smithsonian Magazine, accessed on January 19, 2023 at https://www.smithsonianmag.com/history/the-fox-sisters-and-the-rap-on-spiritualism-99663697/

Delgado, Ann L. "Bawdy Technologies and the Birth of Ectoplasm," University of Colorado Boulder, accessed on January 19, 2023 at https://www.colorado.edu/gendersarchive1998-2013/2011/09/01/bawdy-technologies-and-birth-ectoplasm

Dunn, Barnaby D. "Trust your gut...but only sometimes." Association for Psychological Science. 2011. https://www.sciencedaily.com/releases/2011/01/110104114307.htm

Elliot, Ruth Lisa. "Suffrage and Spiritualism," Found San Francisco, accessed on January19, 2023 at https://www.foundsf.org/index.php?title=Suffrage_and_Spiritualism

Espin, Antonio M., Antoni Bosch Doménech, and Pablo Brañas. "Can Exposure to Prenatal Sex Hormones (2D:4D) Predict Cognitive Reflection?" Psychoneuroendocrinology, no. 43 (May 2014): 1-10. https://www.eurekalert.org/news-releases/682082

"Fear: Men vs. Women." Fearless Psychology online, May 25, 2018. https://fearlesspsychology.wordpress.com/2018/05/25/fear-men-vs-women/

Lowry, Elizabeth Schleber. "Women in Nineteenth-Century American Spiritualism," WRSP World Religious and Spirituality Project, accessed on January 19, 2023 at https://wrldrels.org/2018/06/25/women-in-nineteenth-century-american-spiritualism/

McGreal, Scott A. "Why Women Are More Likely To Believe in the Supernatural." Psychology Today. 2022. https://www.psychologytoday.com/us/blog/unique-everybody-else/202203/why-women-are-more-likely-believe-in-the-supernatural

Nutter, David. The X Files. Season 3, Episode 4, "Clyde Bruckman's Final Repose." Aired on October 13, 1995 on Fox.

Silva, T., & Woody, A. "Supernatural Sociology: Americans' Beliefs by Race/Ethnicity, Gender, and Education. 2022. https://doi.org/10.1177/23780231221084775

BIBLIOGRAPHY

Strickland, Nicole. "The Afterlife Chronicles: Exploring the Connection Between Life, Death, and Beyond." California: Kayli Max Books, 2023.

Swedenborg, Emanuel. Heaven and Hell. A & D Publishing, 2007.

Taylor, Troy. "The Lincoln Theater: The History and Mystery of Decatur's 'Most Haunted.'" 2006. https://www.hauntedillinois.com/realhauntedplaces/lincoln-theater.php

Taylor, Troy. "Waverly Hills Sanatorium: Kentucky's Hospital of the Damned." https://www.americanhauntingsink.com/waverlytb

Weisberg, Barbara. *Talking to the Dead: Kate and Maggie Fox and the Rise of Spiritualism.* New York: HarperCollins Publishers, Inc., 2004, 146.

"Why Men and Women Handle Stress Differently," *WebMD* online, June 6, 2005. https://www.webmd.com/women/features/stress-women-men-cope

Yukooct, Elizabeth. "8 Famous Figures Who Believed in Communicating with the Dead: Spiritualism's Popularity Waxed and Waned Throughout the 19th Century and the First Decades of the 20th Century, and Surged on the Heels of Major Wars and Pandemics," *History,* accessed on January 19, 2023 at http://www.history.com/news/spiritualism-communication-dead-figures